D0394057

THE SECRET EMPIRE

How 25 Multinationals Rule the World

THE SECRET EMPIRE

EMPIRE

How 25 Multinationals Rule the World

Janet Lowe

BUSINESS ONE IRWIN
Homewood, Illinois 60430

This publication is designed to provide accurate and
authoritative information in regard to the subject matter
covered. It is sold with the understanding that neither the
author nor the publisher is engaged in rendering legal, accounting,
or other professional service. If legal advice or other expert
assistance is required, the services of a competent
professional person should be sought.

*From a Declaration of Principles jointly adopted by a Committee
of the American Bar Association and a Committee of Publishers.*

Senior editor: Jeffrey A. Krames
Project editor: Karen J. Nelson
Production manager: Bob Lange
Designer: Laurie Entringer
Cover designer: Tim Kaage
Compositor: TCSystems, Inc.
Typeface: 11/13 Electra
Printer: Book Press, Inc.

Library of Congress Cataloging-in-Publication Data

Lowe, Janet (Janet Celesta)
　　The secret empire: how 25 multinationals rule the world/Janet
　Lowe.
　　　　p.　　cm.
　　Includes index.
　　ISBN 1-55623-513-5
　　1. International business enterprises.　I. Title.
　HD2755.5.L676　1992
　338.8′81—dc20　　　　　　　　　　　　　　　91–44600

Printed in the United States of America

1 2 3 4 5 6 7 8 9 0 BP 9 8 7 6 5 4 3 2

Dedication

To my entire clan, which is vast. They include the Fairbanks family descendants of the west, the latest generation in a long line of American pioneers. Additionally, this is dedicated to the Lowe and Lynas branches of the tree, who prove that a diverse collection of individuals can stand together as a family.

Foreword

While this book was being written, history dashed past like a high-speed chase in an action/adventure movie. Matsushita Electric Industrial bought MCA Inc. for $6.6 billion, a stunning Japanese inroad to the U.S.-dominated entertainment industry. The Bank of Credit and Commerce International fell to an undignified fate; though the recession repeatedly was declared moribund, it refused to die.

The Kuwait/Iraq war erupted and ended, and even more significantly, a coup in the Soviet Union collapsed and the Soviet bloc came apart at the seams. From their very beginnings, it seemed completely likely that the Kuwait war would be a cakewalk for the allied forces and that the Soviet coup plotters had nowhere to go. Both Saddam Hussein and the USSR "emergency committee" were working against a wave that was sweeping the world. The old world believed in political ideology; the new world believes in economics. The new theology is capitalism, and the high priests of the religion are the multinational corporations. Through a natural process of business evolution (a conspiracy isn't the least bit necessary), a select group of multinational corporations—we will call them the meganationals—lead the procession.

Because their missionaries already were walking the streets of the Soviet Union and had received a remarkable degree of acceptance, it was unlikely that the coup plotters could keep in place any plan that uprooted the wave toward free enterprise. Fiat's $1.5 billion contract to assemble 300,000 automobiles a year; General Motors' $1 billion deal to supply auto parts; Daimler-Benz's $140 million plant to build buses; the IBM pact to provide 40,000 personal computers for schools—the long-term benefits of these arrangements for an economically deprived populace were too juicy to pass up. So that these deals and others would stay on track, *glasnost* and *perestroika* had to survive.

For the orderly operation of the petroleum industry and to secure the oil that greases the wheels of big business (not to mention for the protection of the Kuwait Investment Office, which has extensive investments in such meganationals as British Petroleum and Daimler-Benz), Saddam Hussein had to go.

While researching and writing this book, several dozen interviews were conducted, many in person, others by telephone, fax, or mail. Public relations, investor relations, and other departments of all of the corporations were pestered for information and most were very helpful. Government records were examined, and securities analysts were questioned.

I traveled extensively throughout Europe, Africa, the Caribbean, and the Far East. Not one day passed that I didn't read about one of the key meganationals (I came to think of them as *my* companies) in some newspaper somewhere. On a single day on the front business page of the *New York Times*, it was announced that American Telephone and Telegraph would build a telephone link to Armenia; that Exxon would invest millions of dollars in new plants to produce cleaner fuel; and that Citicorp might be forced to sell its consumer banking business in Italy and France. At the same time, a securities scandal was unraveling in Japan, involving Matsushita, Dai-Ichi Kangyo Bank, Hitachi, and dozens of other Japanese companies. The banking industry the world over was under pressure to strengthen capital reserves. Most major European corporate leaders were granting interviews on their strategies for a unified European economy after 1992 and on a more entertaining note, *Vanity Fair* ran a lengthy feature on the glamorous life of Fiat's Giovanni Agnelli.

The stories of how the 25 most powerful companies are consolidating their hold on the business world kept evolving as the book progressed. IBM had been chosen more than a year earlier as a key meganational. But during the very week I was writing about its role in antitrust controversies, IBM announced a bombshell alliance with Apple Computer, followed by a half dozen other brilliant joint ventures. While browsing through a computer data base that same week, I discovered a tiny announcement in *The Wall Street Journal* that Mitsui Taiyo Kobe Bank was changing its name to more user-friendly "Sakura" or cherry blossom bank.

Above all, the biggest and most powerful companies kept growing. Dai-Ichi Kangyo Bank's assets leapt from $352.4 billion in 1989 (the year my research began) to $470.3 billion in 1991. During the same time, Exxon's sales grew from $87.3 billion to $116 billion; Philip Morris from $31.7 billion to $51.2 billion; Royal Dutch Petroleum/Shell, $78.3 billion to $106.5 billion; Matsushita, $38.5 billion to $44.2 billion; and Daimler-Benz, $41.4 billion to $57.3 billion. The sales and assets of some of the consumer-oriented corporations, such as General Motors, were flat during that recessionary stretch but, historically, sales snap back smartly during a recovery. Some of the companies who were constantly the subject of bad-news stories, such as Citicorp and Siemens, increased assets and sales anyway.

Keeping current with the news wasn't the only difficulty. Figures for foreign corporations, when expressed in dollars, are vulnerable to changing exchange rates. A European or Japanese company may have experienced real growth in a given year, but if the value of the U.S. dollar strengthened, their financial results may seem weaker than the year before (or the reverse).

Take this example from the Unilever 1990 annual report. "In Europe operating profit moved ahead strongly, up 35 percent when expressed in dollars, 25 percent when expressed in sterling, and 16 percent when expressed in guilders." Later, when describing performance outside Europe and North America: "In the rest of the world operating profit was 13 percent higher in dollars and 4 percent higher in sterling, but 4 percent lower in guilders. At constant rates of exchange the gain was 14 percent."

Whenever possible and when it made sense, figures are stated in dollars. In certain cases, however, local currencies are used.

As this work was in progress, several books were published about the internationalization of business, the decline in relevance of the nation-state, and the emergence of the rather nebulous "new world order." The idea of a new industrial state is not novel, as John Kenneth Galbraith can attest. What is new is the statelessness of industry, and the expanding breadth of its reach.

A small group of authors are discussing the growing dominance of big business and how governments are struggling to adjust to their own loss of power.

Invariably, many journalists and academicians react to these ideas with hostility. Not only are these impassioned attacks natural, they add credence to our claims. There is a familiar theory in academic circles describing the path of new ideas. First the paradigm is rejected and attacked by the old guard, next it has a few upstart supporters, then it becomes an accepted principle. Eventually the new concept becomes outdated and in turn is uprooted by new precepts. The world changes, and someday the big business bloc also will crumble and give way to a newer "new world order." That eventuality, however, is many generations away. In the meantime, the world must adapt, and individuals—indomitable as ever—will strive to maintain their integrity and individuality. The goal of this book is to facilitate that process.

Janet Lowe

Acknowledgments

Special thanks to my editor Jeffrey Krames and literary agent Alice Martell for their encouragement; D.W. Lowe, Celesta Lowe, and Austin Lynas for reviewing the manuscript; to Dr. Chalmers Johnson, Dr. Lester Thurow, Dr. Noam Chomsky, Nancy Cleland, Barry D. Wood, Elizabeth Mitchell, Keiji Moto, and Tadahiko Teramoto for their technical assistance; and to a whole army of librarians at the San Diego Public Library and the University of California at San Diego libraries who never failed to be patient, helpful, and cheerful.

J. L.

Contents

Chapter One

Marx Was Right About One Thing

"I don't think we can do entirely without capitalism, but the extremes are disagreeable and dangerous."

Graham Greene

Alfred Herrhausen left his home in the elite spa town of Bad Homburg at the usual time on the morning of November 30, 1989. His armored, chauffeur-driven Mercedes-Benz 500SE was protected by two escort vehicles with four bodyguards. Nevertheless, just 550 yards along the tree-lined street where Herrhausen lived, a fireball blasted the limousine into charred, tangled debris. Alfred Herrhausen, chief executive of the mighty Deutsche Bank and chairman of the supervisory board of the esteemed Daimler-Benz, died instantly.

A wooden box containing a bomb detonator was discovered in a nearby park. Beneath the carton was a slip of paper bearing the ominous five-pointed star superimposed over the image of a Kalashnikov submachine gun, the calling card of West Germany's ultraleftist urban terrorists, the Red Army Faction. The Red Army Faction—successor to the Baader-Meinhof gang—had struck Europe at various times. But never before had a business leader of Herrhausen's stature been the target of a political assassination.

Dubbed Germany's "Lord of Money" by the weekly *Der Spiegel*, the 59-year-old Herrhausen was the consummate image of the new industrial leader. A suave and regal personage, he was a youngster during World War II. After assuming leadership at Deutsche Bank in 1988, Herrhausen aggressively began transforming the bank from an insular, European institution into a global financial power.

In the three years before his assassination, Herrhausen engineered the buyout of 10 other commercial and investment banks.

In the perverse way of publication deadlines, the same week other news magazines were running Herrhausen's obituary, *Business Week* featured a story of Deutsche Bank's $1.5 billion acquisition of the British investment bank, Morgan Grenfell Group plc. The story included a photograph of Herrhausen with the caption, "Instant Giant in European M&A." The piece went on to say, "The move adds a key building block to the dominant European position and growing global presence of Deutsche Bank, whose $168 billion in assets place it first among German banks and 20th in the world."[1]

Further evidence of Herrhausen's brilliance and the burgeoning potency of Deutsche Bank appeared again in *Business Week* just one month later. That report told of the purchase of a controlling interest in Nixdorf Computer for $350 million by German electronics giant Siemens.

The deal shut out French and Italian rivals for Nixdorf, keeping it in the hands of Germans. "Everybody wanted to buy Nixdorf," French Industry Minister Roger Fauroux was quoted as saying, "but Deutsche Bank said, 'Don't touch.'" Deutsche Bank, as it turned out, is one of Siemens' major lenders and a representative from Deutsche Bank sits on Siemens' board.

The accumulation of this much power has been an impressive feat for a bank that after World War II was forced by the Allies to close its head office and all of its branches in Germany's Eastern Sector. Deutsche Bank itself was carved up into 10 separate institutions, and only after 1957 was the bank able to reclaim its historic name.

In Germany, Deutsche Bank managers hold more than 400 seats on the supervisory boards of other German groups. Politicians in Bonn, understandably, have complained of the bank's stranglehold on German finance.

Deutsche Bank, however, conducts business everywhere. Its powerful reach extends to Moscow, Tokyo, Curacao, Montevideo, Jakarta, Toronto, Sydney, Hong Kong, Luxembourg, and other world financial capitals. It advertises itself in American publications as "Your European Investment Banker in the United States." It has substantial holdings in Banco Comercial Transatlantico in Spain and in H. Albert de Bary in the Netherlands. Herrhausen even served on the board of supervisors of the prestigious Anglo-Dutch food and soap company, Unilever. Despite the loss of Herrhausen, Deutsche Bank advanced from 20th to 19th place in world ranking the year after his death.

Deutsche Bank not only has considerable muscle in the business world; its leaders hold sway in political circles as well. A champion of German reunification, Herrhausen served as a personal economic advisor to West German Chancellor Helmut Kohl and maintained close ties with Soviet and East European officials. As post-World War II political arrangements began to unravel, Herrhausen's influence was palpable. "It's not Kohl who decides how much aid Poland will get," observed a German chief financial officer, "but Herrhausen."

According to *Euromoney*, the European financial publication, when Herrhausen was asked to name an organization in any other industrialized country that had the same concentration of economic power as Deutsche Bank had in Germany, he answered, "I don't know of any." He quickly added, however, that this did not mean the bank was too powerful in the context of German society.

With Herrhausen's brutal murder, the Red Army Faction had thus made good its threat of years earlier that corporate chiefs, along with military and political commandants, would be held accountable for what the radical group considered sins against the people and the earth. The awesome power of the captains of business was thus pronounced by the terrorists to be equal to that of kings, presidents, and popes.

The Red Army Faction's appalling attack on Alfred Herrhausen, and through Herrhausen on the political-industrial-military complex of Europe, bespeaks a fear that has racked the world for more than a century. The suspicions first germinated with the spread of the British colonial empire and festered with the Industrial Revolution. Economic thinkers with philosophies as dissimilar as Karl Marx and Adam Smith recognized the danger of domination by powerhouse business interests.

"The question is obvious," wrote economists Robert Heilbroner and Lester Thurow in *Economics Explained.* "How does a market society prevent self-interested, profit-hungry individuals from holding up their fellow citizens for ransom? How can a socially workable arrangement arise from such a dangerously unsocial motivation as self-betterment?"

Adam Smith believed that balancing forces would be found

within the market system. Producers or workers who overcharge would be forced out of the market by more competitive agents. Undesirable products would fall by the wayside as consumers flock to those goods they need and want. An "invisible hand" would direct the progress of civilization.

Karl Marx held small faith in the better nature of mankind. In *Das Kapital*, he described capitalism as a murky, clumsy evolutionary process. He said, "The size of business firms will steadily increase as the consequence of the recurrent crises that rack the economy. With each crisis, small firms go bankrupt and their assets are bought up by surviving firms. A trend toward big business is therefore an integral part of capitalism."

Marx muttered darkly, "One capitalist always kills many."

More recent economists such as the late Professor Joseph J. Spengler of Duke University can look back over an extended period of capitalism and the market system. They recognize the vast capabilities of the capitalist structure.

"But (Spengler) was no idealogue of the market as the ideal allocator of goods or dispenser of justice," wrote Leonard Silk in the *New York Times* on the occasion of Spengler's death in 1991. "Though the market spurs and rewards efficiency and innovation, he held, it often neglects those aesthetic, intellectual, and moral qualities essential to the good society. And it may despoil the earth's irreplaceable resources."[2]

Early on, Britain and the United States recognized that a market system wasn't entirely trustworthy. For one thing, free enterprise focuses only on functions that earn money for the company. Public services are neglected because they are notoriously unprofitable. Roads will be built and sewer lines laid to a factory, for example, and to the home of the factory owner who can afford the cost. But the rest of a region may not get paved streets or a sanitation system. Public transportation may be ignored entirely, since there is no financial reward for these activities. Therefore, states must provide essential public services on behalf of all members of a society.

For the most part, the market system has worked well in economies that have the courage to first adopt it and then allow it to function. Free enterprise has served the world well in many ways, and will be with us for a long time even if Smith's Invisible Hand sometimes is shaky. But the flaws are undeniable. Wealth is spread unevenly and recessions occur from time to time. Most important of all, there is plenty of evidence to indicate that Marx's warning of world dominance by corporate giants is coming to pass.

The first billion dollar merger occurred in 1901 when J. P. Morgan combined Carnegie Steel with its opponents to form U.S. Steel. This launched the first of several merger waves, both in the United States and worldwide, that continue into the present.

In the most recent surge of mergers, that of the 1980s, $1.3 trillion was spent in the corporate acquisitions game. That is a sum roughly equivalent to the annual output (in the 1980s) of West Germany. It all started modestly in 1980 with 798 deals totaling $59 billion. By 1989, there were 3,120 acquisitions for a yearly total of $150 billion.

By the end of the decade, billion dollar deals were commonplace, and mergers were uniting companies across the hemispheres. In 1987, British Petroleum paid $7.8 billion for the 45 percent interest in Standard Oil (Sohio, U.S.) that it did not already own. In 1990, Philip Morris purchased the Swiss candy maker Jacobs Suchard for $3.8 billion. In December of that year, following the lead of Sony Corporation and Columbia Pictures, the Japanese conglomerate Matsushita shook the U.S.-dominated entertainment industry when it acquired MCA, owner of Universal Studios and MCA Records, for $6.59 billion.

Despite a slowing in the number of mergers and acquisitions during the recession of the early 1990s, growth by merger is far from over. At the end of the 1980s, the Japanese alone had $18 trillion at their disposal for buying business assets.

Add to the merger trend the fact that the best-capitalized companies can afford to be aggressive in the development of new products and in the pursuit of market share, and you reach an inescapable conclusion: The mammoth corporations keep getting more so.

Many of today's massive corporations are larger than most nations in which they do business. Of the 213 nations on the earth, there are only eight—the United States, Japan, (the former) USSR, France, Germany, Italy, the United Kingdom, and Canada—that report gross domestic products greater than the assets of the world's leading banks. Dai-Ichi Kangyo Bank had 1989 assets of $358.2 billion; Canada, the smallest of these eight countries, had a GDP that year of $363.6 billion. In reality, there are only seven countries that stand above the most massive of the corporations. The former USSR is in such economic disarray that its numbers are no longer relevant.

Japanese banks are not the only enterprises that can overwhelm the governments of the world. General Motors, the largest industrial corporation, had revenues ($110 billion) greater than the GNPs of 191 or 89.7 percent of all the world's nations.

Not only are massive corporations becoming bigger, most of the business in the world is done by big business. Heilbroner and Thurow point out that 85 percent of all corporations do less than $1 million worth of business a year. The 15 percent that do more than $1 million, however, take in 85 percent of the receipts of all corporations. The most powerful among these companies, the ones discussed in this book, are more than multinational in scope. They can better be described as "meganationals." They are leviathans, and they sometimes dominate several world markets at once.

The market system becomes especially ineffective when faced with monopolies or, as is more commonly the case, oligopolies. The problem with a concentration of power by one or a few owners is that the correcting function of supply and demand is interrupted. Companies of inordinate size can keep prices unnecessarily high when it suits their needs, or can set prices unnaturally low to drive out competition.

Despite antitrust enforcement and a general watchfulness by European and U.S. governments, the multinationals continue to swell in girth. Monopolies or oligopolies that once threatened a country or region now can wrap around the planet itself.

Furthermore, while it has always been difficult to deal with antitrust issues, the U.S. government now is beginning to view some restrictions as futile. In a world where competitors are global—and countries such as Germany and Japan allow close relationships among their most powerful companies—being too touchy about monopoly issues seems self-defeating.

There are, of course, many advantages to big business. Though they search the world for cheap labor, these companies usually offer higher salaries and greater job security than other employers in the same market. After all, they want to get and hold the best workers. Certainly some of the greatest accomplishments of the 20th century, from the electrification of the world to the launching of spacecraft to the triumph over many diseases, could not have been achieved without the research, development, and operational expertise of the meganational corporations.

The presence of these companies is seen as so desirable that governments everywhere compete for the $150 billion a year world corporations invest across national borders.

This fact, plus a whole set of emerging economic circumstances listed below, have created a free-wheeling global business climate in which big business can operate almost at will.

• In the 1980s, 7 to 9 million refugees flooded into the United States, hoping to share in the financial wealth of North America. Many of them were economic refugees from Mexico. Poverty at home and the fleeing of its citizens pressured the Mexican government to create more jobs by courting the meganationals.

• At the dawn of the 1990s, Communism collapsed in Eastern Europe, to a large extent because the system was an economic failure. It appears that the East German revolution and that of other communist bloc countries was less about a yearning for democracy and more about a lusting to join the consumer society.

It is hardly surprising that political leaders have come to see their responsibilities to their citizens mainly in terms of economic issues. When American President George Bush and Mexican President Carlos Salinas de Gortari met in 1991, the encouragement of Mexican business development was foremost on the agenda. Mexican citizens in the past fiercely defended themselves from encroachment by their powerful northern neighbor. But President Salinas declared an end to the country's isolation. One year earlier, a Japanese delegation visited Mexico, insisting that laws regarding labor unions be modified, making Mexico an even more profitable home for off-shore assembly plants. This demand was made, despite the fact that the average Mexican worker was paid less than a dollar an hour, about one fourth the minimum wage in the United States.

The ancient question remains. What price will Mexicans, Eastern Europeans, and other emerging economies pay to share in financial wealth? In today's world, to be disenfranchised economically is to be without the most basic human needs. Yet the transition from a dysfunctional or controlled economy is not easy. Being hard workers is not enough. At the very least, citizens of economically aspiring countries must also become avid consumers. At the most, they must give up valued cultural traditions, risk damage to their environment, and expect social upheaval.

Even in developed countries citizens have begun to realize that corporate power may be beyond their control. In California in the mid-1980s, a group of foreign corporations, led by Japanese companies, pressured the state to abandon its unitary tax policy. The tax structure had been formulated many years before to prevent movie companies from transferring profits to another state or another country with a more favorable tax rate. Foreign corporations objected to the law because it required that they reveal more accounting information than was required in their home countries. Japanese companies informed state officials that they would build no new plants in the state until the tax practice was changed. Even so, after the policy was modified some Japanese manufacturers expanded into other states that offered land, tax incentives, and other benefits for relocating.

Corporations have become so formidable that even federal government regulation may not be a sufficient means of control. In fact, corporations have become increasingly influential in setting government policy. In Europe, for example, business interests, Deutsche Bank among them, are the driving force behind the formation of the European Economic Community.

Traditionalists, and some academics in particular, find the demise of the nation-state a difficult concept to accept. The whole idea that the state could be superseded goes against both their training and their idealism. Yet many others, ranging from hourly workers to radical groups such as the Red Army Faction, have no difficulty in grasping the trend. Neither do some corporate leaders.

Editorial columnist Alexander Cockburn frequently harangues big business. His point of view was inserted into a newspaper column that claimed that the Kuwait/Iraq war was all about oil, and waged solely to protect international petroleum interests.

"With the internationalization of capital," Cockburn wrote, "corporations owe loyalty to no one and will seek out the cheapest labor and most beneficial tax codes available. Emblems of the state such as presidents and prime ministers have long since relinquished any supervision or regulation of these corporations."[3]

As a result, he implied, state armies become corporate armies for the execution of corporate policy.

Linguist and philosopher Noam Chomsky is a popular speaker at liberal gatherings around the country. That so much of the United States is owned by a small group, mainly the big corporations, bothers him as well.

"I'm an old-fashioned conservative," Chomsky said in a 1990 newspaper interview. "I think the 18th century libertarian ideals were basically correct: There shouldn't be concentrations of power. Power should be under popular control. The centers of power that people thought about in those days were the church, the feudal system, and the absolutist state. And so they said, 'Okay, let's dissolve that.'

"But in the 19th century a new center of power developed: corporate capitalism. Corporate capitalism destroyed liberalism. Liberal thought kind of broke on these rocks of rising corporate capitalism. A new center of control and concentration of power developed, out of public control. The same standard libertarian ideal that made you opposed to an absolutist state made you opposed to capitalism. And it's always corporate capitalism, because it's going to concentrate."

This concentration of power, he continued, determines "what is produced, what is distributed, what is consumed, what you see, what you read, where you work, whether you work, and what happens in the political system. Virtually everything is traceable back to that centralization. And until that's overcome—until the power in the system is diffused—there isn't going to be any operative political freedom."[4]

In the end, Chomsky believes, it is individual rights that are threatened.

Cockburn and Chomsky might be described as aging liberals unwilling or unable to give up the radical notions of the 1960s. But scribblers, scholars, and off-beat intellectuals aren't the only ones to sound the alarm.

"In this sense, there has been a reversal of roles between government and the corporation. Governments act as if they are fully sovereign within their own borders on economic policy, but stateless corporations have increasingly learned to shape national climates by offering technology, jobs, and capital," wrote *Business*

Week in a 1990 article called "The Stateless Corporation."

Unisys Corporation Chairman W. Michael Blumenthal responded to that assertion.

"I wouldn't say the nation-state is dead," Blumenthal said. "But the sovereignty has been greatly circumscribed . . . even for a country as large as the United States."[5]

Kazuo Inamori, founder of Kyocera Corp. of Kyoto, Japan, reaches beyond Blumenthal's tentative admission. A lifelong industrialist, Inamori's thinking falls closer in line with Chomsky's.

"Multinational corporations operate on a global scale, manufacturing and selling goods everywhere and obtaining personnel, funds, and resources from all over the world," Inamori wrote in *Intersect* magazine. "In business and industry, the role of the government has receded into the background, and the recognition that national borders are actually a hindrance to economic development is behind the planned integration of the European Community and the creation of other regional common markets."

Capitalism and communism, Inamori wrote, have a similar failing. "Communism broke down because it neglected the spirituality of human beings. Its demise was accelerated by the irreversible tide of times, the rising power of the people. But these are not only issues pertaining to communist societies in crisis; they are the concerns of capitalist societies as well."

Inamori isn't simply worried about religion. He refers to the human need for a connection to place and family, a love of nature, and a sense of self-worth, self-determination, and fair play.

Government, Inamori claims, is in collusion with big business in failing to respect the individuality and the potential of the individual.

"'Maintaining order' has become a pretext for protecting existing interests, and the interests of the public are low on the list of priorities," he said. "Control by officialdom over the past hundred-odd years has, by now, lost virtually all of its legitimacy."[6]

In unusually strong terms for one who makes his way in the world of international business, Inamori scolded large corporations on ethics and business practices. Yet Inamori must know all too well how difficult it is to direct and control a multinational corporation. Kyocera came under attack and was sued in California after laying off workers who claimed that, like their Japanese counterparts, they had been promised lifetime employment.[7]

Kyocera, though its annual sales top $3 billion, is merely a pebble compared to the scope and size of other worldwide corporations.

"Vast" and "influential" are among the words that describe the new corporate "super class" that is evolving from the mergers and acquisition trends of the 20th century. As has been the case with princes of power throughout history, it will be by control of money, trade routes, and command over goods and services that these new super-class meganationals will exert their prerogatives.

Just as the murder of Alfred Herrhausen by the Red Army Faction no more than momentarily restrained Deutsche Bank, even extreme action may not be able to halt the march of the multinationals.

Yet this worldwide transformation must be understood. We must know what the changes mean and think about how we will live in the new world that is being created. One place to begin is by naming the principal contenders in this new arena. What are these companies like? Who are their leaders? What kind of a world do they envision and strive for? We must ask how individuals—and the governments that we invent to represent us—will fare in this new-fashioned world. And, finally, we must again ask the old question: Will Marx be right? Will corporate corpulence bring about the death of capitalism, the strangulation of the free enterprise system?

Chapter Two

The Companies

"Power protects itself. Is that any big surprise?"

Noam Chomsky.

Cable News Network gained worldwide notoriety for transforming news into theater verité during the 1991 Kuwait/Iraq war. But to connoisseurs of confrontational television, CNN proved its news mettle a year and a half earlier when it captured the combativeness of a corporate annual meeting. War is a garden party for television, compared to covering traditionally sleepy shareholders' meetings.

The annual meeting in question was that of Exxon Corporation, just a month after the March 1989 Exxon Valdez oil spill in the Alaskan wilderness. Exxon Chairman Lawrence G. Rawl was compelled to face a mob of riled shareholders, not to mention a cadre of environmentalists who gained entrance as stockholders by purchasing a few shares of Exxon. Iron-jawed and red in the face, Rawl fielded questions like a beefy major league batter reaching desperately for a home run world record. He swung hard at every injury and, in the opinion of most witnesses, he struck out. It was embarrassing to watch a forceful and unrepentant chief executive use a bully's tactics to defend the largest oil company in the world to a roomful of enraged, but otherwise seemingly powerless individuals.

It didn't play well to the cameras. The tanker ship accident fouled more than 700 miles of Alaska's shoreline, wildlife refuges, and national parks. Countless birds, about 3,500 sea otters, and 200 harbor seals perished in a disaster that will cost $2.5 billion to $5 billion before it is put right. Even if the dumping of 11 million gallons of North Slope crude oil into the magnificent Prince William Sound was the result of a series of unfortunate decisions, even if the accident occurred without malice or excessive negligence, the buck had to stop somewhere. Rawl made it sound as if he intended to fight long and hard to take as little responsibility as possible. Within the year, 330-odd lawsuits had been filed against Exxon in connection with the mishap, including those by salmon fishermen and more than a dozen Alaskan native tribes. Fifty thousand disgusted Exxon credit card holders sent their cards back to the company.

Even as public relations experts the world over were calling it the most mismanaged corporate disaster in business history, Rawl did not seem to grasp the point. He angered Alaskans by sending lower level executives to manage the cleanup. At first Rawl didn't even go to Alaska to survey the situation; at the very least to scrape some sludge off a puffin and soothe the public's ruffled feathers. This was a curious turn of events for the company that is credited with inventing corporate public relations when John D. Rockefeller, Jr. hired publicist "Poison Ivy" Lee to help the company through the image-battering 1914 Colorado Fuel and Iron Company strikes. Though Exxon was spending millions of dollars for personnel and equipment to attack the filthiest spill in U.S. history, it struck many observers that Exxon's CEO didn't much care.

In fact, even after the federal government stepped in to negotiate a $1.2 billion out-of-court settlement (much of it tax-deductible for Exxon), Rawl couldn't get his tone right. After telling news reporters that he had been "disappointed and angry" since the day of the spill, Rawl insisted, apparently for the purpose of stabilizing Exxon's share price, that the settlement wouldn't hurt the company. "The settlement will have no noticeable effect on our financial results," he said. Exxon's profits for 1989, after spill costs were accounted for, topped $3.5 million. Exxon's share price actually rose $1 the day the settlement was announced.

Many Alaskans, including Governor Walter J. Hickel, favored the negotiated settlement for two reasons. They wanted cash up front to pay for the cleanup and they hoped to avoid lengthy, costly court battles. Other Alaskans, though, were irate at Exxon's attitude.

"How arrogant," said Representative Gene Kubina, a Democrat who represented the town of Valdez, of Rawl's reaction. "He should be ashamed of himself. He should be replaced and sent to jail."[1]

It's probably no surprise that the agreement eventually went the way of the oil-soaked sea otters. A federal judge and the Alaska state legislature rejected the agreement, on the grounds that Exxon's contribution was too small. Both the company and the state and federal governments were compelled to go back to the negotiating table or to fight it out in court. The day the story of the collapse of the agreement ran, Exxon's 1991 first quarter earnings also were reported. Exxon's three-month sales jumped 15 percent and its profits soared 75 percent to $2.24 billion, directly attributable to the circumstances surrounding the Kuwait/Iraq war. Settling the Exxon Valdez lawsuits could take five or more years of court haggling, but the company appeared financially prepared to face the music.

Rawl, of course, eventually did go about the country apologizing. He had to. The campaign, led by the Bush administration, was underway to open the Alaskan Natural Wildlife Refuge to onshore drilling. It was crucial that Exxon be seen as sensitive to environmental carnage. Rawl was right not to worry about the settlement, however. Exxon is so big that it can survive catastrophe, and since Rawl himself is answerable only to shareholders, nothing short of disastrous financial losses could dislodge him from his job.

In fact, while all this was going on, Exxon's troubles compounded. On Christmas Eve, a Louisiana refinery blew sky high. Two workers were killed. A few days later the company discharged another 567,000 gallons into a public waterway, the Arthur Kill between Staten Island and Linden, New Jersey. That New Year's Day, 1990, accident cost the company $10 million to $15 million for environmental restoration.

Exxon, like all huge oil, chemical, and mineral conglomerates, walks in a mine field, where one misstep could set off an explosion of public animosity. Since the company's inception, it has encountered sundry attacks on its policies and reputation.

For those who may have been baffled by a company name change back in 1974, Exxon began life as Standard Oil of New Jersey. Standard of New Jersey itself had been spun off from John D. Rockefeller's massive Standard Oil Company in one of the bloodiest antitrust brawls ever fought.

The Standard Oil story began in 1863 when Rockefeller entered the oil refining business in Cleveland, Ohio. Rockefeller at first was a silent partner, but later took control of the company. Soon,

Rockefeller entered into a secret agreement with railroad companies that would destroy many of his competitors. The railroads agreed to rebate large sums of money to Rockefeller and several other major refiners if they would guarantee a steady stream of oil shipments. The shipments meant an orderly flow of profits for the railroads, not to mention for Rockefeller himself. Eventually, the company evolved into Standard Oil, and through similar bone-crushing moves, Rockefeller swallowed up even more rivals, including his own brother's firm. By the turn of the century, Standard Oil controlled three quarters of the oil market in the United States.

Rockefeller's company became one of the most feared and despised in the United States. The *New York Times* charged that even shareholders didn't know about the company's business practices, which were cloaked in dark secrecy. Employees dared not talk about their work publicly, for fear of losing their jobs. In 1911, Ida M. Tarbell, the infamous journalistic muckraker, published *The History of Standard Oil*, an exposé that sparked a monumental snit among American readers. That same year, culminating a fight that went all the way to the Supreme Court, the federal government enforced the Sherman Anti-Trust Act of 1890. Standard Oil, which by then controlled nearly 90 percent of the refining capacity in the United States, was split into 34 separately owned companies.

Already established in Canada, Jersey Standard continued to prosper, outperforming most of the other Standard Oil spin-offs. In the 1920s it branched into the West Indies, South America, and the Middle East. In the 1930s it moved into the Far East and Australia. In the 1960s the company diversified into nuclear energy, nonoil minerals, office products, and electronics.

Exxon today operates in the United States and 79 other countries. The majority of its income is derived from oil and natural gas exploration, refining, and marketing. Yet Exxon has tentacles in many sidelines. Exxon owns minimarkets in Guatemala, Esso gasoline stations in Canada, copper mines in Chile, carries out plastics research in Belgium, and helps provide electricity to Hong Kong. It vies with Royal Dutch Shell for the title of the world's largest oil conglomerate, and it is the third-largest industrial company in the United States.

No one understands the power or prerogative of Exxon better than the residents of Northwestern Colorado. Even a decade after it happened, the local economy staggers and many individuals carry scars from Exxon's abrupt exit, in the early 1980s, from its oil-shale operations there. Within hours of Exxon's announcement that it would abandon the project, ancillary businesses closed and property values crumbled. Yet few economic analysts fault the company. From a business point of view, which is by necessity focused on profits, Exxon did the right thing.

Despite its sullied reputation, Exxon views itself as a conscientious corporate citizen. It provides 104,000 people in various parts of the world with good-paying jobs. After the Alaskan calamity, an oceanographic scientist was added to the board of directors. In 1989, even before the big spill, Exxon contributed $51 million to educational and public service activities throughout the countries in which it conducts business.

Exxon, with its contentious history and remarkable reach, is a member of an elite international club of corporations. It is among the most powerful companies in the world, enterprises that move across national and cultural borders. In stride with more than two dozen preeminent corporations, Exxon flexes its muscle with a prowess that until the second half of the 20th century was relegated to the imagination of fiction writers.

These companies are the meganationals. Members of an exclusive club, they operate in a cluster of key industries, and they have much in common.

• *They are among the 100 largest banks and industrial corporations in the world.*

Each of these companies lists its assets and revenues in the billions of dollars. But size alone isn't enough to qualify as a true meganational. Japan's Nippon Telephone and Telegraph, for example, is not on the list. Though it dwarfs many worldwide corporations in terms of assets, sales, and capitalization, it remains a partially nationalized telephone company. Though in the past few years it has experienced a reenergization, NTT still operates with much of the cumbersome parochialism of a government agency. Until recently, it was better compared to the U.S. Post Office than to Exxon, Deutsche Bank, or any of the Japanese giants that flash the meganational badge.

Fiat, on the other hand, is overshadowed by other carmakers. Nevertheless, with its farm equipment, publishing, and other multitudinous operations, Fiat has grown beyond a simple manufacturer of automobiles. It has a unique position in world markets, and reigns supreme in the Italian economy.

• *The meganationals are well-established enterprises, with a management arrangement that transcends the leadership of any single individual.*

How many Americans, much less persons from other parts of the world, remember the name of the chief executive officer of American Telephone and Telegraph? Very few indeed, despite the fact that AT&T is in the news almost daily. Yet AT&T traces its heritage back to Alexander Graham Bell and can be credited with one of the most amazing and transforming changes of the 20th century—the leap into an era of instant communication. Now more than ever, AT&T touches the lives of people around the globe. Though Robert E. Allen is among the highest paid executives in the United States, AT&T is not a company that relies heavily on charismatic leadership. As visionary as he may be, when Allen is gone, there still will be an AT&T.

• *Each of the meganationals has a distinct corporate culture that sustains it through times of crisis and uncertainty.*

The $438.6 billion Mitsui Taiyo Kobe Bank Limited was created in 1990 in a merger between Mitsui and Taiyo Kobe banks. Its bloodline, however, weaves intricately into Japan's legendary past. The Mitsui family traces its lineage to A.D. 1100 when for several generations they produced dauntless Samurai warriors. Over time, the family became merchants and money lenders and, eventually, the official Meiji government banker. In 1683 they established the Mitsui Money Exchange House. In 1876 Mitsui became Japan's first private bank.

Like the other meganational Japanese banks, Mitsui derives its real power from its alliances. Following an ancient tradition of *zaibatsu*, or "money cliques," Japanese businesses are sequestered into *keiretsu*, a system of quasi cartels. Dominated by lead banks that are committed to provide financing and see them through troubled times, the companies also act as preferred suppliers to one another. These business "families" meet regularly and obey a set of unspoken rules that generally exclude foreigners from the business club. To stabilize share prices and to fend off unwelcome takeover attempts, the companies own shares of one another's stock.

The zaibatsu were disbanded and declared illegal after World War II, and the conglomerate companies split up. However, the groups continued to meet quietly and unofficially as lunch clubs. Eventually, under the new label "keiretsu," they reorganized, following their prewar patterns fairly closely. The old banks assumed their previous names, and business carried on as it had in the past.

Mitsui Taiyo Kobe is lead banker for the keiretsu that includes about 40 companies, many with Mitsui in their names. These companies also include Toshiba, Oji Paper, and Sapporo Breweries.

• *The meganational companies have a profound international presence. They command deference and attention wherever they do business.*

At 125-years-old, Nestlé SA is the eminent industrial corporation in Switzerland. Yet as the world's largest food processor, 98 percent of Nestlé's sales are outside Switzerland. Chocolate, coffee beans, wine, milk products, and fruit juices (and an endless list of other things) are collected from diverse regions of the globe and sold in other far-flung geographic areas. The company buys about one tenth of the world's green coffee beans for its Nescafe, Taster's Choice, Hills Bros., MJB, and Chase & Sanborn brands. Nestlé manufactures in every market in the world, with 197,000 employees and 421 factories in 61 countries. The company's U.S. operation alone produces sales of $7 billion.

How is it possible to run a company that big? Organized in a highly decentralized way, Nestlé can be described as a "confederation." Its 200 operating units enjoy a great deal of autonomy. They function within the guidelines of long-term policies that are established by the directors, but meant to be adapted to local conditions.

• *The world's most influential companies are at the vanguard of essential, forward-looking technologies or services.*

Whether it is providing a commodity as fundamental as food, medicine, and money, or a technology as complex as space-based communication, transportation, and electronics, there are certain tasks the meganational performs better than any other company.

Two American corporations, Merck & Co. and Bristol-Myers Squibb, compete for the title of the largest pharmaceutical company worldwide. In terms of assets and sales that include consumer products, Bristol-Myers was 1990 champ; measured by market value and profits, Merck took top honors. There is little doubt that, together, they dominate the ethical drug business.

Merck holds the largest share—almost 5 percent—of the international market for prescription drugs. Faced with that size of competition, Bristol-Myers and Squibb, separate companies and way back in the pack, decided to merge in 1989. Bristol-Myers Squibb, which vows to become "Number 1 by 2001," holds 3.5 percent of the prescription drug market. It also sells a familiar range of over-the-counter medicines (Excedrin, Bufferin, Mineral Ice, etc.) and consumer products (Ban deodorant, PreSun sunscreen lotion, Infamil, and more).

As the global population expands and the populations of the industrialized world grow older, the pharmaceutical businss is destined to prosper. With the advent of biotechnology and the development of genctic engineering, the drug business is even more science driven than it has been in the past. It takes either very large companies, or smaller companies funded by sponsoring organizations, to stay in the race, much less at the lead. Competition in this industry is keen, since both national government and industry leaders know that biotechnology, in particular, is a key growth industry of the future.

Compiling a register of the 25 most powerful companies in the world is an ambitious task. It is also fraught with danger. We are naming those corporations that will dominate business bcyond the turn of the century. They very likely will stand capitalism on its ear. There is always risk in such predictions. Since big companies have been known to fail, there always is the question of survival. Almost every company on the following list has been threatened with extinction at one time or another, yet they endure. They have the staying power of trees that have been grafted from ancient roots. Names may change, old ways must be thrown over for new, but these corporations go on. Each of the companies chosen for this compendium has a tradition of transformation, adaptation, rebirth, and revival.

Besides the dangers of inclusion, there is the question of exclusion. Why embrace Citicorp and reject American Express? Why choose General Motors, often characterized as a sluggish giant that sometimes has equally enormous financial losses, and overlook Ford? American Express and Ford are likely to be around and doing well for some time into the future, as will thousands of other companies. The difference between those included and those excluded is their ability to influence personal lives and public policy—and the potential for that leverage to extend far beyond the end of the century.

The search for the most powerful corporations in the world did not begin with a predetermined number of winners. The roll could have been longer or more brief. In the course of research, however, the following companies emerged at the pinnacle. They are likely to stay at the top of the heap because of their unique combination of qualities. The selection, in short, was based on observation, thoughtful analysis, and logical conclusion. Added to that was the sense that with these corporations we indeed are in the presence of titans.

The companies on this register have a singular air of self-confidence that comes from their unyielding economic grip. They are the aristocrats of the business world. Their chief executives, whether we like the idea or not, will stand with presidents and prime ministers in determining how fast and in what direction the world turns. Like the Medicis and Rothchilds and other great commercial families of the past, however quiet or low-keyed they may be, the voices of the new meganationals will be heard.

While there are more U.S. and European companies on the meganational roll than Japanese, the Japanese banks tend to rank highest on the list. Their elephantine size is derived from the keiretsu system. Because antitrust laws are different in Japan, these banks have been allowed alliances with the customers that U.S. banks cannot enjoy. Likewise, Deutsche Bank holds shares in many German companies it serves and, according to German law, is not required to disclose the details of those holdings.

Germany's other contenders base their prowess on the German reputation for engineering excellence. Likewise, the United States shows its strength in manufacturing and high technology. The British and Dutch corporations on the roster reflect the early, world-trader status of these nations. The European companies, taken as a group, represent the predominant companies of the emerging European Economic Community. If the EC lives up to its highest expectation and the Eastern European countries take their place in the free market system, these European giants will grow even more prodigious. The meganational mix reflects the emerging new world economic order. In all, there are 11 U.S.; 6 Japanese; 3 German; 2 Anglo-Dutch; and 1 each British, Swiss, and Italian meganational corporations.

The Meganationals
(Ranked by size: industrial sales or bank assets)

Name	Country	Size
Dai-Ichi Kangyo Bank	Japan	$470.2 billion

The lead financier for dozens of keiretsu companies including Shiseido, Kawasaki Heavy Industries, Isuzu, and Fujitsu.

Mitsui Taiyo Kobe Bank	Japan	$438.6 billion

The nucleus of an industrial organization that includes Toyota Motor Corporation, Toshiba Corporation, and Showa Aircraft Industry.

Sumitomo Bank	Japan	$428.6 billion

The primary lender to an industrial group that includes all the Sumitomo companies, plus electric giant NEC. Owns a major part of Goldman Sachs, an old-line New York investment bank.

Mitsubishi Bank	Japan	$419.7 billion

This bank is an important supplier of funds to the many Mitsubishi companies, Kirin Brewery, and Nikon camera.

Deutsche Bank	Germany	$266.5 billion

Following the creation of a single European Community market in 1992, Deutsche Bank is key contender for the title of pan-European superbank.

Citicorp	United States	$217.3 billion

In terms of presence and range of services, Citicorp is the premier global financial service company, despite its 1991 financial crisis that required an infusion of capital.

Exxon Corporation	United States	$116 billion

Concerned about inflation? Check Exxon's oil and gas pricing policy. The single largest influence on consumer prices is wielded by big oil companies, of which Exxon is king.

| General Motors Corporation | United States | $107 billion |

Still the largest industrial corporation in the world, GM has diversified, modernized, and built foreign markets.

| Royal Dutch Petroleum/Royal Dutch/Shell | United Kingdom/ Netherlands | $106.4 billion |

RDP owns 60 percent of RD/S, and has no other function. The Shell companies handle about one tenth of the non-Communist world's oil and natural gas.

| International Business Machines | United States | $69 billion |

Only IBM can force other computer makers to conform to its standards. Few other companies can jolt the entire stock market when its share price takes a dive, as IBM did when it announced disappointing results in 1991.

| British Petroleum Company plc | United Kingdom | $63.6 billion |

British Petroleum owns Standard Oil of Ohio, and the Kuwait Investment Office owns nearly 10 percent of BP, Britain's largest industrial concern and the world's third-largest oil and natural resource company.

| General Electric Company | United States | $58.4 billion |

Evolving from the wizardry of Thomas Edison, GE is now diversified into television broadcasting, medical technology, financial services, and numerous other shrewdly chosen fields.

| Daimler-Benz Group | Germany | $57.3 billion |

In addition to Mercedes-Benz vehicles, Daimler is involved in electronic, aviation, and space manufacturing. It owns Messerschmitt-Bolkow-Blohm GmbH.

| Hitachi, Ltd. | Japan | $52.1 billion |

Hitachi is Japan's leading manufacturer of electrical machinery. Somewhat independent because it is new by Japanese standards (founded in 1910), Hitachi belongs to several keiretsu.

| Philip Morris Companies, Inc. | United States | $51.2 billion |

Philip Morris's product line isn't particularly healthy (cigarettes, Velveeta cheese, pastry goods, Jello, coffee, and salty snacks) but consumers gobble them up. Tobacco sales are booming in Third World countries and Philip Morris remains the industry leader.

| Fiat Group | Italy | $50 billion |

One of Europe's leading car makers, Fiat has telecommunications, robotics, bioengineering, aerospace, and financial services. It dominates the Italian economy.

| I.E. du Pont de Nemours | United States | $40 billion |

Du Pont, which started out in gunpowder and explosives, has become synonymous with brilliant organic chemistry. Du Pont tells shareholders it seeks to be "the premier global partner."

| Unilever plc and N.V. | United Kingdom/ Netherlands | $39.6 billion |

In 1989, Unilever acquired 55 companies at a total cost of $3 billion. True to the early days of soap and margarine, most of Unilever's products smell and taste good.

| Matsushita Electric Industrial Co. Ltd. | Japan | $44.1 billion |

With its Panasonic and National brands, Matsushita is pacesetter in the consumer electronics field, ranging from semiconductors to bread machines. In the Japanese tradition of ancestor worship, Matsushita employees are encouraged to venerate the founder.

| Siemens AG | Germany | $42.1 billion |

Once thought of as stodgy, Siemens went on an acquisition spree and changed its image. The electronics and telecommunications leviathan will profit from German unification.

| American Telephone & Telegraph Company | United States | $37.3 billion |

Ma Bell once had the last word when it came to telephones, but few Americans wanted to see the company split up. Never mind. AT&T recovered and gets noticeably bigger every year.

| Nestlé SA | Switzerland | $36.2 billion |

The leading food company in the world, Nestlé's brand names are ubiquitous: Carnation, Quik chocolate mix, Lean Cuisine, Taster's Choice, Nescafe and other coffees, Friskies dog food, and on and on.

| Bristol-Myers Squibb Company | United States | $10.3 billion |

Newly united Bristol-Myers and Squibb own an impressive list of proprietary drugs and beauty and household products, and new ones are in the pipeline. Also a leader in baby formula.

| The Coca-Cola Company | United States | $10.2 billion |

Coca-Cola tried diversification, but its soft drinks and juice business does so well there didn't seem much point. Coke is the most recognized brand name in the world.

| Merck & Co Inc. | United States | $7.6 billion |

Considered one of the best-managed and innovative pharmaceutical companies, Merck produces more than 1,000 products for human and animal health. More than half of Merck's business is international.

* Ranking is subject to change from year to year.

Data Chart—Companies

Company Name	Nation	Date Founded	Latest Assets ($ billion)
AT&T	U.S.	1885	43.7 (90)
Bristol-Myers Squibb	U.S.	1887	9.2 (90)
British Petroleum	U.K.	1909	59.2 (90)
Citicorp	U.S.	1812	217.3 (91)
Coca-Cola	U.S.	1886	8.2 (89)
Dai-Ichi Kangyo Bank	Japan	1873	470.2 (90)
Daimler-Benz	Germany	1926	10.3 (89)
Deutsche Bank	Germany	1879	266.5 (90)
Du Pont	U.S.	1802	38.1 (89)
Exxon	U.S.	1882	83.2 (89)
Fiat	Italy	1899	46.3 (89)
General Electric	U.S.	1892	180.3 (90)
General Motors	U.S.	1916	96.7 (89)
Hitachi	Japan	1920	49.3 (90)
IBM	U.S.	1911	87.5 (90)
Matsushita	Japan	1918	49.4 (90)
Merck	U.S.	1891	8.01 (90)
Mitsubishi Bank	Japan	1880	419.7 (90)
Mitsui Taiyo Kobe Bank	Japan	1876	438.6 (90)
Nestlé SA	Switzerland	1866	28 (90)
Philip Morris	U.S.	1847	46.5 (90)
Royal Dutch Petroleum/Shell	Dutch/U.K.	1890	28.9 (89)
Siemens	German	1847	40.1*
Sumitomo Bank	Japan	1895	428.6 (90)
Unilever	Dutch/U.K.	1930	14.3

* Approximation based on Jan. 1991 exchange rate.

Data Chart—Companies, con't.

Co. Name	Latest Sales/Assets ($ billions)	Industries	Brand Names
		<and keiretsu connections>	
AT&T	37.3	Information movement, management, and products	AT&T Paradyne Istel Unix
Bristol-Myers Squibb	10.3	Medical, household, beauty, infant formula	Clairol, Bufferin, Drano, Windex, Endust, Enfamil
British Petroleum	63.6	Petroleum, chemicals, coal, minerals	BP, Standard Oil
Citicorp	217.3	Consumer and global financial services	Citibank
Coca-Cola	10.2	Soft drinks, juices, and other beverages	Coke, Fanta, Minute Maid, Hi-C
Dai-Ichi Kangyo Bank	470.2	City bank, lottery, Fujitsu, etc.	Heart Finance, CIT Group
Daimler-Benz	57.3	Autos, trucks, aircraft, medical, office and communications equipment	Mercedes-Benz, Dornier, Messer-schmitt, etc.
Deutsche Bank	39.3	Commercial, mortgage, investment, international banking, leasing	Morgan Grenfell, Banco-trans, H. Albert de Bary, etc.
Du Pont	40	Chemicals, petroleum, explosives, coal	Dacron, Lycra, Orlon, Teflon, Conoco Oil, Remington, Kevlar
Exxon	116	Oil, gas, coal, minerals, petro-chemicals, electric power	Exxon, Esso, Hong Kong Power

Data Chart—Companies, con't.

Co. Name	Latest Sales/Assets ($ billions)	Industries	Brand Names
Fiat	50	Autos, trucks, aviation, insurance, retailing	Fiat, Alfa Romeo, Lancia, Ferrari,
General Electric	58.4	Aerospace, aircraft, consumer electrical products, appliances, communications, financial services	GE, Hotpoint, NBC, Calma, RCA, Monogram
General Motors	107	Autos, trucks, aircraft, defense products, computers, finance	Pontiac, Buick, Olds, Cadillac, Chevrolet, GMC, Opel, Saab, Lotus, EDS, Hughes Aircraft and Electronics
Hitachi	52.1	Electric machinery, nuclear power, TVs, VCRs, semiconductors, computers, automotive products	Hitachi, Maxell
IBM	69.02	Information technology, computers, software, chips	IBM
Matsushita	44.1	Audio and video equipment, home appliances, electronics,	Panasonic, JVC, Quasar, Victor, National,

Data Chart—Companies, con't.

Co. Name	Latest Sales/Assets ($ billions)	Industries	Brand Names
		batteries, entertainment	Technics, MCA
Merck	7.6	Pharmaceutical, chemical, food and consumer products	Calgon, Mylanta
Mitsubishi Bank	419.7	City Bank, corporate and international banking, trade financing, foreign exchange	Mitsubishi Bank, Bank of California, Diamond
Mitsui Taiyo Kobe	438.6	Universal Bank, Toshiba, Toyota	Mitsui Manufacturers Bank
Nestlé S.A.	36.2	Food, pharmaceuticals, cosmetics	Carnation, Hills Bros., Nestlé, Stouffer, Alcon, L'Oreal
Philip Morris	51.2	Cigarettes, Food, Beer, Real estate	Marlboro, Virginia Slims, Merit, Benson & Hedges, Kraft, Miller Beer, Oscar Mayer, Mission Viejo
Royal Dutch Petroleum/Shell	106.4	Petroleum, chemicals, coal, metals	Shell, Euroshell, Repsol, Billiton
Siemens	42.1	Electrical machinery, power supply, medical, computer, communications, and	Siemens, Nixdorf, Stromberg Carlson, Plessey, Plaisir,

Data Chart—Companies, con't.

Co. Name	Latest Sales/Assets ($ billions)	Industries	Brand Names
		defense equipment, transportation	Osram
Sumitomo Bank	428.6	Global bank, NEC	Goldman Sachs
Unilever	39.6	Food, drinks, detergents, personal products, chemicals, agribusiness	Flora, Country Crock, Lipton, Elizabeth Arden, Pears, Cutex, Ponds, Pepsodent

Meganationals Ranked by Size	($ billion)
Dai-Ichi Kangyo Bank	470.2
Mitsui Taiyo Kobe Bank	438.6
Sumitomo Bank	428.6
Mitsubishi Bank	419.7
Deutsche Bank	266.5
Citicorp	217.3
Exxon Corporation	116
General Motors	107
Royal Dutch Petroleum/Shell	106.4
IBM	69.02
British Petroleum	63.6
General Electric	58.4
Daimler-Benz	57.3
Hitachi	52.1
Philip Morris	51.2
Fiat	50
I.E. du Pont de Nemours	40
Unilever	39.6
Matsushita	44.1
Siemens	42.1

Data Chart—Companies, concluded

Meganationals Ranked by Size	($ billion)
American Telephone & Telegraph	37.3
Nestlé S.A.	36.2
Bristol-Myers Squibb	10.3
Coca-Cola	10.2
Merck	7.6

Chapter Three

The Men behind
the Money

*"Whoever sits down behind a desk begins to think differently;
his vision of the world and his hierarchy of values change. From
then on he will divide humanity into those who have desks and
those who do not, and into significant owners of desks and
insignificant ones. He will now see his life as a frenzied progress
from a small desk to a larger one, from a low desk to a higher
one, from a narrow desk to a wider desk. Once ensconced behind
a desk he masters a distinct language and knows things—even if
yesterday, deskless, he knew nothing. I have lost many friends
for reasons of desks. . . . The desk, after all, has one more
dangerous property: It can serve as an instrument of self-
justification."*

Ryszard Kapuscinski

As wife of the president of the United States, Nancy Reagan's appearance clearly was important to her. With the help of some of the nation's leading designers, she sported marvelously stylish clothes. Her hair certainly deserved no less attention. According to *New York* magazine, Julius, a hairdresser from Beverly Hills, California, flew to Washington every three weeks to color Mrs. Reagan's hair with a mixture of Clairol's Chestnut and Moonlight Gold hair dye. During that time the stylist, the magazine said, heard a rumor that Clairol would be dropping his consulting fee. Very sad, for it was this contract that made the trip to Washington affordable for him. According to the magazine, Mrs. Reagan had an approach made to someone at Clairol, and the company decided to keep Julius on the payroll.

Julius told *New York* he had heard a rumor about his contract and had been worried enough to mention it to Mrs. Reagan. "But I don't think she intervened," Julius said. "All I know is Clairol didn't discontinue me."[1]

Certainly if the White House wanted to pull strings, they knew whom to call. Richard Gelb, chairman and chief executive of Bristol-Myers Squibb, the company that owns Clairol, has close ties to the Republican Party. He had, in fact, known then-Vice President George Bush for years. His brother Bruce Gelb, who was president of Bristol-Myers, also is a major Republican party fundraiser. Bruce Gelb left the company in 1989, first to head the U.S. Information Agency and eventually to serve as Ambassador to Belgium in the Bush administration. Thus are built the Washington contacts so important to a company that must petition federal agencies for product approval and that sells millions of dollars worth of its output to government programs.

The Gelbs came to Bristol-Myers through a merger with Clairol decades earlier. The brothers can best be described as corporate aristocrats. Their parents founded Clairol, then prepared their sons properly for an inherited role in business. The young Gelbs attended the Phillips Academy in New England when George Bush was a student there. Bruce Gelb, in fact, said that the president has been his hero ever since Bush rescued him from a bully in prep school. The Gelb brothers, like Bush, then moved on to Yale. Bush and Richard Gelb graduated with the class of '48. Finally, both Gelbs went on to Harvard for MBAs. They joined dad's company, and less than a decade later Richard became president and Bruce was elevated to executive vice president.

It is Richard Gelb who runs the show, and though one might say he was handed the job on a silver platter, he directs the show with considerable skill. Richard Gelb helped sell Clairol to Bristol-Myers, a much larger firm, in 1959. Then, on the basis of his marketing expertise, he rose to the top of that corporation. Even before the Squibb merger, the company had an impressive line of well-known consumer products, including Drano, Windex, and, of course, Clairol hair supplies. It also sells infant formula, patent medicines, and pharmaceutical drugs.

Though Richard Gelb traces his lineage from the cosmetics side of the business, paradoxically, he strove to lessen Bristol-Myers dependence on over-the-counter remedies and pushed the company into prescription drugs. The company has made cancer cures one of its specialties. Richard Gelb, interestingly enough, in 1986 won a battle of his own with stomach cancer.

Even before Gelb engineered the much-admired merger with Squibb, shareholders had every reason to be pleased with his stewardship. A $1,000 investment made at the end of 1977 in Bristol-Myers, if dividends had been reinvested, was worth $5,940 by mid-1988. By that time, Bristol-Myers had a market value of $12 billion, putting it safely outside the reach of corporate raiders. However, the company was not big enough to satisfy Richard Gelb. It was not a leading contender. Throughout the 1980s, mergers were rampant, and Gelb spied an opportunity.

Through a mutual pal he contacted another long-time friend, Richard Furlaud of Squibb Corporation and proposed a friendly corporate union. It turned out to be one of the savviest business deals of the 1980s.

The $11.5 billion merger was accomplished with an old-fashioned stock swap. "There is no cash, there are no mortgages, no rinky-dink, no junk bonds, no special deals," Furlaud said. Eventually, of course, there was to be no Furlaud, but we'll get to that later.

By combining the 12th and 14th largest pharmaceutical companies in the world, Bristol-Myers Squibb leap-frogged to second place. When all of the corporate elements are taken into consideration, Bristol-Myers Squibb is slightly weightier than Merck, the world's largest ethical drug producer. Yet even in the high-stakes game of pharmaceuticals where Merck leads, it is Gelb's goal to make Bristol-Myers Squibb "Number one by 2001."

Considering Richard Gelb's track record, that goal has an honest chance of becoming reality. Though he is described as gentlemanly, Gelb has not achieved success without making difficult decisions that have touched and changed the lives of many individuals.

As Bristol-Myers and Squibb moved through the merger process, about 2,000 people lost their jobs, and another 2,000 jobs were being considered for elimination. To abolish duplicate effort, the company shuttered half of its 60 pharmaceuticals plants worldwide, as well as 6 of 18 consumer product plants. Plans for a new 1.1

million square foot, $240 million Squibb corporate headquarters planned for Plainsboro, New Jersey, was put on hold indefinitely.

Communities in New Jersey felt a difference on the very day the Bristol-Myers Squibb merger was announced. While Squibb was an independent company operating out of Princeton, Richard Furlaud was normally available to the press. It was relatively easy to get information on research programs, building projects, hirings and layoffs, personnel changes, and so forth. The Princeton area felt comfortable with Squibb as a corporate citizen. That changed with the merger. Though Furlaud became president of the combined companies, he also became unavailable to reporters. Even on the day of his retirement in 1991, according to reporters in the area, company spokesmen said Furlaud was not reachable for comment. "Too busy to talk," said the corporate handlers. Furlaud's retirement came two years before he had been expected to leave the company.

In most cases, the only people at Bristol-Myers Squibb with the time to chat were in the public relations office, and their offerings primarily were limited to press releases, annual reports, and other prepared company literature. The curtain on the corporate stage, as far as Central New Jersey was concerned, had snapped shut.

The loftier level of news and information management to which Bristol-Myers Squibb had ascended is of particular concern, considering the critical medical, nutrition, and other products with which the company is involved. Bristol-Myers, for example, has developed an alternative AIDS drug, called Videx or ddI. It also is a key manufacturer and distributor of commercial infant formula, a $1.6 billion business in the United States alone. With Infamil and seven other products, Bristol-Myers is one of the top three formula producers worldwide. Those three companies control 95 percent of the U.S. market and distribute products extensively worldwide.

In earlier decades, Bristol-Myers and its competitors were targeted by children's activists, who objected to the way infant formula was marketed, especially in the poorest regions of the world. The critics said the companies were encouraging parents to use formula as a substitute for mother's milk. Aside from being less nutritional and more expensive, there was another serious complaint. Babies in Third World countries were dying as a result, because the formula had to be mixed with water and local water supplies often were contaminated. Eventually, when formula makers were pressured by consumer and religious groups into complying with the World Health Organization's Code of Ethics for the Marketing of Breast-milk Substitutes, the furor subsided. The infant formula battlefront was not quiet for long, as it turns out.

In 1991, Bristol-Myers, along with the two other industry leaders, was charged in a Floida state court with fixing and inflating formula prices in sales to the Special Supplemental Food Program for Women, Infants & Children (WIC). This program provides formula to low-income mothers in the United States, feeding nearly one third of all babies born in this country.

In many states, formula for the WIC program is purchased through competitive bidding, in which the formula makers promise rebates on retail prices. When the 1990 bids came in, rebates were 32 percent lower than the previous year's offers. Oddly enough, the bids of Bristol-Myers and the other two prime manufacturers were within pennies of each other. On top of that, there was a disturbing trend in retail pricing. Infant formula prices had increased 150 percent in 15 years, growing six times faster than the cost of the main ingredient—cow's milk.[2]

Bristol-Myers and the other defendants (Abbott Laboratories, maker of Similac and American Home Products, producer of Nursoy) denied any wrongdoing. In fact, spokesmen pointed out that the companies had spent hundreds of millions of dollars on rebates, enabling the states to add many thousands of infants to the WIC rolls.

Bristol-Myers spokesman Rolland M. Eckles called the antitrust allegations "hogwash," and the similar bids coincidental. He added that WIC had eroded profits for each of the companies. "The infant-formula companies (can't) give large rebates forever," Eckles said.

The practice of companies like Bristol-Myers to donate formula samples to hospitals and childbirth centers is also the subject of controversy. Some health care providers get education and research grants from the formula makers in return for the exclusive right to supply formula. These medical facilities then send the formula home with families in the baby's discharge packet. The parents assume, quite naturally, that this is the formula recommended by the hospital, and hesitate to switch brands. Even if the sample formula costs more, parents stick with it for what they believe is the baby's sake. Sample distribution has been an effective marketing technique. Some doctors and parents have decried the practice as misleading and unethical. Both the price-fixing and the give-away disputes have yet to be settled.

Gelb and other top executives in the health care field hold keys to the availability, quality, and cost of medical care for millions of persons, not only in the United States, but worldwide.

This is an industry where the adage "it takes money to make money" applies. While there is no verification for these numbers, the pharmaceutical companies estimate it costs $200 million to $231 million to bring a new drug into the market. Though costs are high, so are profits. Through the 1980s, earnings grew an average of 13.5 percent per year at Bristol-Myers, and dividends to shareholders increased an average of 19 percent annually. Bristol-Myers in 1990 had a 17.4 percent net profit margin, and Merck had 24 percent.

Though Gelb makes decisions daily that determine what medicines are developed for which illnesses; how a great number of patent medicines, cleaning supplies, and consumer goods will be priced; and what communities get or lose jobs, he seldom talks publicly on these matters or any other subject. Based on his messages in the company's annual reports, Gelb's overriding concern, like that of most other chief executives, is how best to maximize profits for shareholders. It is shareholders, after all, who are the nearest thing to a boss that Richard Gelb has.

Drug and health industry leaders play a profound role in the contemporary human experience. If there is a single trait that binds all people, it is the desire to live and to be healthy. Few events make individuals in the rapidly spreading industrial society more vulnerable than to suffer ill health. In cultures where families are small, scattered, and not self-sustaining—and where social safety nets often are absent or insufficient—people must be capable of paid work.

Most of the meganationals operate in industries that are fundamental, in one way or another, to our comfort, safety, or well-being. Food, medicine, transportation, weapons for defense, communications, and sufficient capital and technology to keep nations strong and employment high—these are the keys to corporate authority. Certainly these powerful company leaders are steadfastly linked to economic stability—not to mention the prosperity, of the globe.

How strange it is that so little is known about the men who make choices so critical to international survival, economic security, and global prosperity.

Throughout the world, government leaders are exposed to public scrutiny. Writers, musicians, and artists reveal themselves through their work. We get to know, face to face, the educators, physicians, and others who influence our daily lives. But somewhere offstage in the darkened wings is a group of men who influence government officials, determine whether a local economy prospers or withers, and, too often, have a say over whether we live or die. They are the meganational corporate leaders. Even employees of these massive operations may know managers only a few rungs up the corporate ladder from where they are. The worker may never see, speak to, or even partially understand the person who can reconfigure her or his destiny with a single telephone call, the dictation of a memo, or a simple lifting of an eyebrow to the appropriate vice president.

Who are these aloof people? How did they get where they are? Why do they do what they do? Can we trust them?

Richard Gelb of Bristol-Myers Squibb could be called the prototype for each of the top executives of the major meganationals, whether the executive is Japanese, British, or any other nationality.

• For the most part, these are company men. The majority— virtually all of the leaders of the six meganational banks, for example—have worked for the same company their entire lives. They have strong identity ties to the corporations they head, and in most circumstances their foremost loyalty is to the corporation. Those who have not served the same corporation in a lifelong tenure invariably have, like Richard Gelb, and like Michael Miles of Philip Morris, come very close. At the very least, they have toiled in the same industry.

• In the same way that Gelb is, they often are isolated from the public. Just as often they even are shielded from their own employees by a Maginot line of corporate "communicators." However much General Motors was able to discredit the independent semi-documentary movie "Roger and Me," the film did accurately depict the inaccessibility of modern corporate dignitaries. Philosopher and linguist Noam Chomsky notes that the public relations function is a 20th-century creation, and amounts to nothing more or less than mind control.

• Some corporate leaders, such as Gelb and Giovanni Agnelli, chairman of Fiat, have blood lines to the company. A few of the corporations, such as Du Pont and Unilever, count descendants of the founders as major shareholders, but family members no longer head the companies.

These ascendants to the seat of power take on many of the trappings of aristocracy, especially of those from when being a royal also meant being rich. Agnelli, for example, is sometimes called the "king" of Italy. And why not? He presides over nearly all Italian automobile production, owns a quarter of Italy's stock exchange, publishes two leading newspapers and numerous magazines, and owns a soccer team.

• While few CEOs can match the social status of Agnelli, like Gelb, most of those at the corporate crest are well connected. They've attended their country's most prestigious schools. And, especially within their own country, they know one another.

Sixteen of the 25 meganationals either have a company representative sitting on a board of another meganational, or have a meganational officer on their own board. Deutsche Bank has representatives on both the Siemens and Daimler-Benz boards. Among the relatively few companies that have cross-national links, Deutsche also has a board of directors affiliation with Unilever plc. Royal Dutch Petroleum shows its internationalism as well by inviting representatives from IBM and Unilever to sit on the supervisory board. IBM and Du Pont have the most ties with other meganationals, four each. The exception to this cross-fertilization of boards is with Japanese corporations. There, the keiretsu or corporate cartels serve the same purpose. Furthermore, Japanese banks have greater control of the management of the companies to which they lend. In Japan the linkage between the largest companies is less visible on paper, but it is more substantive in practice.

Board of Directors Connections

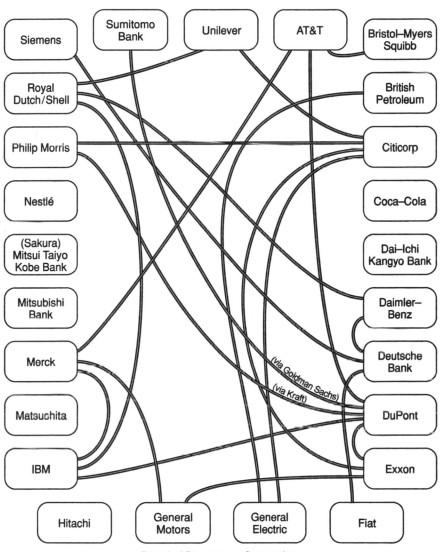

Board of Directors — Connections

For each of the companies, however, these bonds are por-
tentous. Leaders meet other leaders at regular board meetings.
Ideas are exchanged. Attitudes are influenced. In many cases, the
companies end up doing business together.

A study conducted by professors at Dartmouth's Amos Tuck
Graduate School of Business Administration implies that having a
chief executive who enjoys a high standing in the business or
political community, or is on the social register, helps the company
to carry out friendly mergers. It is through mergers, essentially, that
the meganational companies have achieved and preserve their
dominance.

In studying 106 takeover deals announced between 1983 and
1986, the professors found the smoothest mergers involved
wealthy, well-connected managers and directors. There are several
theories as to why this is true. One is that prestigious executives
tend to have powerful roles on the boards. They often control the
board, and thus have the latitude to independently woo a candidate
or to cooperate with a bidder. Certainly stellar connections played a
paramount role in the Bristol-Myers Squibb merger. Richard Gelb
initiated merger discussions through American Express CEO
James D. Robinson. Robinson was friendly with Squibb's Furlaud,
and sat on the Bristol-Myers board as well. Robinson now is a board
member of the merged companies.

• Many of these businessmen, especially in Japan and Europe
where industrial policy is formulated through consensus of the
public and private sector, have close relationships with government
leaders. As mentioned earlier, many retired Japanese bureaucrats
move on to top jobs at Japanese corporations. In any case, by
various lobbying tactics, they all attempt to influence government
action, not only in their home country but in the various other
countries in which their companies operate. Through industrial
associations, private fundraising, or company political action committees, many chief executives, like the Gelbs and like AT&T's
Robert Allen, are generous political contributors.

Though the meganational leaders hardly need an international
cabal to make their clout felt, a surprising number sit on David
Rockefeller's enigmatic Trilateral Commission. Agnelli of Fiat, and
executives from Mitsubishi, Sumitomo, Dai-Ichi Kangyo, Deutsche Bank, AT&T, General Electric, Exxon, General Motors, and

Coca-Cola have been associated with the organization over the years. If they attended meetings long and faithfully enough, they will have rubbed shoulders with members excused for public service, President George Bush; U.S. director of the powerful Office of Management and Budget, Richard C. Darman; chairman of the Federal Reserve Board, Alan Greenspan; U.S. Trade Representative, Carla Hills; and assistant to President Bush for National Security Affairs, Brent Scowcroft.

The stated purpose of the Trilateral commission, by the way, is innocent enough. ". . . far from being a coterie of international conspirators with designs on covertly ruling the world," said Rockefeller, "the Trilateral Commission is, in reality, a group of concerned citizens interested in fostering greater understanding and cooperation among international allies."[3]

Among women, minorities, and other disenfranchised people, this is called networking. The importance and the power of networking are well documented. It was this knowledge that inspired women to force Rotary International to open up its ranks. All the world knew you don't join Rotary Club just to get a good lunch once a month.

• The leaders of the world's most powerful corporations tend to be married and well educated, and most of them either served in World War II, could have served, or at least are able to remember the war.

• This also means that many of the men whose names appear on the directory at the end of this chapter are nearing the twilight of their careers.

While this presents the possibility of a new generation of managers with fresh ideologies regarding business, it is unlikely that the changeover will lead to smaller companies. In fact, in Germany, where the CEOs of about half the top companies are faced with mandatory retirement in the next few years, the incoming leaders are expected to be more global in their outlook. The replacement for Alfred Herrhausen, after his assassination, was eagerly anticipated as a harbinger of what the prospective group of German CEOs would be like. Hilmar Kopper, Herrhausen's strategy adviser and one of Deutsche Bank's representatives on the Daimler-Benz and Siemens supervisory boards, got the job. Kopper is a Deutsche Bank career officer. "There is no doubt that Deutsche will keep to the expansionist global strategy established by Herrhausen," wrote *Euromoney* magazine following Kopper's appointment. "The management board has made the strategy its own."[4]

Though not everyone will concur with their personal philosophies, most of these men are urbane, intelligent, and have iron-clad personalities. Granted, some observers disagree with that appraisal too. Probably one of the harshest critics of corporate management today is Harvard economist John Kenneth Galbraith.

"There is a widespread impression that the association with large sums of money," Galbraith has said, "involves a special intelligence and therefore should be left to the specialists. But anyone acquainted with the top bankers of our day or the leading financial geniuses of Wall Street or our large corporations knows that you can encounter some of the most limited men to be found anywhere."[5]

On the other hand, perhaps the world could do worse than to have the meganational managers grasping at the helm of global destiny. Governments, after all, seldom earn accolades for administering the world efficiently. Business leaders, it is often proclaimed, could easily do a better job at running the public sector. Maybe they could—if you have no objection to an authoritarian form of rule, that is. While it is true that most chief executives have passed through a rigorous selection process while working their way to the top, they are, for the most part, self-selected. These are ambitious men. They fought for their leadership positions, and often will protect their jobs at great cost. Once a chief executive reaches the pinnacle, unelected by any voting body except a small, incestuous board of directors, he can rule unchallenged.

In theory at least, company managers are beholden to the shareholders for their authority. But Galbraith insisted that even shareholder control is an illusion.

"There is a basic anomaly there that was emphasized by such scholars as (Adolph) Burley and (Gardner) Means in the 1930s, not just by myself," explained Galbraith. "That anomaly is that the current corporate system puts into positions of great power people who ultimately are responsible only to themselves. Beyond a certain point in a corporation, there is enough diffusion of the common stock so that management can appoint directors who are under the control of the management."

Only a vital investor or a lender of large amounts of capital can unseat a chief executive. The least clever CEO, therefore, arranges for the board to approve a "poison pill" or "golden parachute" agreement that permits the CEO to fend off threats to his job, and makes certain that he will take a lot of money with him, in the event he is forced to depart. Squibb's Richard Furlaud and 36 other Squibb executives collected $21 million under an accelerated incentive plan, for agreeing to an amicable merger with Bristol-Myers. In addition, these executives carried over generous severance pay provisions, in case they quit or were fired from the merged company. The money, of course, came from the shareholders' pot.

The amazing independence of chief executive officers, especially in the United States, again was demonstrated during the recession of 1990 and 1991. Despite lagging sales and poor earnings by most corporations, salaries for top executives continued to climb. Forty-eight percent of the Forbes 800 chief executives earned more than $1 million in total compensation each in 1991. Of those, 161 were paid more than $2 million, 35 more than $5 million, and 8 made more than $10 million.

The regulatory agencies do little to defend shareholders against abusive pay practices by the corporate elite. In 1990, the U.S. Securities and Exchange Commission was asked by 15 corporations whether the companies were required to present shareholders' proposals on compensation at the annual meeting. The SEC said the corporations did not have to do so.

At a Senate hearing on corporate pay, a compensation expert testified that the average chief executive at a large American corporation received 110 times the pay of the company's average worker. Outside the United States, exploitation isn't so rampant. The top executive at a Japanese company, by comparison, earns around 17 times the pay of an average Japanese worker. In Germany, the gap is 23 times.

When a corporation is growing and shareholders see continued good earnings, few complain. Unfortunately, even in bad times many CEOs continue to feather their nests. In 1991, when IBM was facing its fifth consecutive year of declining profitability and 47,000 workers had lost their jobs, IBM chairman John Akers prospered. In 1990, his pay and bonus leapt 185 percent to more than $2.2 million.

Though the heads of the 25 most powerful meganationals are lavishly compensated for their efforts (in most cases among those earning more than $1 million a year), they do not rank among the most abusive international executives, in terms of pay. Even so, like other corporate leaders, they name their own price.

"Hence the anomaly, an enterprise that is presumed to be maximizing revenues for the stockholders, but in which the stockholders have no power," Galbraith continued. "I've likened this to someone who is expected to maximize the erotic opportunities for someone else, but who forgoes it himself or herself."

To compound the problems presented by concentration of power in a single person or group of people, Galbraith says, "We have a government that of late has backed away from its oversight duties; it has taken a hands-off approach."

Unfortunately, the government has gone beyond averting its gaze. Because they depend upon corporate leaders and business political action committees for campaign funding, and because constituents clamor for economic security, politicians habitually take their instructions from the corporate elite. In fact, many elected officials are de facto representatives of corporate interests in public policy. When all is said and done, the meganational corporate leaders are granted unimaginable control over the only effective means of international power—money.

Chief executive officers/the meganationals

AT&T–Robert F. Allen, Chairman and Chief Executive Officer, born 1935.

Bristol-Myers Squibb–Richard L. Gelb, Chairman and Chief Executive Officer, born 1924.

British Petroleum–Robert B. Horton, Chairman, born 1939.

Citicorp–John S. Reed, Chairman, born 1939.

Coca-Cola–Robert C. Goizueta, Chairman and Chief Executive Officer, born 1931.

Dai-Ichi Kangyo Bank–Ichiro Nakamura, Chairman, born 1926.

Daimler-Benz–Edzard Reuter, Chairman, born 1928.

Deutsche Bank–Hilmar Kopper, Speaker, Board of Managing Directors, born 1935.

Du Pont–Edgar S. Wollard, Jr., Chairman, born 1934.

Exxon–Lawrence G. Rawl, Chairman, born 1928.

Fiat–Giovanni Agnelli, Chairman, born 1921.

General Electric–John F. Welch, born 1935.

General Motors–Robert C. Stempel, Chairman, born 1933.

Hitachi–Katsushige Mita, President and Representative Director, born 1924.

IBM–John F. Akers, Chairman, born 1934.

Matsushita–Masaharu Matsushita, Chairman, born 1912. (Akio Tanii, president, born 1928).

Merck–P. Roy Vagelos, Chairman, President and Chief Executive Officer, born 1928.

Mitsubishi Bank–Kazuo Ibuki, Chairman, born 1920.

Mitsui Taiyo Kobe Bank (renamed Sakura Bank)–Yasuo Matsushita, Chairman, born 1926.

Nestlé–Helmut Maucher, born 1928.

Philip Morris–Michael A. Miles, Chairman and Chief Executive Officer, born 1940.

Royal Dutch Petroleum/Royal Dutch Shell–Lodewijk C. van Wachem, Chairman, Managing Director and President, born 1931.

Siemens–Karlheinz Kaske, Chairman, born 1928.

Sumitomo Bank–Sotoo Tatsumi, Chairman, born 1923.

Unilever–Sir Michael Angus, born 1930 and F. A. Maljers, born 1933, Chairmen

Chapter Four

Worshiping at the Temple of Growth

"A slow sort of country!" said the Queen. "Now, here, you see, it takes all the running you can do, to keep in the same place. If you want to get somewhere else, you must run at least twice as fast as that."

Lewis Carroll, *Through the Looking Glass.*

The western art collection of Japanese trading organization Itoman & Company should have been truly impressive. The company was said to have invested more than $500 million in hundreds of works by such masters as Picasso, Toulouse-Lautrec, and Chagall. Many of the paintings were purchased privately from a gallery that employed the daughter of the then chairman of Sumitomo Bank which, not incidentally, controlled Itoman.

As it turns out, the purchases, which were at highly inflated prices, were not made for the love of things beautiful. Japanese officials suspect the acquisitions were part of an elaborate scheme to conceal transfers of millions of dollars in cash or to evade taxes. The details of these artful exploits are still unraveling in Japan, a country where back-door money exchanges and privacy are part of the fine arts business. However, even by Japanese expectations, the dealings were too much. *Shukan Gendai*, a popular weekly magazine in Japan, described the schemes as the "ultimate zaitech tool." *Zaitech* is Japanese parlance for financial engineering, or the profitable 1980s proclivity for old-line industrial and banking concerns to throw themselves into financial speculation.

The art subterfuge, however, was only part of a broader imbroglio involving Itoman and its main lender, Sumitomo Bank. Sumitomo officials had stepped in to rescue the Osaka trading company when its profitability lagged in the mid-1970s. The company's fortunes revived but, by the end of the 1980s, it appeared that aggressive management and risky real estate investments had led to greater trouble.

Just as Japanese officials were investigating the possibility that the paintings were being bought and sold, among other things, to skirt the government-set yen limits on real estate deals, a top Itoman executive intensified the intrigue by killing himself. Not long afterward, Ichiro Isoda, the Sumitomo chairman whose daughter worked at the art gallery, resigned his position, ostensibly in apology for loans made for stock manipulation by a branch manager. The 77-year-old Isoda, called "the emperor" by his underlings, was considered one of Japan's most powerful bankers. The messy affair reached even more scandalous proportions early in 1991. Contrary to Japan's most revered business traditions, Itoman president Yoshihiko Kawamura was sacked by his board of directors.

Kawamura was the executive who had been dispatched to Itoman by Sumitomo in 1975 to guide the company out of its financial morass. He did exactly that, and by the late 1980s, profits had soared to more than $100 million annually.

But, according to a report in the *Washington Post*, "some of Kawamura's (real estate) acquisitions also were widely viewed as being directed by Sumitomo—and Kawamura's mentor, Isoda—to help maintain the bank's healthy profit performance. For example, Itoman bought a Tokyo condominium company that Sumitomo had helped finance.

"Critics say the takeover of the troubled company (Itoman) was designed to help Sumitomo avoid loan losses. In the eyes of many in the Japanese financial community, Itoman had become a virtual subsidiary of Sumitomo, assuming risks that the bank wanted to shuck off."

The entity at the top of this intrigue of luxury, money, and death was Sumitomo Bank, third largest and frequently the most profitable of Japan's city banks. Sumitomo is among the world's oldest known, continuous business operations, but in Japan it is viewed as something of a maverick because of its emphasis on profits. Sumitomo's prestigious antecedents reach back to the early 16th century and, chiefly on this basis, the bank also is the major player in one of the largest and most influential keiretsu or financial cliques in Japan. Sumitomo's Tokyo and Osaka offices serve 43 of Japan's most prominent companies, including Nippon Electric and all the companies that display Sumitomo in their names. It was this keiretsu or main bank relationship that gave Sumitomo the right and responsibility to appoint management and to act as Itoman's rescuer.

Sumitomo is known as one of Japan's more farsighted banks, and certainly it has been one of the most ambitious and fast-growing Tokyo financial institutions. It made an enlightened, early entry into the United States when it opened a branch in California in 1925. In the past two decades, Sumitomo has pursued the goal of evolving into a global bank, becoming Japan's version of Citicorp. The bank steadily expanded and strengthened its overseas business —particularly with the establishment of Sumitomo Financial International in London in 1973 and the purchase of Banca del Gottardo of Switzerland in 1984. The $144 million Sumitomo paid for Gottardo was the highest amount ever disbursed for a European acquisition by a Japanese company.

In 1986, Osaka-headquartered Sumitomo made two daring moves. First, it absorbed the troubled Heiwa Sogo Bank, a Tokyo-based mutual savings bank that kept long hours and had more than 100 branches near railway stations to collect blue-collar deposits. This acquisition gave the bank a major presence in the Tokyo area, where high real estate prices and entrenched competition make the development of a branch system difficult. However, some observers suggest the deal was evidence of the closeness between the Japanese government and the banking industry there. Heiwa Sogo was in danger of failure and a complex web of insider fraud had been uncovered.

"No sooner had the Ministry of Finance prepared a list of possible merger partners for Heiwa Sogo than Sumitomo volunteered to absorb the insolvent institution," wrote Aron Viner in *Inside Japanese Financial Markets*. "In doing so, it precluded its idol, Citicorp, from pursuing strong acquisitive designs of its own and beat all other banks to the mark. Indeed, before the news regarding Heiwa's insolvency had become public, Sumitomo Bank had already acquired (through its subsidiaries) 34 percent of Heiwa Sogo stock."[1]

Also that year, Sumitomo announced it had bought a $430 million or 12.5 percent interest in the noted New York-based investment bank Goldman Sachs. The venture, as originally envisioned, offered a double advantage to Sumitomo. Sumitomo (along with banks everywhere) eagerly awaits the dismantling of the U.S. Glass-Steagall Act, a U.S. law that separates commercial and investment banking. If and when the Glass-Steagall barriers fall, Sumitomo would be in a superior position to U.S. banks, which would not have been allowed to make the Goldman Sachs acquisition.

As for the second advantage, a Japanese banking regulation also prohibits banks from owning more than 5 percent of a domestic securities company. Goldman Sachs, however, is a member of the Tokyo Stock Exchange, which would have breached the wall into the securities business for Sumitomo.

Ultimately, the merger did not achieve these goals. The U.S. Federal Reserve eventually ruled that Sumitomo's investment was legal, but that the Japanese bank could not increase its interest beyond 24.9 percent, exercise management rights, or make acquisitions in Goldman Sachs affiliates. That ruling squelched plans for a Sumitomo-Goldman Sachs joint venture in London, and virtually rendered the acquisition an arms-length deal. Sumitomo benefits from financial returns only. By 1989 Sumitomo was end-running around Goldman Sachs, doing deals on its own, and the banks's annual report didn't even mention the relationship between the companies.

These surprise Federal Reserve limitations, plus friction in profitably integrating Heiwa Sogo and other operations into the company, led to the replacement of Sumitomo president Koh Komatsu in 1987. At aggressive Sumitomo, the stereotypical image of aging management who move through chairs to the top and stay there no matter what, does not always apply. The guiding principle seems to be similar to the American standard—succeed or step aside.

Despite real estate slumps and rumors of stock market crashes, fumbled deals, and fraud, Sumitomo has proved remarkably resilient. In fact it has maintained a reputation for a reliable, customer-oriented institution. It has achieved impressive growth, despite extremely difficult conditions in most of the world's financial markets. Sumitomo has 373 offices in Japan, compared to 223 before the Heiwa Sogo merger. Overseas, the bank has a network of 1,500 employees working in 46 cities in 31 nations. In the 10 years between 1979 and 1989, Sumitomo's income more than tripled. Net profits grew tenfold. In 1989, a year when Japan was suffering an inverse yield curve and most of the world was slipping into recession, Sumitomo posted an 18.8 percent gain in assets. Sumitomo Bank's California subsidiary reported eight consecutive years of earnings growth, with 1989 besting 1988 by 32 percent.

"Many Japanese bankers think in terms of competing with other Japanese bankers," wrote *Forbes* magazine in a 1989 profile of the bank. "Sumitomo thinks in terms of competing with the world."[2]

Sumitomo's lusting after size is not a singularly Japanese trait. It is the quest of all the meganationals. While aggressive growth gives these companies status and a competitive advantage, it also leads to trouble.

The Sumitomo story is a contemporary corporate parable. While there are many justifiable reasons for financial and geographic acquisitiveness, it is easy to think of company growth in impersonal terms. Success and achievement are attributed to the company. Failure is pinned on an individual. Ultimately, companies are made up of people—individuals who are capable of both strength and susceptibility, of honesty and evil.

Corporate culture, or any organization's standards, invariably flows from the top down. Corporate leaders not only see the growth path as a way of fulfilling responsibilities to investors, employees, and others who depend upon them for leadership, their own egos also come into play. The power and glory of bigness not only translates into corporate pride and partriotism for the workers, it becomes personified in corporate executives. Chief executives insist that their subordinates produce growth, sometimes at any cost, since size is equal to personal power.

Few company officials are dishonest enough or dense enough to overtly insist that their employees push beyond ethical and legal limits. On the other hand, lower-level executives know what it takes to rise in the company. Their dedication to a spectacular performance can eat away at their principles. Nearly every meganational corporation described in this book has experienced some form of public embarrassment, incidents invariably linked to the perpetual push for higher profits and business expansion.

For example, General Electric, a highly respected and thoroughly American establishment, in 1985 pleaded guilty in a federal district court in Philadelphia to bilking the U.S. Air Force out of

$800,000 on a project to upgrade the reentry vehicles on Minuteman missiles. Then, in 1991, three employees of a Japanese medical equipment firm of which GE owns 75 percent were arrested for paying bribes to a hospital official responsible for buying medical devices. The company, Yokogawa Medical Systems, said it did not instruct the salesmen to make the bribes. In Japanese markets in particular, however, GE battles to maintain a competitive advantage.[3]

It is easy and convenient to nail the full culpability for greed and associated misdeeds to the chief executive's door. However, nothing in life is ever that simple. Just as we adore the batter who breaks home run records and idealize the doctor who finds a cure for the killing disease, the CEO who leads his company to championship status is regarded as a hero. This is what he was hired to do. If he does it exceedingly well, he will be sought out for newspaper interviews. He may see his face on the cover of newsstand magazines and be sought for interviews on national and international television programs.

Investors demand growth to guarantee that their investments keep ahead of the inflation rate and perform better than alternate investments. If this doesn't happen, capitalists take their money elsewhere. That "elsewhere" could be virtually anyplace in the world. To meet the challenges of an increasingly global capital and consumer marketplace, companies are driven to ever-greater dimensions.

Granted, General Motors has been a huge company that has dominated U.S. markets for years. Yet GM will not be able to meet the escalating challenge of foreign competition—most of it from Japan but much of it from Germany and other European manufacturers as well—if sales slip behind theirs. General Motors, in fact, has seen its market share sink in the past decade. Japanese companies, which continually nip at GM's 34.5 percent market share, began spending heavily abroad in the mid-1980s, when a strengthening yen gave them enormous buying power. In 1989 alone, Japanese investment in North America totaled $44.3 billion; in Europe, $24.9 billion; elsewhere in Asia, $12.9 billion; and in other areas, $17.9 billion. Like everyone else, the Japanese want to compete effectively.

"In today's world, it is no longer a simple question of quality versus quantity," said Mitsui Bank president Kenichi Suematsu at a 1989 press conference announcing Mitsui's merger with Taiyo Kobe Bank. "You have to have a certain quantity in order to have quality. For us to survive as a universal bank, we have to have a certain size." The Mitsui Taiyo Kobe merger transformed the new financial institution into the second largest bank in the world.[4]

Some companies, by the very nature of their product and corporate history, were entrenched in worldwide markets from their inception. As the world population has grown, demand for their products and services also has expanded. Royal Dutch Petroleum and Unilever began by importing and processing commodities from distant markets. Their ownership is binational as well. Nestlé, considered the most international of all companies, has a similar heritage, since it had to import chocolate from warmer climates than Switzerland.

Other companies are involved in global economics by choice. A domestic telephone system may not seem a likely candidate for globalization. Yet, after the most market-rattling antitrust bust-up in recent U.S. history, AT&T found itself with a reduced business base and laboratories full of valuable technology. AT&T undauntingly leapt into the international business pond and began paddling.

In the company's 1989 annual report, chairman Robert Allen wrote, "The changes we experienced in the 1980s were little short of volcanic as we split apart what was the largest enterprise in the world, the Bell System. We still are changing. But one thing is certain: This isn't a sleeping giant any more. The AT&T of the 1990s will be a leading, customer-focused, market-savvy business with a strong technology base—a business that will be successful in an era of global information movement and management."[5]

Allen reiterated, perhaps to drive his point home to employees, " . . . we will continue to develop into a truly global corporation. It is not sufficient for AT&T to be a U.S. company with aspirations to serve international markets. The concept of globalization must become an ingrained part of the way our people think and view themselves and their work."

In 1983 AT&T had only 50 employees working outside the United States. By 1990, there were more than 22,000 AT&T employees working in 41 countries.

Allowing corporations to grow to massive size is imperative if an economy is to survive in the world today, claims Massachusetts Institute of Technology economics professor Lester Thurow. "In a global economy, small business cannot survive by itself. It can't sell its product in Japan or Germany. Our standard of living depends on our ability to sell things. We've got to have good-sized corporations that can sell products in the rest of the world. Ma and Pa businesses can't do that."[6]

There are three ways in which companies can grow:

1. By internal methods, such as pursuing greater market share and the development of new products through research and development.
2. By acquiring additional assets such as entire companies, segments of companies, or income-producing properties.
3. Through joint venture projects, which are a combination of the first two methods.

The development of new products and new markets is by far the most desirable of these methods, because in this way new jobs and new money are created.

One of the great advantages to a nation of hosting big companies is that these corporations can afford the kind of investments in equipment and technology that build a strong economy and a more efficient world. It is estimated that at least half of America's productivity growth since World War II is attributable to better technology. When companies turn their attention in this direction, the results can be brilliant.

In an attempt to expand its retail business and to improve consumer service in Japan—where banks are notoriously unresponsive to small customers—Sumitomo developed what it calls a "superboard." This multifunctional electronic display board was installed in branches, where it linked several market and interest rate information systems with the bank's on-line computer network. Customers are offered instant access to a wealth of timely financial data. Sumitomo in 1989 spent $240 million on premises and equipment.

Merck & Co. expended a record $751 million on medical research and development in 1989. In the decade from 1980 to 1989, Merck invested nearly $4.5 billion. Each year the company offers new cures for health afflictions. In 1990 Merck was able to introduce a vaccine to protect children against Haemophilus influenza type b infections, a virus that can be fatal. The disease caused nearly 20,000 serious infections a year in the United States, including 12,000 cases of meningitis.

While the level of investment spending in the United States isn't all it might be, American companies did spend $65.2 billion on research and development in 1989, more than all the other industrialized nations combined. Japanese companies spent $26.3 billion, West German $11.4 billion, British $5.7 billion, Dutch, $3.5 billion, Swiss $3 billion, and Italian, $2.3 billion.

Five of the U.S. meganationals, GM, IBM, AT&T, Du Pont, and General Electric were among the top 10 American R&D investors. General Motors and IBM, each with more than $5 billion per year budgeted for research, spent more than most nations do on scientific and technical investigation. Other meganationals—most notably Siemens, Hitachi, and Matshushita Electric Industrial—also are among the heaviest research spenders in the world. As a result these companies also are among the most innovative anywhere. They are likely to maintain their lead in the international race for profits and growth.

Most companies use some combination of all three growth paths—capital and R&D investment, merger and acquisition, and joint venture activities—to achieve their objectives. Though Exxon made impressive direct acquisitions in recent years, much of its growth has been secured by exploration, development, and assembling a vibrantly productive mix of properties.

"In choosing new investments," Exxon's annual report said, "we look for opportunities that offer the greatest quality and most attractive returns, that are most compatible with our overall business goals, and that improve our competitive position. During the past decade, we have invested more than $90 billion in projects that meet these criteria."[7]

This investment, of which no small company would have been capable, is paying off for Exxon. Exxon and a joint venture partner (another meganational, Du Pont) in 1991 announced a large oil and gas discovery in the Gulf of Mexico in a field 4,350 feet beneath the water. That was at about four times the depth of the typical seabottom well at the time, and deeper than any drilling so far attempted. Yet the company believed new technology would allow the capture of the energy source. The oil field, Exxon estimated, contains between 100 million and 200 million barrels of oil.

Though growth by capital investment, research, and development has greater benefit to the economy, it isn't always the simplest way for businesses to expand. In the cyclical manner that business goes, it is often less costly and more efficient for companies to buy the assets and operations of another firm than to develop these things independently.

"These days, greenfield (buying a green field and building a plant) investment isn't practical," Kenji Sugunoya of Yamaichi Securities told *Business Tokyo* magazine in 1989. "Japanese firms don't have time to wait; they must take advantage of high yen and cheap U.S. stock prices now."[8]

U.S. companies felt the same pressures to enter European markets before the 1992 European Community accord closed them out. Euopean companies also find that currency fluctuations and varying world economic conditions encourage them to buy property, equipment, operations, and technology. As a result, despite the difficulties and dangers, corporations are likely to continue to use mergers and acquisitions as the primary vehicle for driving growth.

Twenty-five largest world companies

1. NTT—Japan
2. IBM—U.S.*
3. Royal Dutch/Shell—Netherlands—U.K.*
4. General Electric—U.S.*
5. Industrial Bank of Japan—Japan
6. Exxon—U.S.*
7. Toyota Motor—Japan
8. Fuji Bank—Japan
9. Sumitomo Bank—Japan*
10. Dai-Ichi Kangyo Bank—Japan*
11. Mitsui Taiyo Kobe Bank (renamed Sakura Bank)—Japan*
12. Mitsubishi Bank—Japan*
13. Philip Morris—U.S.*

14. AT&T—U.S.*
15. Sanwa Bank—Japan
16. Tokyo Electric Power—Japan
17. Wal-Mart Stores—U.S.
18. Merck—U.S.*
19. Bristol-Myers Squibb—U.S.*
20. British Telecom—U.K.
21. Hitachi—Japan*
22. Coca-Cola—U.S.*
23. Long-Term Credit Bank-Japan
24. British Petroleum—U.K.*
25. Matsushita Electric—Japan*

*The 25 meganational corporations.
Ranked by market value as of June 30, 1990, as determined by Morgan Stanley Capital International Perspectives. Source: *The Wall Street Journal*, September 21, 1990.

Twenty-five largest U.S. exporters

1. Boeing
2. General Motors*
3. Ford Motor
4. General Electric*
5. International Business Machines*
6. E. I. du Pont De Nemours*
7. Chrysler
8. United Technologies
9. Caterpillar
10. McDonnell Douglas
11. Eastman Kodak
12. Hewlett-Packard
13. Unisys
14. Motorola
15. Philip Morris*
16. Digital Equipment

17. Occidental Petroleum
18. Allied-Signal
19. Weyerhaeuser
20. Union Carbide
21. General Dynamics
22. Raytheon
23. Textron
24. Archer Daniels Midland
25. Dow Chemical

*Indicates Meganational
Note: Many of the 25 most powerful companies in the United States do not appear on this list because, rather than export, they manufacture abroad by foreign subsidiary.
Source: *Fortune,* July 16, 1990.

Chapter Five

Growing by Merger

Question: What does a six-ton elephant eat? Answer: Anything it wants.

Worn Out Children's Joke

The appetite of a true meganational is insatiable, and no corporate creature suffers more voracious hunger than Unilever plc. In 1990 Unilever chairman Sir Michael Angus pointed out that the company was acquiring "something like three businesses a month around the world." A company spokesman later said Angus may have been too modest: At the beginning of the new decade acquisitions were running more than one a week. In 1989, Unilever bought 55 businesses at a total cost of $3 billion. To be sure, some of the purchases were too insignificant and in countries too small to catch the attention of the financial press. But not all of them. During the 1980s, Unilever captured Chesebrough-Ponds Inc., Fabergé/Elizabeth Arden fragrances and cosmetics, and about a dozen European food companies. In aggregate, the Unilever feeding frenzy solidified an awesome business base. Sales nearly doubled between 1984 and 1989 and profits more than tripled. In 1989 alone, earnings per share rose 15 percent.

In a daunting three-volume set of books, the history of Unilever is traced into the 1960s, starting from 1870 when the company's founders sailed distant seas and carried on trade with tropical plantations. The recurring theme in the annals of Unilever is the word *merger*. Unilever itself wasn't actually created until 1930, when Lever Brothers in the United Kingdom and Margarine Unie, of both the U.K. and the Netherlands, joined forces. Lever produced soaps and personal grooming products, while Margarine Unie dealt in butter substitutes. As dissimilar as their product lines may seem, the companies shared something in common. Their original products were based on animal and vegetable fats. In a series of amalgamations and mergers that have yet to cease, the company steadily extended its influence.[1]

Unilever's familiar brand names now include Flora margarine; Lipton tea and soup; Ragu sauce; Lux, Dove, and Pears soaps; Pepsodent and Close Up toothpastes; Vaseline; Q-tips; Prince Matchabelli and Calvin Klein perfumes; and much more. Unilever manufactures medical products, does fish farming in Scotland and Chile, and trades in textiles and beer. In India, it also makes clothing. Raw materials are collected from remote corners of the earth. Palm oil plantations are located in Colombia, Ghana, Malaysia, Thailand, and Zaire. There are coffee and tea estates in East Africa and India.

Unilever participated in all four of the great merger waves of this century. The first surge came about the turn of the century, and saw the creation of such great combinations as Standard Oil (Exxon) and Du Pont. In 1908, the Dutch forbear of Unilever was created when Van den Berghs and Jurgens pooled interests in an effort to make the best of the impoverished economic situation that plagued most of the world. The second merger torrent swept through from World War I until the beginning of the Great Depression. In this era, Lever and Margarine Unie realized that an "alliance wasted less of everybody's substance than hostility," and joined forces. The company continued its expansion through the third merger wave of the 1960s, but launched its most lavish buying spree during the 1980s.[2]

In reaction to a stodgy reputation and declining profitability, Unilever examined its structure. The decision was made to sell off anything that was peripheral to its main line of business—foods and consumer cleaning and grooming products. The company's various divisions made acquisitions in Mexico, Chile, Venezuela, Spain, Germany, Ireland, the United States, Canada, and other countries. The company may well go on spending to fill in gaps in its product lines. For example, it now has no snack foods. The company may have had no choice. Its competitors were amassing size as well.

In 1984, an unprecedented $122 billion was spent on all corporate mergers and acquisitions. In 1985, another worldwide record of $179 billion was set. A grand total of $1.3 trillion was allocated during the 1980s' shuffling of corporate assets. In the first half of 1991, merger activity fell to half of what it had been in 1990, but there were still nearly 2,000 deals at a value of $51.7 billion.

Unilever is the number one food supplier in Europe. Meganational Nestlé remained in second place, but it was growing as well. Philip Morris assured itself a solid third place when in 1990, for $4.1 billion, it purchased the Swiss chocolate and coffee purveyor Jacobs Suchard. These three companies also battle it out in the United States, where Philip Morris's Kraft subsidiary dominates. Along with Philip Morris and Procter & Gamble, Unilever is the largest advertiser in the United States.

Growth by internally generated means was not neglected at Unilever, which allocated $615 million in 1989 and $728 million in 1990 to research and development in dozens of laboratories in Britain, India, the United States, and other countries. Generally about 2 percent of sales is directed to R&D.

In the company's 1989 annual report, Sir Michael and co-chairman F. A. Maljers asserted, "We approach the new decade committed to a strategy for growth."

Though Unilever is a conservative and well-established company, it often is at the forefront of new trends. It has harkened to the consumer call for low-calorie, low-fat-content food. "We now offer varieties ranging from milk-based products to complete meals, and from biscuits to breakfast drinks," the company boasted. Microwave meals, nonpolluting packaging, and products from renewable resources are among its advances.

As the 1990s dawned, Unilever was negotiating to extend its activities to Eastern Europe and to make a greater inroad into Japan. Though the company's Timotei has become one of the most popular shampoos in Japan, Unilever wasn't satisfied with its presence there. In the intensely competitive and notoriously protected Japanese market, Unilever was losing money.

Unilever juggles 500 operating groups in 75 countries. Even today, the company has dual nationality with boards of directors on each side of the English Channel. The logistics of managing such a company seem mind-boggling. How does a company keep track of such a massive organization, much less get all the parts working in harmony and at maximum efficiency?

Originally, Unilever granted enormous autonomy to its numerous divisions, but in the past decade power has again become more centralized. Managers are brought to training centers in Britain to learn the Unilever philosophy, and are recalled at regular intervals for reindoctrination. Some of the company's divisions have had problems, like a British meat subsidiary that had botulism in some of its meats. But, says Sir Michael, "if a business is central to our core strategy we take a lot of time and attention putting it right when things go wrong."

Restructuring is an intermittent occurrence in a capitalist economy. Its function is to facilitate adaptation to economic and technological change.

According to conventional thinking, merger activity catches fire when the economy is in crisis. In bad times, nearly bankrupt owners are willing to sell companies at slashed prices or, like Lever Brothers and Margarine Unie, companies see a greater chance of survival if they cooperate rather than compete. As shown in an earlier chapter, these mergers may benefit the corporations themselves, but they do little to advance economic progress in general.

Heilbroner and Thurow said in *Economics Explained*, ". . . when the market is very low, companies with large retained earnings may be tempted to buy up other companies, rather than use their funds for capital expenditures. Financial investments, in other words, may take the place of real investments. This helps successful companies grow, but does not directly provide growth for the economy as a whole."

Then, in the 1980s, a peculiar thing happened. The United States celebrated the longest, strongest, uninterrupted period of growth in its history, and most other developed countries prospered as well. Yet mergers and acquisitions were being consummated at a pounding pace. Part of the reason was the advent of high-risk or so-called junk financing that allowed previously underqualified buyers to get hold of valuable assets. But even when a network of insider trading was unveiled and junk bond king Michael Miliken went to jail, merger activity did not abate. The best-financed corporations marched on.

For example:

- Siemens of Germany spent DM 2.7 billion acquiring new companies and parts of companies in its 1989/90 fiscal year, and another DM 3.8 billion in the 1988/89 fiscal year.
- During the 1980s, General Electric bought companies worth $17 billion, notably RCA, investment banker Kidder Peabody, and half of the appliance business of Britain's General Electric Company.
- Already the largest U.S. cigarette company and the second-largest brewer (Miller Brewing Co.), Philip Morris pushed deeper into the food industry with the 1988, $12.6 billion purchase of Kraft Inc. and the $4.1 billion acquisition of Jacobs Suchard in 1990.

What was happening? The major corporations of the world were aligning themselves for increased competition in the global marketplace. They were doing this in a special way.

Psychologists suggest that, throughout their lives, people arrange themselves in hierarchal orders based on deeply ingrained perceptions of their personal abilities and importance. Often, an individual's view of whether he should be a general, a lieutenant, or a foot soldier is formed early in life. It evolves from birth order, or perhaps from favored status with a parent. If it is possible to assign human characteristics to a corporation, it appears that in recent years something similar is going on in the corporate world. Companies that formerly enjoyed power and prestige on a national scale are moving up to the international sphere. Here they confront establishments that have operated on a worldwide basis for many decades. In a mesmerizing global dance, each of these companies is realigning itself, carving out territory, establishing relative strength, and building power bases.

The whole process is accompanied by verbal challenges, intellectual justifications, and general braggadocio. The Japanese insist that their international sorties are intellectually motivated by long-term, strategic planning. American companies charge forward with a mandate to maintain national competitiveness and to satisfy demanding capitalist shareholders. European companies proceed along the lines of entitlement. Some European companies only recently have reclaimed their pre–World War II birth rights. Like Japanese companies, they have been tireless in their compulsion to return to their proper positions. They were born to greatness and regaining that status is a matter of honor.

Whatever the rationale, the corporate behavior is the same. European and Japanese companies see openings in U.S. markets, and corporations from all three regions make tracks to position themselves for the economic union of Europe in 1992. Those companies with massive resources have been able to use their advantage to secure powerful positions in multiple markets through internal growth, acquisition, or joint venture.

Much of the attention is focused on Europe, where the entire economy is in flux. In the second half of 1989, more than $50 billion worth of European companies were sold, with American buyers grabbing $15.2 billion or 27.6 percent. German companies acquired assets worth $7.3 billion; British, $6.1 billion; Italian, $1.85 billion; and Japanese, $1.63 billion.

Though the Japanese are latecomers to the international acquisition game, they are making up for lost time. In 1984 Japanese firms orchestrated only 44 mergers or acquisitions of foreign companies. That number jumped to 315 by 1988.

"Doing acquisitions is a part of Japanese firms' internationalization," M&A attorney Toby Myerson explained in a 1990 *Business Tokyo* interview. "They realize they don't have time to access certain strategic markets. They're also trying to leapfrog the problem of protectionism. Japanese companies are driven by market and economic forces, and by political forces as well."[3]

Currency fluctuations often are cited as a reason that companies expand into foreign markets. For example, in the late 1980s the yen was strong against other currencies, especially the U.S. dollar. Suddenly there was a rash of real estate, corporate, and technological purchases by Japanese. The currency advantage was not the *reason* that the Japanese went after attractive U.S. assets; it was simply the circumstances that made those acquisitions possible. U.S. assets and the massive U.S. market had always appealed to Japanese investors, but it was the weak dollar that made some merchandise not only attainable, but irresistible.

Analysis of the nature of business aside, corporate leaders have pragmatic reasons for playing the mergers-and-acquisition game. They are hired to lead companies in the direction that corporate constituencies believe they should go. Most of these star coaches succeed because they play to win and growth by acquisition is sound strategy on the corporate game field.

Why? Acquisitions can help a company overcome the rigors of old age; secure a technological edge; and to a very important extent, keep pace with their competitors. Finally, some of the companies are growing larger to satisfy the urges of a gifted (and perhaps obsessive) chief executive. This creative individual builds a company for the same reason a mountain climber climbs, a painter captures a flower arrangement, or a landscaper creates a lovely garden.

PUTTING THE BLOOM BACK ON A MATURE COMPANY

Because so many of the meganational companies are of venerable age, they operate in mature, slow-growing industries or in areas of the world with stable or declining populations. Author Robert Heller, writing in an AT&T in-house magazine, pointed out that "New growth means new geography. That's largely because mature markets have become oversupplied and insufficiently profitable." Food, household appliance, and other consumer goods companies are particularly adept at saturating their established markets.[4]

Most companies go on the prowl when they find themselves in that predicament. Others are spurred into action when they get tossed out of their comfortable niches. AT&T could have continued operating in a mature but profitable industry segment had not the break up of Ma Bell shoved it out of the nest. Suddenly, AT&T was better able to optimize its technology and it became highly motivated to be an international contender.

AT&T made lightning quick inroads into the global marketplace. Its international sales of network equipment grew from zero in 1983 to approximately $1 billion in 1989. By 1990 sales were up to $1.5 billion. In 1991, 15 percent of AT&T's revenues evolved from international sales. It is the company's goal to derive between 20 and 25 percent of its revenue from international markets by 1995. AT&T's acquisition of NCR was an essential part of achieving that objective.

SEIZING AND MAINTAINING A TECHNOLOGICAL EDGE

Often the most valuable technology is developed either by accident by a company unable to make the best use of it, or it is developed by design by small companies without the management expertise or marketing structure to compete in global markets. For well-capitalized companies it is quicker and easier to buy expertise than to develop it.

The purchase of the entertainment giant MCA by Matsushita and Columbia Pictures by Sony represented an effort to complete a vertical structure by these two companies. They already produce much of the high-technology equipment used in the entertainment industry; the companies wanted to add to that the technology of programming that was transmitted by their own equipment. Even as industry experts were decrying the creation of an international entertainment cartel, rumors spread that Hitachi and other electronics manufacturers were shopping for an entertainment subsidiary.

Meganationals often use the acquisition track to gain an advantage in the industries with the greatest potential for future development—biotechnology, microelectronics, new material science, telecommunications, advanced civil aviation, robotics plus machine tools, and electronics plus software.

Chalmers Johnson, author of *MITI and the Japanese Miracle*, points out that high technology particularly is subject to accumulation into the hands of a few owners. Young, energetic, high-tech companies usually are underfinanced. They cannot survive a recession, or even overbearing competition, because they must have profits to meet payrolls, buy materials, and bankroll marketing campaigns.

Like AT&T, which at considerable trouble and expense ($7.4 billion) acquired NCR, many of the big league players are situated in several hot technologies at once. Though AT&T did buy NCR during a recession, the acquisition was no bargain. After five months of haggling, AT&T paid 22 percent more than its original offer.

BECAUSE THE COMPETITION IS GROWING BIGGER AND TOUGHER

General Motors and Ford Motor Co. locked horns over who would claim Jaguar plc in the ongoing consolidation of the world auto industry. Ford won (again, by probably paying too much) and in 1990 acquired glamorous Jaguar for $2.38 billion. Earlier, GM had linked up with Group Lotus, and Ford bought 75 percent of Aston Martin Lagonda. Chrysler picked up a portion of Maserati and Lamborghini. Each of the car companies felt compelled to strengthen its position in Europe and to fend off the Japanese in the luxury car market. But the tussle didn't end with Ford's Jaguar victory. GM beat out Fiat for a $600 million, 50 percent stake in Saab-Scania's automaking arm. A year later GM and Fiat vied to be White Knight to Poland's bankrupt auto manufacturer, FSO.

Growth by acquisition is addictive. Investors and analysts look for growth stated in percentages. The bigger the company becomes, the more sales it must generate to maintain the same percentage of growth. A 10 percent growth in sales is easier for a $40 million company than for a $400 billion company. When companies cannot achieve their earnings objectives with current property, they must add new ones. It isn't yet clear how heavy a company can become before it implodes, but it seems reasonable that mergers come in waves to give the economy (and the companies) an opportunity to rest, digest, and adapt to the changes before consolidation takes off again.

Seeking growth by acquisition sometimes can be a mistake. It is estimated that one out of three acquisitions later unravels. Certainly many companies that expand through acquisition also regularly divest themselves of lagging performers or mismatches. On the other hand, the business press often is too anxious to declare an acquisition a failure. For example, just one year after GM bought into Saab, *Business Week* ran a story with the headline, "GM's

Swedish Fling Is Causing Headaches." The deal may indeed turn sour, but even by impatient U.S. standards, a year isn't much time for manufacturing companies to mesh gears. On the whole, because they tend to buy high-quality enterprises, the meganational corporations have a greater success rate with acquisitions than do other companies.[5]

UNDISGUISED AMBITION

"Jumping Jack" and "Neutron Jack" are two of the nicknames pinned on Jack Welch, CEO of thriving General Electric. No wonder. Welch, who assumed the chairmanship in 1981, has said his plan is to make GE the largest company in the United States. In the first six years of his chairmanship, he bought 338 companies for a total of $11.1 billion. While GE also sold operations worth $9 billion during the 1980s, during the decade the company invested a total of $17 billion in acquisitions.

GE's purchase of RCA, the giant electronics firm, catapulted the conglomerate from 10th to 6th on *Fortune's* list of the 500 biggest industrial companies in the United States.

"In 1980, we had a total market value of $12 billion, which ranked us 11th among American companies. We left the decade ranked second, with a year-end market value of $58 billion, and that $46 billion increase during the 1980s was the largest of any company in the United States," Welch told shareholders in GE's 1989 annual report.[6]

Welch started out with a good company, but saw that it could be a blockbuster. His success has made him a corporate celebrity.

The end of the merger wave of the 1980s has been heralded several times, and the early 1990s did bring something of a slowdown. Yet many a corporate colossus can continue to buy if it wants to, since it likely has cash on hand. Philip Morris, in the third quarter of 1990, reported an astounding $2 billion cash reserve. The food business tends to be recession-resistant—people turn to macaroni and cheese in hard times, so Philip Morris's Kraft foods thrives. New acquisitions are likely to be international. Analyst Sarah A. Sheckler of Duff & Phelps Inc. told *Business Week* that because of Philip Morris's large U.S. holdings, " . . . they'd have difficulty finding a business to buy that doesn't overlap with their existing operations."[7]

While the meganationals avariciously seek mergers worldwide, they in turn are shielded from such unpleasantries. Their very size usually protects them from becoming merger targets. In Japan, keiretsu alliances serve as a double shield. Members of the financial cliques hold shares in one another's stock, which are seldom traded. This trading block creates a barrier for any unwanted outside investor who may attempt to accumulate a majority position in the company. The 10 largest shareholders of Sumitomo Bank stock, for example, are some of the bank's largest customers, and have been for many years. They include the Sumitomo Life Insurance Company, Sumitomo Trust and Banking Co., Matsushita Electric Industrial Co., Sanyo Electric, Kajima Corporation, and Nippon Steel Corporation.

Daimler-Benz continues to grow substantially by acquisition, and it will invest more than $1.11 billion to expand into eastern Germany. Yet Edzard Reuter, Daimler's chairman, obviously is sensitive to the nervousness that the company's burgeoning size creates in Germany and elsewhere in the world. In his 1989 message to shareholders, Reuter made a commitment to free competition:

"We will allow ourselves to be guided by the conviction," Reuter said, "that Germany as a whole needs a balanced assortment of company sizes. It remains to be seen whether independence of company sectors or collaboration with appropriate medium-sized companies in West Germany or abroad is appropriate. At any rate, we will have the obligation to contribute to the strengthening of market competition." Shortly thereafter, Daimler acquired a $233 million share in Metallgesellschaft A. G., a metal recycler.[8]

Selected mergers and acquisitions

Here is a sampling of the merger activity conducted by the world's most powerful meganationals after the mid-1980s, when experts were claiming that excessive leveraged financing had brought the merger wave of the 1980s to an end. When available, acquisition prices are given.

AT&T

1991–NCR Corporation—$7.4 billion—U.S.
1989–Istel—U.S.

1989–Paradyne—U.S.

1989–Eaton Financial Corp.—Swap for 2 million shares AT&T—U.S.

1989–Italtel—Italy

1989–Compagnie Industriali Ruiniti S.p.A.—Italy

1988–Sun Microsystems—$555.4 million—U.S., sold in 1991 to avoid antitrust problems with NCR purchase.

Bristol-Myers Squibb

1990–Orthoplant GmbH—Germany

1990–S+G Implants GmbH—Germany

1990–UPSA Group of Rueil-Malmaison—France

1989–Squibb—$12.6 billion—U.S.

1986–Genetic Systems (Oncogen)—$290 million—U.S.

British Petroleum

1989–Repurchase of 11.7 percent of BP shares from Kuwait Investment Office (KIO still owns 9.9%)—2.4 billion pounds sterling.

1988–Britoil—2.8 billion pounds sterling—U.K.

1988–Lear Petrolcum

1987–Remaining 45 percent of Sohio—$7.6 billion—U.S.

Citicorp

1990–Bank of New England (credit card operations)—U.S.

1986–Quotron—U.S.

Coca-Cola

1989–Oasis Industries Ltd.—$38 million—New Zealand

1989–Coca-Cola Amatil Ltd.—$491 million—Australia

1989–Pernod Ricard—$140 million—France

1989–Coca-Cola Bottling Co. of Arkansas—$232 million—U.S.

1989–Coca-Cola Bottling Co. Consolidated (30%)—stock swap–U.S.

1988–H. P. Hood Inc.—$45 million

Dai-Ichi Kangyo Bank

1990–Unibanco (11.72 percent)—$64 million—Brazil

1990–Large Commercial Bank, Hong Kong

1989–Manufacturers Hanover Corp., 60 percent—$120 million?—U.S.

1989–CIT Group (60 percent)—$1.3 billion—U.S.

Daimler-Benz

1991–Sogeti SA (34 percent)—$400 million—France

1991–Metallgesellschaft A. G. (10 percent)—$233 million— Germany

1989–Messerschmitt-Bolkow-Blohm—$859 million— Germany

1988–Modicon (division of Gould)

1986–AEG—$820 million

1986–Modular Computer Systems

I. E. du Pont de Nemours

1989–Venture Coke Co. (50 percent)

1989–Howson-Algraphy—U.K.

1989–prepress printing operations of Crosfield Electronics (in a joint venture with Fuji Photo Film)—U.K.

1986–Inland Steel Coal Co.—U.S.

1986–Sierra Coal—U.S.

1986–Tau Laboratories Inc.—U.S.

1986–U.S. Crop protection assets of Shell Agricultural Chemical Co.—U.S.

1986–paint operations of Ford Motor Co.—U.S.

1986–American Critical Care—U.S.

1986–Elit Circuits

Deutsche Bank (unless noted, the companies are German)

1989–Morgan Grenfell Group—$1.5 billion—U.K.

1989–Roland, Berger (management consulting firm)

1989–Banco Comercial Transatlantico, SA,—Spain

1989–Grunelius (private bank)

1989–Schiffshypothekenbank zu Lubeck AG

1989–Antoni Hacker & Co.—Austria, name changed to Deutsche Bank, Austria

1988–H. Albert de Bary & Co.—Netherlands

1986–Bank of America, Italian operations—$603 million—Italy

Exxon

1989–Texaco of Canada—$4.15 billion—Canada

1984 to 1990–2 billion oil-equivalent oil reserves—$7 billion

Fiat Group

1991–Ford New Holland (farm equipment)—U.S.

1990–Alcatel-Alsthom (6 percent interest)—France

1990–Nycoa (nylon)—U.S.

1989–Cogefor (civil engineering)

1989–Autoflug and Sepi (industrial components)

1989–Sifind (financial and real estate)

1989–Innocenti—Italy

1989–Incstar Corp. (Immunodiagnostics, U.S. 51 percent)

1988–Ferrari (remaining 40 percent)—Officially $13.7 million, perhaps as much as $36.1 million—Italy

1986–Alfa Romeo—Italy

1986–Maserati—(49 percent)—Italy

General Electric

1991–Financial News Network—$154.3 million—U.S.

1990–GE-Thorn Lamps—U.K.

1989–General Electric Co. plc (50 percent of the appliance division)—$575 million—U.K.

1988–Borg-Warner—$2.3 billion—U.K.

1987–Thomson, SA (medical diagnostics)—France

1986–RCA—$6.3 billion—U.S.

1986–Kidder, Peabody (80 percent)—$600 million—U.S.

General Motors

   1991–SD Scicon (British, computers)—$194.2 million
   1991–Infocel (data processing)—U.S.
   1990–Saab autos (50 percent)—$600 million—Sweden
   1986–Group Lotus—U.K.
   1984–Electronic Data Systems (EDS)—U.S.

Hitachi, Ltd.

   1989–National Advanced Systems—$398 million—U.S.

IBM

   1990–Perkin-Elmer (bought by Silicon Valley Group Inc.,
      which is partly owned by IBM)—U.S.

Matsushita Electric Industrial Co.

   1991–MCA Inc. (largest acquisition ever by a Japanese
      company)—$6.1 billion—U.S.

Merck & Co.

   1991–Woelm Pharma GmbH by the 50–50 Johnson &
      Johnson—German Merck joint venture—$90 million
      (est.)
   1986–Vestal Laboratories Inc.

Mitsubishi Bank

   1984–Bank of California—U.S.

Mitsui Taiyo Kobe Bank

   1989–Taiyo Kobe Bank—Japan

Nestlé

   1990–Alco Drumstick (ice cream)—U.S.
   1990–Curtis Brands (chocolate candy)—U.S.
   1990–Superior Brands (pet accessories)—U.S.
   1988–Rowntree plc (chocolate)—$4.5 billion—U.K.
   1988–Buitoni SpA (Italy, pasta)—$1.2 billion—Italy
   1987–Herta Group—Germany and France

1987–Sanpareil (paté)—Belgium

1987–Vittel (52 percent, mineral water)—France

Philip Morris

1991–Jacobs Suchard (coffee & chocolate)—$4.1 billion—
France

1990–Rothmans International plc—U.K.

1988–Kraft—$12.6 billion—U.S.

1987–Melrose Foods Co.—Canada

1987–Dickson's Food Service Co.—Canada

1987–Jacob Leinenkugel Brewing Co.—U.S.

1986–General Foods Credit Corp.—U.S.

Royal Dutch Petroleum Co.

1989–Nigerian National Petroleum Corp. (additional 10
percent acquired, bringing total to 30 percent)—
Nigeria

1989–Les Minues Selbaie (35 percent)—Canada

1989–Calamcrck (agrochemicals)—German

1987–Coal mining properties in Australia from CSR

Siemens

1990–Nixdorf Computer—$959 million—German

1990–Duewag Aktiengesellschaft (rolling stock)

1990–Krauss-Maffei Verkehrstechnik GmbH (rolling stock,
minority interest)

1989–Plessey Co. (joint venture with GE of Britain)—$1.68
billion—U.K.

1989–IN2 SA—France

1989–Rolm Systems—U.S.

1988–Bendix Electronics Group—$250 million

Sumitomo Bank

1986–Goldman Sachs (12.5 percent)—$500 million—U.S.

1986–Heiwa Sogo Bank—Stock swap, value not disclosed—
Japan

Unilever

> 1989–Fabergé personal products division—$1.55 billion—
> U.S.
> 1989–Shering-Plough's European perfume business
> 1989–Calvin Klein—U.S.
> 1987–Chesebrough-Ponds—$3.1 billion—U.S.

Chapter Six

Growth by Joint Venture

"Come now, let us reason together."

Lyndon B. Johnson

"When Gianni Agnelli climbs into his chauffeured Croma Automatic Turbo—the executive Fiat—heading toward his corporate offices in downtown Turin, he's inclined to take the wheel and then to drive fast. Very fast. Speed is second nature to this 'king' of Italy . . . " bubbled *Lear's* magazine in a profile of the chairman of Fiat. The whole point of the piece was to report that an opinion poll showed Agnelli was "the man the greatest number of Italian women would like to have an adventure with."[1]

The magazine did not indicate the 71-year-old Agnelli's reaction to the survey, but it did make it obvious that the Italian industrialist fears neither adventure nor dangerous relationships. Fiat, Italy's largest private company, once saved itself from collapse both by defying terrorism in its auto plants and by accepting help from Libya's Colonel Moammar Khadafi. Several years after extricating itself from the controversy-ridden Libyan alliance, Fiat was staking much of its future on the development of political and commercial joint ventures.

Fiat Group has so many corporate and foreign-government affiliations that it is almost impossible to recount them all. Fiat's automobile operation, by itself, has more joint ventures than any other automobile manufacturer. It is seeking more.

The company's experience with joint ventures goes back many years and illustrates Fiat's remarkable diversity. Among Fiat's U.S. partners have been Ford Motor Co., Chrysler, Pratt & Whitney, Sikorsky, General Electric, Westinghouse, Motorola, and Foster Wheeler. Fiat has joint venture ties with Hitachi to produce farm equipment parts and Nissan to design a more-efficient, less-polluting diesel engine. In partnership with French-owned Alcatel-Alsthom, Fiat created a European holding company to develop a business in new composite materials, artificial intelligence, and telecommunications. Other subsidiaries have cooperative under-takings for civil engineering in Spain and Greece.

The Economist in London pointed out that Fiat is building on ties with the Soviet Union and Eastern Europe that go back more than 50 years. With about half of Soviet cars already Fiat deriv-atives, the company "is planning a huge expansion. It aims to build new cars in Russia, Poland, and Yugoslavia, both for local markets and to export to the West. Fiat has committed itself to nearly doubling the Soviet Union's production capacity in a joint venture to build what may be the world's biggest car plant in Yelabuga, 600 miles east of Moscow. It is supposed to have a final production capacity of 900,000 cars a year."[2]

Agnelli announced to shareholders in 1990, "If there are to be cars in the Soviet Union, they will be Fiats." Agnelli meant that. By mid-1991 the company was considering buying a share of Lada, the Soviet state-owned automaker.

The joint ventures are an attempt to reclaim Fiat's impressive sales of the 1980s, which by 1990 were sagging. Not only was Fiat hit by weaker West European auto demand but, due to an easing of government protection of Italian markets, Fiat is losing domestic sales. In the first eight months of 1990, Fiat's share of the Italian new car market fell to 53.7 percent from 57.6 percent a year earlier, and 60 percent a decade earlier. Yet Agnelli views more compe-tition at home and declining market share simply as part of a natural economic evolution.

" . . . few dispute the widely held belief, today, that a mature automobile industry has only limited future growth potential (with the exception of East Europe), and that high-tech industries and financial services will represent an increasingly important share of tomorrow's advanced economies," proclaimed Fiat in its official corporate history.

Sometimes called Fiat's "constitutional monarch," Agnelli is the grandson of the company's founder. A family-controlled holding company, IFI (Industrial Fiduciary Institute) owns almost 40 per-cent of Fiat's shares. The remaining shares are traded on 10 Italian and 8 German exchanges, the Paris Bourse, London's SEAQ, and by American Depositary Receipts on the New York Stock Exchange.

In 1899, four years before Henry Ford founded his automobile company in Detroit, ex-cavalry officer Giovanni Agnelli and a group of entrepreneurs organized Fabbrica Italiana di Automobili Torino (F.I.A.T.) to build motor-driven vehicles.

The company grew briskly, moving into mass production of models that sold for as little as $5 and $8. By 1903 Fiat was exporting cars to the United States, and in 1908 licensed a plant in Poughkeepsie, New York. That plant produced automobiles for nearly a decade. By 1915, the company had expanded into military aircraft and soon was building commercial airplanes.

Because of Fiat-supplied planes, cars, trucks, and armored vehicles for Mussolini and the Axis powers' World War II effort, the company's plants were targets for relentless Allied bombing raids. Though the company was badly scarred after the war, the U.S. government understood that Fiat's survival would be crucial to the rebuilding of Italy. With the help of a $10 million Marshall Plan loan, reconstruction began immediately, and by 1947 the war-damaged factories were restored and humming along at 300 cars a day.

Giovanni Agnelli II took control of the company in 1966, but didn't find it an easy go. The oil crisis of 1973 halted more than a quarter of a century of uninterrupted growth at Fiat and the company went into a tailspin. Italy was racked with inflation and internal turmoil. Wildcat strikes, excessive absenteeism, militant unionism, and even terrorism erupted at Fiat plants. Four Fiat managers were killed by terrorists and 27 others were seriously wounded. Agnelli confronted the unions, fired all workers with a history of violence, and announced that 20,000 workers would be laid off. The company's reputation in the United States for cars that needed frequent, costly repairs (hence the epithet, Fix It Again Tony) forced Fiat eventually to withdraw from the U.S. market.

The company edged close to failure in the mid-1970s. Cash flow was at a alarmingly low level, with earnings of less than $200,000 on sales of about $4 million. Fiat was dipping into reserves to pay dividends.

In a pact with Colonel Khadafi in 1976, Libya acquired a 10

percent interest in Fiat. Though the purchase included no management control, the wedge of Fiat cost Khadafi $415 million, almost triple the market price of Fiat's shares. Though Khadafi's long-term motives were questioned, Fiat shares immediately rocketed on the Milan stock exchange. It took several years for Agnelli to convert the capital into a turnaround, but it eventually happened.

Though the Libya/Fiat relationship ended under pressure from Libya's enemies, Khadafi turned out to be an astute investor. Fiat had not only diversified its business base but modernized operations and automated plants. Annual worker output was only 14.8 units in 1979; in 1983 output had improved to 25 units per worker.

By the mid-1980s, Fiat's farm equipment, telecommunications, and other subsidiaries were competing in the U.S. high-technology and manufacturing fields. The company sent key executives to Washington, D.C., to compete for Star Wars business and Fiatallis, the heavy-equipment subsidiary, bid on a contract to sell 178 bulldozers to the U.S. Marine Corp. However, Defense Secretary Caspar Weinberger stepped in and suspended the $7.9 million deal.

"Our concern is that Libya might get some money out of this contract," said one Pentagon official.

Very likely it would have. In 1985, Libya received $21 million in dividends from its Fiat holdings. Ironically, selling the Fiat shares would serve Khadafi even more. Because of the rebound, shares were trading at an all-time high. In just a decade, Khadafi's $415 million had proliferated to $2.95 billion.

In 1986 Fiat did buy out Libya's interest, and in 1987, Fiat was designated a prime contractor by the U.S. government for a $2 billion Star Wars project.

Despite the admittedly dubious way Fiat found the capital it required, the company's turnaround lifted the entire Italian economy in its wake.

Fiat's central role in the Italian economy is beyond debate. By 1948 Fiat's holdings represented 6 percent of Italy's industrial capital. Since that time Italy has grown and its economic base diversified, but Fiat still generates 3.7 percent of gross national product and employs 4.2 percent of the labor force. The northern Italian city of Turin, sometimes called "Italy's Little Detroit," was nourished with Fiat money. Half of Turin's population, either directly or indirectly, rely on Fiat for a living. General Motors, the largest industrial company in the United States, by contrast, represented only 2.2 percent of the U.S. economy, and employed only about 0.6 percent of the labor force.

Today, Fiat operates through more than 900 companies employing 303,500 workers on six continents in 58 countries. Its core businesses remain automobiles, commercial vehicles, and farm and construction equipment. However, Fiat has diverged into dozens of related sectors including metallurgical products, aviation, bioengineering, chemicals, fibers, retailing, insurance, newspapers, and other publishing.

Fiat's diversification-by-joint-venture strategy was put to the test in the recent recession, and will face even greater trials as trade and economic barriers are dismantled in Europe in the 1990s. If Agnelli has it figured right, however, these experiments not only will bring financial reward, they will forge ties that ensure Fiat a pivotal role in a global economy. Indeed, in the first half of 1991 Fiat's exports increased 7.5 percent.

In 1988, Agnelli made changes among his top management that signaled the direction in which Fiat would be headed. Vittorio Ghidella, described in *The Economist* as "a cars man," was replaced with Cesare Romiti, a financial expert. Agnelli told a gathering of executives that Ghidella had "an auto-centric vision, while I see Fiat as an industrial holding group." Romiti shared that vision, wanting to push the company into armaments, banking, and telecommunications. *The Economist* spat at Agnelli for a decision the influential British magazine perceived as short-sighted. Yet one writer's poison is another's passion. Just a year earlier *Fortune* magazine—ignoring any skill Agnelli may have used in choosing his lieutenants—heralded Romiti as Fiat's unsung hero, and gave him credit for getting Fiat "firing on all cylinders again.

"Don't give Giovanni Agnelli, Fiat's famous chairman and principal owner, the credit," *Fortune* scoffed.[3]

Joint ventures are the mercantile madness of the late 20th century. Many companies either have found what they consider appropriate alliances, or they are courting attractive confederations.

"We seek to be the premier global partner," Du Pont chairman Edgar S. Woolard, Jr. told shareholders in the company's 1989 annual report. Some of Du Pont's ventures take advantage of the company's imposing stature in the business world. They offer the company extraordinary potential for future growth. For example, it was a joint venture company established with Exxon that discovered a huge, deep-water oil and gas patch in the Gulf of Mexico in 1991.

Du Pont is especially proud of an agreement with another meganational, Merck. The joint venture links the world's premier chemicals and fibers producer and the world's largest pharmaceutical manufacturer. It was expected that Du Pont Merck in 1991, just two years after its inception, would have sales of $700 million. Turnover of that magnitude would place the joint venture as one of the top 50 drugmakers in the world. It would take an entrepreneurial, start-up company decades to achieve sales of that level.

Both Du Pont and Fiat have joint venture agreements with another meganational—AT&T. AT&T executive Victor Pelson says such agreements are crucial to AT&T's goal of internationalization.

"We've learned, for instance, that we can't go it alone in a global marketplace," Pelson said. "There's a critical need for international collaboration to gain access to markets, especially restricted ones, to ensure access to technology, and to share financial risk." By 1990, AT&T had arranged 15 joint ventures.

"Obviously we're committed to international agreements," Pelson continued. "Indeed, I expect us to accelerate the number and variety of our alliances and cooperative agreements. It's an investment in our future that we're prepared to make, but it's not an investment without drawbacks."[4]

The hazards are considerable, and not every meganational feels the same enthusiam for joint ventures. During a panel discussion in San Francisco for The Conference Board, the chairman of Unilever explained his distaste for the practice.

". . . we prefer to have 100 percent ownership of subsidiaries," Sir Michael Angus said. "The reason for that, essentially, is not just to have total control. It's because using your research and development and putting it freely into enterprises that are not wholly owned clearly has a cost. You give part of it away if you're not careful.

"Nonetheless, there are some countries where you have to be prepared to live with outside ownership. I mentioned India, where our subsidiary (Hindustanlever) has 130,000 other shareholders besides ourselves. In Korea, and to some extent in Taiwan, we find ourselves in joint ventures; indeed, we've had one or two in this country. They are less satisfactory in the end. There is an inhibition about dealing with part of your business that is not totally owned.

"Worst of all are 50–50 joint ventures," Sir Michael continued. "You probably all know the story about the pig and the hen who went into a 50–50 joint venture to produce the English breakfast, bacon and eggs. When they got down to the actual operation, the hen said: "Fine, I've laid my egg. Now you go about making the bacon." To which the pig replied: "I've just realized that 50–50 joint ventures don't work."[5]

Perhaps Sir Michael had in mind the plight of the U.S. computer chip industry.

Business Week described what happened to it. "When Intel and Motorola licensed NEC and Hitachi to build low-end microprocessors in the late 1970s, their partners snared so many customers that America's global market share tumbled. When chip-design leaders LSI Logic and VLSI Technologies swapped their software skills for Japanese production technology, they helped make world-class rivals out of partners Toshiba and Hitachi."

While hard work and capital investment no doubt also helped Japanese chip makers, " . . . the real secret is a dense, crisscrossing network of strategic alliances the Japanese have woven with foreign designers and makers of every conceivable species of the chip," said the article.[6]

From that, it would seem likely that more executives would share Sir Michael's reluctance. It appears, however, that other corporations think they've learned something from the chip industry experience, and some hope they can replicate the techniques Japanese companies used to seize possession of a globally important industry.

Most of the meganationals seek strategic alliances, and they do it for a variety of reasons. In certain countries, such as India and Japan, joint ventures may be the only way to enter a protected or a culturally exclusive marketplace. In some endeavors, such as deep-ocean oil drilling, it is a way to share expenses and to disperse financial risk.

In the medical drug business, which becomes more science-driven as time passes, it takes either very large companies, or smaller companies sponsored by well-funded organizations, to keep research alive. When small companies team up with the giants, there is little threat to the competitive nature of business. In fact, competition often is reinforced. By working with a larger company in one segment of its business, the lower-tier company may be empowered to develop other parts of its business. But when one massive organization teams up with another, survival becomes even more slippery for small competitors. Eventually, there will be fewer and fewer contenders in the global market, creating worldwide oligopoly conditions.

Some joint ventures obviously are intended to create an unbeatable dominance in a particular field. For example, to defy Kellogg's commanding presence in ready-to-eat cereals, Nestlé formed a joint venture with General Mills to produce and market cereals in Europe. A year later, Nestlé formed a strategic alliance with Coca-Cola to cooperate in bottling and distributing Nestea iced tea, Nescafe iced coffee, and other beverages in cans. General Motors joined with Ford and Chrysler to develop new technology in plastics, batteries, transmissions, electronics, and the environment—but most of all to fend off Japanese competition. Partially because corporate alliances are commonplace in other regions of the world, the U.S. Justice Department sanctioned the automaker's arrangements.

These joint ventures differ from acquisitions in an important way. They are not outright purchases of another company or technology. Each joint venture tends to involve a relatively small portion of a meganational's resources. In some cases the agreements are between manufacturers and either a supplier or a key customer. Though many of them skate very close to antitrust issues, the companies in most cases have been able to avoid anticompetitiveness complaints. More and more, joint ventures are being formed between competitors—though not those competitors who must have strategic alliances to survive. The following chart does not represent all the joint ventures that the 25 most powerful meganationals have orchestrated; rather they are those they have established among themselves.

In a nearly cryptic social web, the meganationals are becoming extremely well acquainted: Merck has a relationship with Du Pont, which in turn has joined with AT&T, which in turn is associated

Joint Venture Links

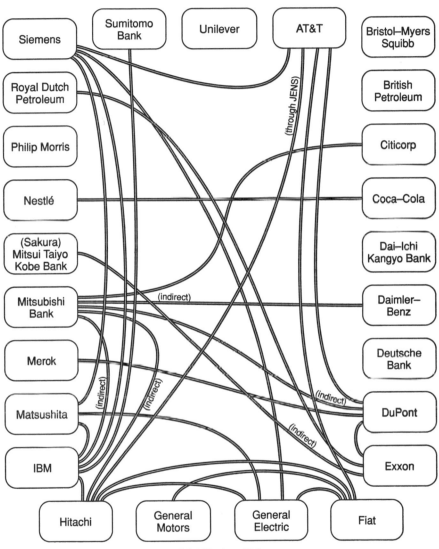

Joint Venture Links

with Fiat, which has ties with General Electric, which has linked up with Hitachi, which has relations with IBM, which is working with Siemens. Citicorp and Mitsubishi Bank cooperated on a construction project in the Far East, and both have many lending and service arrangements with the other meganationals. And so it goes.

Corporate executives often draw analogies between mergers and marriage. (" . . . we've learned that in all joint ventures—from marriage to mountain climbing—finding the right partner is vital," AT&T's Robert Allen.) Strategic alliances can more aptly be compared to dating—and holding hands a lot. It's usually acceptable to date more than one person at a time. Nevertheless, relationships are built and, in a good dating experience, mutual benefits evolve.

The networks cross international borders and industry frontiers. The chain of cooperation and communication is shrewd and sophisticated. But in the fashion of private clubs, school fraternities, or royal families, the relationships bind together a group, a class, or a stratum that has interests to protect. In this case, they promote and safeguard links between global barons.

Chapter Seven

Globalization—The Death of Antitrust?

"Imperialism is the final stage of capitalism."

Lenin

The news from International Business Machines in 1991 slammed in as fast and hard as aces from tennis pro Martina Navratilova. Twice the company shocked the stock market by announcing that quarterly earnings would be less—much less—than anticipated. "IBM Is Losing Ground in Japan," trumpeted one newspaper headline. Word spread that IBM chairman John Akers was dressing down both company executives and employees for the poor performance he was getting from those entrusted with upholding the reputation treasured by the world's largest computer maker. IBM, Akers charged, had "too many people standing around the water cooler," and that he would tolerate no further loss of market share.

"The only question now," said the *New York Times* after a report of Akers' tirade leaked out, "is whether the accidental release happened on purpose." Actually, there was another question—that of whether Akers was taking advantage of temporary market conditions to enlarge IBM's overwhelming presence in the computer industry.[1]

At the time this drama was unfolding, other news—sometimes tiny little stories—was running on inside pages. These pieces indicated that people at IBM were exceedingly busy.

- IBM would be licensing program design software by Borland International and would be working with Borland on other software technology.

- IBM would market Lotus Development Corporation Notes and electronic mail software.
- IBM would invest $100 million in Wang Laboratories Inc., which would resell some IBM products under the Wang name. In turn, IBM had a shot at winning access to Wang's advanced optical and imaging technology.
- In Japan, IBM offered licensing rights to 11 major Japanese computer makers to combat NEC Corporation in the personal computer market. Among its own competitors that signed on with IBM were Toshiba, Fujitsu, Hitachi Ltd., and the Matsushita Electric Industrial Corp.
- IBM would build mainframe computers for another rival, Mitsubishi Electric Corp.

A year earlier, IBM teamed up with the German meganational Siemens to develop high-capacity, 64-megabit memory chips. In July of 1991, IBM and Siemens said they would remodel the IBM plant near Paris to make advanced 16-megabit dynamic random access memory (DRAM) chips.

Big Blue also formed a partnership with Diebold Inc. to manufacture and market automated teller machines worldwide.

As early as 1989, IBM had established more than 75 equity alliances worldwide with more than 43 joint ventures in Japan alone. The partners ranged from long-established meganationals such as Siemens and Hitachi to small entrepreneurs who brought along innovations IBM hadn't thought of or did not choose to develop itself. In the early 1990s, the company pressed ahead with its international network of alliances.

The real revelation came in July of 1991 when IBM reached an agreement with the second-ranking U.S. computer manufacturer, Apple Computer Inc., to jointly develop and market a new personal computer. That move could effectively cut out Microsoft, creator of IBM's PC operating system Ms-DOS, not to mention Intel Corporation and other manufacturers with which the two industry giants had previously worked. IBM had lost patience with Microsoft and Intel's feisty, freewheeling styles. Each company insisted on selling its products on the open market, though IBM preferred exclusivity.

In a memo to his senior executives, Microsoft chairman William

Gates expressed his horror. "Our nightmare—IBM 'attacking' us in systems software . . . is not a scenario, but a reality." Of course nothing in the business world ever is simple. Microsoft and 40 other computer companies had joined in an alliance called ACE, that hoped to set new industrywide standards for personal computers.

As a result, several things were going on at IBM at once.

Number one, for the first time in decades some real competition had risen in the computer industry, and IBM, the undisputed leader in the world of computers, was experiencing a decline in sales and profits. Those market inroads were made much more dire by the worldwide recession that hurt the sales of practically every participant in the computer industry. The repressed state of the industry meant that competitors, especially smaller ones, were open to alliances with companies they once had challenged. And finally, IBM had navigated the shark-infested waters of antitrust a decade earlier, had come head to head with government lawyers, and had won. The company felt confident that it could consolidate its intimidating world position with impunity.

To be sure, some of IBM's troubles were real and some were of its own making. For decades, IBM had basked in the admiration of business leaders everywhere who envied the way IBM vanquished the computer industry.

Then in the mid-1980s, at the height of its triumph, IBM made several mistakes that led to slowing growth and creeping loss of share in certain key markets. Though it was one of the creators of the personal computer, IBM used someone else's products to make the machine. In fact, most parts of IBM's PCs were built by others, which made it possible to legally "clone" or make affordable duplicates of the stand-alone computer. Clone sales and competition from the Apple Macintosh PCs meant that IBM at last had genuine competition.

Additionally, because of a commitment to the large computers and to exclusivity of its systems, some customers were abandoning IBM. Again, Digital Equipment, Fujitsu, and other adversaries in the commercial market strengthened. About the time IBM sailed the world looking for alliances, it also abandoned the policy of obstructing other brands from having total compatibility with IBM. The company set out to reclaim lost market share through many different strategies.

As often is the case when a star loses some sparkle, public reaction to IBM's changing position was outrageous. "For six years now," wrote *Business Week*, "IBM has been struggling to recover from an unprecedented earnings slump." While it was true that profits were flat, from 1985 to 1989 IBM revenues had increased every year. IBM's 1990 profits remained among the biggest in the world—$6 billion on revenues of $69 billion. Yet at the height of IBM's headline storm, a strange dichotomy existed. The headlines screamed that 1991 second-quarter profits plummeted 92 percent, and therefore more employees would lose jobs. Careful reading of the story, however, made it clear that sales were off only 11 percent. Profits were being slammed by acquisitions and reorganization costs, actions that would position IBM nicely for post-recession growth.[2]

Still, investors were distressed by horizontal net earnings, indicating that either the company's overhead was too high, or that it was making big investments in the future. IBM, which had operated by a no-layoff policy, knew its work force was too big, and vowed to cut up to 50,000 jobs from its peak of 405,500. Even so, in 1991 the company employed around 370,000 people.

Measured by its own standards, the company was in crisis. IBM watchers had become to believe that Big Blue would grow at 15 percent per year forever. Yet by 1990 the company hadn't topped a record $11.2 billion in operating income that was set in 1984. IBM's shares, long the market bellwether, still traded 40 percent below their 1987 zenith.

Even though IBM's total market share slipped from a mind-boggling 37 percent, the company still controlled 21 percent of the worldwide computer market. IBM remained larger than all of its computer-making competitors combined and had the second largest market capitalization in the world. In 1990 it ranked second in world stock market value, bested only by one of its venture partners, Japan's NTT.

IBM had dominated its markets since Thomas Watson Sr. adopted the company name in 1924. Nevertheless, as IBM swept in to claim part of the operation of one competitor after another in the 1990s, no one complained about anticompetitive practices. Most commentators pooh-poohed IBM's plans as unlikely to succeed. In its glee over the prospect of beating out Japanese computer makers, the *Los Angeles Times* even printed an editorial lauding the alliance as "bold and strategic."

Taking psychological advantage of a recession, a war, a cyclical slump in its own industry, and some poor choices by its own management, IBM made the most of the American terror of losing competitive advantage. IBM created a network of agreements that, in another climate, certainly would have been viewed as anticompetitive. The central seam holding the networks together was alliances with IBM's largest and toughest competitors in the United States, Asia, and Europe.

IBM had little reason to fear antitrust action in a national climate that looked kindly upon the high-tech colossus. However, some observers had been critical of IBM practices. Only a few years earlier, IBM had come under scathing attack in Richard T. DeLamarter's *Big Blue: IBM's Use and Abuse of Power* for what were described as "monopolistic" practices.

In that book, DeLamarter described his years at the U.S. Department of Justice working on a 13-year antitrust campaign against IBM. "During the case," he said, "IBM portrayed itself as the underdog, asking, 'Who are we against the vast resources of the U.S. government?' In fact, IBM was, and still is, the most powerful corporation in the world and fought tooth and nail for the continuation of that power. It spent lavishly on its defense, on a scale the government trial team was never able to match."[3]

In 1982, the Reagan administration's hands-off policy took hold. The assistant attorney general in charge of the Antitrust Division, William Baxter, declared the IBM case to be without merit and ordered the Justice Department to withdraw its efforts.

"In the first year following Baxter's decision," DeLamarter wrote, "IBM rose three positions, from eleventh to eighth, in the annual *Fortune* magazine survey of firms with the largest worldwide revenues. In the process of securing sales of $34 billion in that year, it increased its 70 percent plus share of the large computer business and also expanded into new areas—areas where other firms already had established positions."

Challenges to IBM's dominion in foreign markets also came to nothing. The company's policy of establishing a headquartered company in each country provided protection. In 1985, Japanese computer makers unsuccessfully protested a joint venture between

IBM and the recently privatized Japanese telephone company NTT. Between them, the two companies controlled about a 30 percent share of Japan's $68 billion installed base of computers. Japan was allowing various joint ventures in an attempt to break up telecommunication monopolies, and the country's traditionally languid Fair Trade Commission viewed the IBM venture as no different from any other.

In late 1988, IBM negotiated a deal with the European Commission, which viewed IBM with slightly more suspicion. In return for EC surrendering a long-standing legal action against IBM for abusing its predominant position in the computer industry, IBM agreed to make available to EC competitors certain technical information.

So what's the problem, laissez-faire proponents ask. If government regulators in Japan, Europe, and the United States can't make antitrust allegations against IBM stick, maybe there isn't any problem. "It is that IBM monopolizes the computer business," insisted DeLamarter in *Big Blue*, "which is arguably the most important industry in the world. IBM's power is such that all of its competitors, large and small, exist entirely at its sufferance. IBM is nothing less than the most powerful corporation in the world and, thanks to (attorney general) Baxter's decision, it is now virtually unrestrained by the antitrust laws or meaningful public scrutiny."[4]

As a consequence of acquisitions and alliances that IBM made several years after DeLamarter wrote those words, the company is practically assured of maintaining its lock on the computer market. New IBM products are said to be the best they have been in decades and even more-dynamic products are in the pipeline. "IBM compatible," may not have the caché it once did, but the universality of IBM computers will continue to set industry standards. As computerization infiltrates every industry segment and sweeps the globe, few consumers will want to risk buying equipment that can't interface with everyone else—especially when most "others" are using IBM products.

Next to a deeply held certainty that they trust in democracy, Americans believe that they stand for free trade. For decades, although federal officials were given meager funds for investigation and prosecution of companies that imposed unfair competition in the marketplace, the United States paid lip service to the concept of open, freewheeling competition. The idea that big business must be watched has been a difficult concept to reconcile, given American impatience with government for meddling in efficient business practices. If the government interferes, how free can trade be? Furthermore, there exists an extremely thin line between playing to win and playing unfairly. On top of that, Americans, like everyone else, love winners.

Nevertheless, by choosing its targets well and prosecuting egregious violators when they were found, the Justice Department for decades was able to discourage many companies from anticompetitive practices. Then suddenly in the 1980s, following the split up of AT&T, antitrust enforcement piddled out. Announcements of new mergers swept the news worldwide.

"What had happened to bring about this earthquake?" asked Robert Slater in *The Titans of Takeover*. The answer? Reagan was elected, abandoned antitrust efforts, and gave the green light to big business.

"A nine-year government effort to break up Kellogg Co., General Mills, and General Foods was dropped," Slater said. "Most importantly, when the large-scale takeover wars began in the 1980s, rather than serve as a referee and halt the big companies from consolidating, Washington acted like a cheerleader. Du Pont and Conoco, Chevron and Gulf, Texaco and Getty: none of these deals could have been contemplated in the past. By the early 1980s, as the investment bankers would say, they were doable."[5]

Antitrust watchdog Baxter maintained that mergers and takeovers are part of a natural evolutionary process. Baxter explained to Congress that mergers are "a very very important feature of our capital markets by which assets are continuously moving into the hands of those managers who employ them most efficiently and interfering in a general way with that process would, in my judgment, be an error of substantial magnitude."

Economic theory wasn't the only reason for the new attitude in Washington. The Reagan administration was driven by fear—the fear that the United States would become a secondary player in the international economy. Globalization was sweeping the world. U.S. companies found themselves in close competition with huge foreign corporations, many of which operate under different, less-restrictive rules. In recognition of the reality that the United States faced in world markets, the Bush administration proposed the National Cooperative Production Act, which will make joint production by U.S. companies easier.

A number of experts have agreed that a change in rules regulating free competition was in order. "We have antitrust laws that are obsolete," said MIT economist Lester Thurow. "They apply to American corporations but cannot apply to foreigners. You could file an antitrust suit against Ford and GM for having a joint facility, but Toyota and GM have a joint operation. The Mitsubishi Group is illegal under our law, but all (members of the Mitsubishi keiretsu) are in the United States. If our corporations are there and theirs are here—what makes sense?"[6]

Crossing national borders wasn't the entire problem. Crossing cultures had a lot to do with it. The Japanese keiretsu system (cooperative coteries) mentioned in earlier chapters was one major culprit. Since the end of World War II, the six largest keiretsu have accounted for about one fourth of Japan's booming gross national product.

The economic reach of these keiretsu is staggering, noted *Fortune* magazine in a 1991 article. "When the *Sankin-kai,* or president's council of the DKB group, gets together for its monthly lunch, the presidents of the world's largest bank (Dai-Ichi Kangyo), the world's largest textile company (Ashi Chemical), and the world's second largest computer company (Fujitsu) are at the table, along with the heads of Kawasaki Steel, Isuzu Motors, cosmetics maker Shiseido, and a couple of dozen other important companies."[7]

Though Japan has perfectly good antitrust laws left in place at the end of the U.S. occupation, the Fair Trade Commission seldom enforces the laws. " . . . like the rest of Japan," *Fortune* explained, "the commission believes in *wa,* or harmony."

As usual, the problem isn't solely centered in the United States and Japan. European countries also have antitrust rules, but there is disagreement on how they should be interpreted and enforced.

The West German economics minister, overriding the direction of his own antitrust panel, in 1989 allowed automaker Daimler-Benz to buy an arms maker—an acquisition that made Daimler one of Europe's largest companies. The Cartel Office contended that Daimler-Benz already controlled a big share of the arms, technology, and aerospace business in West Germany. The combination of Daimler and Messerschmitt-Boelkow-Blohm would be so powerful that it would distort competition among key domestic industries. Not only was Daimler allowed to proceed, a condition of the Messerschmitt purchase was that Daimler buy a greater share of the German government's stake in Airbus Industries.

Daimler isn't the only expanding German meganational. Siemens AG, Germany's largest electronics firm and manufacturer of everything from electric teakettles to nuclear power plants, in the early 1990s went on a buying spree. It acquired several companies, including Nixdorf Computers, without undue regulatory objection. "In western Germany," the *New York Times* said, "Siemens completely dominates some market sectors, including telecommunications, where its market share is 40 to 50 percent." Siemens, perhaps needless to repeat, was to become one of IBM's largest venture partners.[8]

What *is* the problem, as long as a company like IBM, Daimler-Benz, Siemens, and Dai-Ichi Kangyo Bank contribute something important to society, and do a good job of it?

Some business executives simply accept industrial leviathans as the price of efficiency and advancement.

"For certain European industries to grow to the level of the United States and Japan," Martin Waldenstrom, president of Paris-based Booz Allen Acquisition Services told the *New York Times*, "Europe must have a more enlightened merger policy."[9]

On the other hand, Michael Porter, Harvard professor and author of *The Competitive Advantage of Nations*, doesn't believe that easing antitrust restrictions is necessarily in a country's or an industry's foremost interest. Allowing rivals to collaborate blunts their aggressiveness, he contends, and thus makes them less competitive globally.

Others claim that a nation's total economy is less proficient when there are fewer competitors. "Efficiency is a multifaceted concept," explained Adams and Brock in *The Bigness Complex*. "There is operating efficiency. Here the question is whether giant corporations are producing mousetraps at the lowest possible cost. Then there is innovation efficiency. Are corporate giants in constant quest for a better mousetrap? Finally, there is social efficiency. Perhaps mousetraps should not be produced at all. Perhaps rodent control should be effectuated through superior pesticides or a greater investment in feline capital."[10]

The most extreme example of what can happen when monopoly

exists was in the former communist bloc nations. There was only one company—the government. Therefore efficiency was extremely low, consumer choice was virtually nonexistent, and the economy literally fell to pieces.

Kazuo Inamori, chairman of Kyocera Corporation, contends, "Capitalist societies cannot function properly unless overexpansion of business and monopolistic activity are prohibited; they work best in a climate of healthy competition. Many Japanese companies have become very large, even by international standards. The world's top 10 banks are all Japanese. In every industry—from steel to automobiles to electrical appliances—Japanese corporations are among the largest and the fastest growing anywhere, but it is hardly a trend we can delight over."[11]

Japan also is a good example of what transpires when massive business interests, with the backing of a compliant government, begin to encroach. In that country, citizens often pay twice as much for consumer goods as Americans or Europeans.

"Prices here are far too high," wrote Taro Yayama, a Japanese political analyst. "Last year the exchange rate fluctuated between Y120 and Y130 to the U.S. dollar. But the Economic Planning Agency estimates that it actually took Y200 to obtain $1 worth of goods and services in Japan.

"Under free competition," Yayama continued, "domestic prices should reflect international trends." Otherwise the consumer becomes the victim.[12]

All kinds of choices are limited in such a society. While Japanese workers may feel secure with lifetime jobs, they also may feel stuck with their company, whether they like it or not. Big Japanese corporations discourage mid-career switches.

Ultimately, antitrust is about fair play. When a company becomes big enough that there are no viable competitors to set them straight, they can play any way they want to. In a *Business Week* interview, management consultant Thomas J. Peters described a discussion he'd had with one of IBM's top dozen customers. In scalding terms, the client told Peters, " . . . they don't shoot straight—on when the products are going to be available and how well they are going to work. They're heavy-handed in controlling you. A hundred little arrogances still."[13]

Most economists agree that the concentration of power in big business presents a perpetual dilemma. But they have different ideas of what to do about it. Some believe that big business is under constant siege by aggressors, innovators, and new technology. The vast companies lose their controlling positions eventually, in the natural course of events.

Others, like John Kenneth Galbraith, accept power gathering as inevitable but would subject it to public surveillance and management.

Galbraith isn't very hopeful, however. He already believes that the dominance of big firms in America means that the U.S. system is not much different from socialism in that risk taking has been replaced by the bureaucratic planning of the "corporate technostructure."

Indeed, antitrust abuses, price-fixing, and the problems that have plagued the United States since early in the 20th century will be center stage again in the 21st, except that now the theater will be global rather than merely national. Almost every nation (and emerging economic entities such as the European Community) knows they need strong laws to deal with issues of competition. But just as is the case in Japan and the United States, the laws will do no good unless they are enforced energetically.

In theory, most government officials realize that close adherence to antitrust rules is necessary. The European Community agreed to jointly review mergers that exceed approximately $6 billion. Previously, such mergers were scrutinized by each member country. Unfortunately, some members of the EC suspect that centralized investigation will mean a less critical eye on monopolies, rather than a more stringent approach.

It is heartening that, under pressure from the U.S. government, Japanese officials recently have pursued and enforced some antitrust abuses. The government also published new directives prohibiting companies from fixing prices, driving competitors out of the market, and blocking certain types of exports. However, it is feared that the Japanese "amakudari" or "descent from heaven" system, in which retired government officials are appointed to positions with Japan's most significant companies, will guarantee that the regulations are taken lightly.

It seems that in recent years antitrust disputes, rather than pure in intention, have become an arena in which competitive nations act out their trade feuds.

Antitrust proponents were pleased with reports that the Justice

Department under President George Bush would increase antitrust operations. However, the department's most notable suit was filed against a Japanese company that planned to buy a U.S. manufacturer of semiconductor equipment. The purchase of Semi-Gas Systems Inc. would give Nippon Sanso a 48 percent stake in the U.S. market and a third of the world market for equipment to handle the hazardous gases used in semiconductor manufacturing. The Justice Department didn't think IBM's more than 30 percent of the world computer market was excessive nor a 40 percent combined share with Apple was out of line. But it did object to a Japanese company controlling a lesser U.S. market.

Without question, it is wrong for a single Japanese company to entrap a key element of a U.S. market, but it is equally wrong for any company from any nation to have a viselike grip on any market.

There is always hope that governments will reclaim their right to halt the march toward monopolization—and to develop antitrust mechanisms suitable for the new world of globalized business in which bigger business is inevitable.

The U.S. Justice Department had considered extending its own antitrust laws to foreign companies that engaged in price fixing, the carving up of markets, or other anticompetitive practices in their own markets—if the practices damaged American companies. That threat didn't go over well with foreign governments, who understandably do not relish the idea of their citizens being dictated to by another government. Since then, the United States has been studying a joint agreement with Great Britain on antitrust matters.

Though business becomes increasingly transnational as this book is being written, there is no effective international convention for handling competitiveness issues. Rather than leave this important issue to be controlled by the country with the most contentious methods, the majority of nations would no doubt encourage the establishment of international guidelines through the General Agreement on Tariffs and Trade (GATT), the Organization for Economic Cooperation and Development, or such other international bodies.

"A system of social checks is needed to ensure that the immense power of corporations is not taken advantage of or used solely for the interests of certain people, or that actions counter to the public interest and the spirit of the times are not taken in the name of corporate profits," wrote Kyocera's Kazuo Inamori. "Corporations must be operated in a fair manner for the benefit of society as a whole."[14]

If all else fails, consumers and citizens alike can hope that Justice Louis Brandeis, writing in *The Curse of Bigness*, was correct when he said "there is a point where (the organization) would become too large for efficient and economic management, just as there is a point where it would be too small to be an efficient instrument. The limit of efficient size is exceeded when the disadvantages attendant upon size outweigh advantages, when the centrifugal force exceeds the centripetal." Perhaps it is that overwhelming centrifugal force that would cause a company to implode.[15]

What is antitrust?

By U.S. standards, antitrust violations exist in several circumstances:

- When a contract, combination, or conspiracy restrains trade.
- In all monopolies or attempts to monopolize.
- When mergers and acquisitions—horizontal, vertical, and conglomerate—substantially lessen competition or tend to create a monopoly.
- When any unfair methods of competition are utilized. The unfair tactics may include price fixing, predatory pricing, dumping, and so on.

Chapter Eight

At Issue Is Money

"The management of a balance of power is a permanent
undertaking, not an exertion that has a foreseeable end."

Henry Kissinger

Tom Fox, with his open-neck shirt, cotton pants, and his Normal
Heights storefront office, hardly seems a serious threat to Mitsui
Taiyo Kobe Bank of Japan, the second largest bank holding company in the world. Yet he intends to be the fiercest community
watchdog possible, and in that spirit Fox launched an assault that
could stand in the way of the U.S. expansion plans of many international banks.

Fox is the executive director of Normal Heights Community
Development Corporation, a citizen-based organization in an aging, moderate-income neighborhood of San Diego, California. It is
Fox's assignment to make Normal Heights (which got its name
from a normal school, or old teacher's college, that once had a
campus there) as vital a community as possible. His organization
holds meetings to discuss community needs, assess problems, and
find solutions. They even publish a newspaper. "We're a lightning
rod for community issues, a mini city hall," Fox explained. Because
small business operators in the neighborhood complained that they
were routinely refused access to credit, his organization investi-
gated. Three business people submitted their loan applications to
several banks that advertised for deposits in the area. "Mitsui
wouldn't even take the application on one loan, and the other two
were denied," Fox said. "All three loans have since been funded."
One loan was to a small restaurant, which later opened in two
additional locations.[1]

Fox's group subsequently challenged Mitsui Manufacturers

Bank (a Mitsui Taiyo Kobe Bank California subsidiary) on its compliance to the U.S. Community Reinvestment Act (CRA), which requires that banks make a suitable balance of loans in the constituencies that they serve. The purpose of CRA is to prevent "redlining" or discriminatory lending practices to minority or low-income borrowers and neighborhoods. Before long, 13 other California citizens groups joined the protest. They picketed Mitsui Manufacturers' Los Angeles office and eventually succeeded in delaying regulatory approval for parts of Mitsui Taiyo Kobe's postmerger reorganization to achieve international integration.

Fox and other community activists were particularly rankled by Mitsui Manufacturers' refusal to involve its parent bank in the negotiations. The protesters wanted Japanese officials to hear their concerns and hoped for a policy statement that would embrace fair treatment of low-income and minority borrowers. Mitsui Manufacturers officials refused to call upon their parent company, saying that it was Mitsui Manufacturers, not Mitsui Taiyo Kobe, who held the U.S. banking license. It was the American subsidiary's problem to deal with.

"When we started our challenge," said Gilda Haas, organizer of Communities for Accountable Reinvestment in Los Angeles, "(Mitsui Manufacturers) said 'We're just a $1 billion bank, a little bank, and we can only do so much.' Then they launched an advertising campaign, telling people that they were backed by the $400 billion Mitsui Taiyo Kobe Bank. Obviously there is a lot of confusion about accountability."[2]

Each Mitsui foreign subsidiary, incidentally, is headed by an officer assigned from Japan.

While Mitsui Manufacturers' management was insisting that their Japanese parent had no responsibility in the matter, the community groups launched a similar protest against Security Pacific Bank of Los Angeles. Security Pacific wanted to acquire 20 percent of Mitsui Manufacturers to cement long-term relations with Mitsui Taiyo Kobe Bank. Security Pacific's president and other high-level executives met with the community groups. They promised to cooperate in setting up an equitable lending program that would preclude risky loans for the bank. An agreement was hammered out, and the community group's challenge to Security Pacific was dropped.

"They (Mitsui) are still resistant," Fox said. "They believe in their heart of hearts that they should not have the regulation, should not have to comply with CRA."

For both Fox and Haas, the central question is protecting their community from exclusionary banking practices. Japanese banks now own 25 percent of bank assets in California, and 12 percent of the U.S. banking assets. As the 1990s progress, the foreign ownership issue looms even larger. President George Bush's administration pushes for full interstate banking, which would allow banking and branch expansion across all state lines. The community activists fear that only the largest banks will be able to meet the capital requirements necessary for the interstate scope of business, and not many of those banks will be American owned. There are misgivings that individuals and businesses will be forced to deposit funds in the big banks because there will be no other choices. Conversely, the big banks won't be interested in lending to small organizations. Such practices would drain the financial blood from communities like Normal Heights.

"We want to make international banks the focus of our attention," Fox went on, "because we don't think the regulators or the politicians have thought this through. Mitsui is the tip of the iceberg.

"We are in competition with the world for cash," Fox continued. "We're going to see German, Italian, South American, and Japanese banks in here. Whether or not a farmer in Iowa gets a loan should not be decided in Japan."

The bank eventually dropped the regulatory application on which the Normal Heights protest was based, but Fox expects to keep up the fight for community access to financing. "We're not going to get off their case," he insisted. "We're not going to get off their case ever. Groups like ours are not going to go away. We have a constituency, and we have needs that must be met."

Mitsui Manufacturers Bank insisted it had done nothing wrong, and said in fact it does lend in moderate- to low-income communities. But not even the subsidiary would deny that Mitsui Taiyo Kobe Bank *is* an iceberg among international banks. It is massive, has many facets, and moves freely in the seas of both high- and individual-level finance.

This stately institution was created by the 1989 merger of Mitsui

Bank of Tokyo and the Taiyo Kobe Bank of Kobe. The aristrocrat of this union is Mitsui, which dates back more than 300 years to 1683 when the Mitsui Exchange House was founded in the ancient city of Edo. Edo later became Tokyo and the Mitsui Exchange House became the first private commercial bank in Japan. A pioneer in international banking, in 1906 it was the first Japanese bank to transact foreign exchange business. In the next two decades, Mitsui established branches in Shanghai, New York, London, and Bombay.

Despite its blue blood, Mitsui was Japan's ninth largest bank before the merger; Taiyo Kobe was ranked twelfth. Together, they moved to number two in assets—in the world. Ken-ichi Suematsu, who took the operating helm of the merged institutions, admitted that fear was the exegesis for the union. "We were worried about being a weakling," he said when the merger was announced. "In order to survive as a commercial bank, we cannot afford to remain in the middle rank. It's too insecure a position."[3]

It is the ambition of Mitsui Taiyo Kobe, said Chairman Yasuo Matsushita, to be a "universal bank," one that goes everywhere and does everything. "Everything" already ranges from consumer services to trust banking to commercial loans in China to underwriting Euroyen offerings. With 103 offices in 31 countries outside Japan, Mitsui has the geographic wherewithal to reach its goal.

Additionally, reads Mitsui's annual report, " . . . the bank's strong overseas network is an extremely effective competitive weapon in building relationships with the growing number of Japanese corporations setting up operations overseas."

In that simple statement lies the explanation for the daunting size and influence of the bank. The message has been—where go our keiretsu members, so goes Mitsui Taiyo Kobe. It has been the Japanese way. Mitsui is the leading bank in a formidable keiretsu led by the auto manufacturer, Toyota Motor. The group also includes Toshiba, Mitsukoshi department stores, Japan Steel Works, Oji Paper, Mitsui trading company, Mitsui Mining and Smelting, Mitsui OSK Lines, and the other Mitsuis.

More than half of all the Japanese-affiliated manufacturing facilities in California are owned fully or partially by keiretsu. They also account for 68 percent of U.S. high-technology investments since 1989. One of the reasons California has so many Japanese banks is that it has numerous Japanese manufacturing facilities, not to mention an enormous amount of Japanese real estate investment. There are several Mitsui-affiliated companies operating in San Diego, where the Mitsui Manufacturers' protest began. The investment of Japanese money in California began accelerating in the late 1970s and early 1980s, a trend that later made its way through the rest of the United States.

Another unforgettable member of the Toyota/Mitsui keiretsu is Koito, the headlamp manufacturer where T. Boone Pickens made a noisy, Texas-brash quest for a board position. Because other members of the keiretsu held large blocks of Koito's shares, Boone bombed. He did, however, shine the spotlight on how Japan does business, which may have been his only intention anyway. Pickens was appalled at the way the Japanese system closed ranks to protect one of its own, and Japanese business barons were no less appalled at Picken's impudence.

Banks worldwide are under enormous stress, not only from recessionary times, but also because of their own expansionary notions. Mitsui is no exception. It has struggled since the merger with what appears to be an overly large bureaucracy. Chairman Matsushita, in an interview with the author in his high-rise office overlooking the Imperial Palace grounds in Tokyo, explained that Mitsui intends to become better known internationally, and that the bank intends to be a good corporate citizen.

Mitsui Taiyo Kobe also has had to call upon its vast resources to meet the new, higher capital requirements the Bank for International Settlements has demanded of all international banks. Yet, since American, European, and other Japanese banks also are having difficulties with new capital requirements (and since German banks have had to deal with reunification costs), Mitsui is in the same boat with competing financial institutions.

As a postscript, in mid-1991 Mitsui Taiyo Kobe Bank announced it would simplify its name to Sakura Bank. There was talk of Mitsui Manufacturers Bank following suit. Sakura means cherry blossom, the logo symbol Mitsui has long employed. The whole point, apparently, is to evoke the image of Japan's most beloved flower and therefore render the bank more user-friendly.

Money is the *reason* business exists, but it also is the *way* business exists. Without cash—a medium of exchange, a measure, and a storehouse of value—businesses could not operate. Money was invented for business, and banks were invented by business interests to take care of money. As the guardians of money, what happens in the banking industry usually mirrors the evolution of the economy and of the societies that rely on that economy for their well-being.

For example, the rise of Japan as an international economic power is reflected in its banking industry. Eight of the 10 biggest banks in the world are Japanese, though not all of them wield the same enormous influence as the four described in this book as meganationals. The 12 largest commercial banks in Japan—described as city banks—control assets worth $3.2 trillion, roughly equivalent to the total assets of the entire U.S. commercial banking industry. Japanese banks, according to the Bank of International Settlements, commanded a 36 percent share of the 1990 worldwide lending market.

Despite the enormous control of private banks over the money that businesses and individuals use, actual currencies (at least in the past) have belonged to governments. Governments traditionally have manufactured currencies, as an infrastructure mechanism for trade but also to facilitate taxation. Currency management has been a means of financing governmental activities and a way to meet those needs of society that could not be provided by individual or commercial enterprise.

One of the great failings of Russian Communism was its inability to cultivate a viable currency that was convertible into other national currencies. Without that tool, major western countries were unwilling to invest in the republics. They had no way of earning profits, except in rubles. Yet, outside the USSR they couldn't use the rubles. Nobody knew how much of the currency circulated even inside Russia, and nobody could figure what the ruble was worth. Therefore it became virtually worthless.

The great enthusiasm in the USSR and the Eastern European nations to split into their ethnic or nationalistic parts, no matter how dear to its proponents, will soon pass. Most Eastern Europeans are seeking greater, not less, economic security. They eventually will be forced to face the new world reality: Sustenance and stability are to be found in league with others. They will shortly discover that the global capital markets, where banks, governments, and corporations trade $400 billion a day in currencies, is where economic decisions are made. In today's world, wrote *Los Angeles Times* columnist James Flanigan, "Global investment markets give orders to governments." It may be a sad and painful lesson, but it will be learned quickly by peoples who have been left at the back end of economic development for far too long. Unfortunately, global economic participation comes at a price. Even a money base as large and strong as the U.S. dollar is vulnerable to outside influence.[4]

A press release, circulated to the news media on behalf of a California-based real estate company that was a 50 percent subsidiary of Nomura Securities of Japan, made clear what the price is. The press release, and others like it sent out over several months in 1990, issued a warning to the American public not to be overly critical of Japanese investors.

"Despite competitive real estate markets throughout the country and recent setbacks in the Japanese economy, Japanese investors remain eager to provide long-term capital for the U.S. real estate industry. But they have become increasingly anxious about making these investments with the current wave of public sentiment running against them." The press release quoted Roy March, executive vice president of the Normura subsidiary, Eastdil Realty Inc.

"Within 12 months, however, a decline in Japanese–U.S. real estate investment could trigger dramatic increases in domestic interest rates felt by consumers in the form of higher home mortgage, car, and credit card payments. The U.S. real estate market already is feeling the withdrawal of capital from Japan.

"We need Japanese capital to maintain liquidity in our economy and keep interest rates down and will eventually welcome their investments once again," March said.

Not long afterward, when the United States threatened to apply sanctions against the Japanese construction and financial markets unless they were opened further to foreign competition, the Japanese government retaliated by threatening to cut off U.S. credit. The tiff was settled before it erupted into full-blown trade warfare.

With nations, as with families, money is an emotionally charged topic. After all, money presents power, control, and privilege. No wonder former British Prime Minister Margaret Thatcher thundered at the British Parliament as they debated a common currency for the European Community. "If you hand over your sterling, you hand over the powers of this Parliament to Europe."

Thatcher literally was shouting into the wind. The march of economics had passed her by, and soon she was forced to step down from a post she had held longer than any prime minister in British history. Her opponents understood something that Thatcher was unwilling to concede. Business has outgrown many nation-states, and therefore has outgrown many currencies.

"That the world economy is being internationalized through increases in world trade and the spread of multinational corporations is a truism," wrote Peter Grier in the *Christian Science Monitor.* "The easy flow of capital across borders is eating away at the ability of governments to exercise control over their own interest rates and fiscal policy."[5]

The economists also agreed that an important manifestation of the outflanking of governments by big business is the unmanageability of inflation.

"The emergence of massive institutions of private power makes an important contribution to our inflationary propensity," Heilbroner and Thurow wrote in *Economics Explained.* "A striking difference between today and yesterday is that in the past inflationary peaks were regularly followed by long deflationary periods. Prices tended irregularly downward over most of the last half of the 19th century. Why? One reason is that the economy was much more heavily agricultural in those days, and farm prices have always been more volatile, particularly downward, than the prices of manufactured goods."[6]

Chronic inflation should be expected, the authors continued, for it "comes about because capitalism exerts its nervous, threatening, expansive energy in a changed social environment. Capitalism is now government-supported capitalism, power-bloc capitalism, a capitalism of high public expectation."

Probably no country exemplifies inflationary anguish more strikingly than Argentina. Once the most affluent and productive country in South America, Argentina has been plagued by hyperinflation in the past decade. In spite of several years of intense government efforts, in 1990 annual inflation raced along at 1,344 percent.

Because Argentina has suffered chronic inflation, the biggest businesses in the country (and individuals who were able to do so) amassed hordes of U.S. dollars. Many prices came to be quoted in dollars; the dollar came to exist as a parallel currency. When Argentina's australs and the U.S. dollar were counted together, there was too much money afloat in Argentina, adding to an already difficult situation. though government officials made an effort to force dollars out of the system, they failed and the less stable austral could not hold its own. The government intermittently considered abandoning the austral in favor of the dollar, and partially did so when dollar-denominated checking accounts were legalized.

Argentina is not the only small country with its currency under siege. In certain countries, such as Panama, the dollar is a de facto currency. Liberia uses the U.S. dollar exclusively.

Though the United States has been able to deal with inflation in a reasonably competent manner, market trends are more powerful when the exchange rate, or the dollar value versus other currencies, is concerned. Balance and stability among the dominant currencies is essential for the effective management of trade. When market forces drive the price of the U.S. dollar too high (too much demand) or allow it to slip too low (too little demand), it often requires coordinated action between the Group of Seven. These seven most industrialized countries—the United States, Japan, Germany, Britain, France, Italy, and Canada—meet at regular summits in an attempt to synchronize economic activities. When the dollar strengthened to the point that it further damaged the U.S. balance of trade in the summer of 1991, the Group of Seven coordinated a wave of selling that knocked the dollar down 2.4 percent in a single day.

Exchange rates are of vital importance to business, as indicated in the 1990 annual report of Mitsui Taiyo Kobe Bank. "As a result of the fall in the yen's value and the rise in interest rates, stock prices dropped sharply in early calendar 1990 and remained stagnant through the end of the fiscal year," it read. These two events, the rise in both the yen's value and interest rates, also harmed the banks' domestic profits. However, some of those problems were offset, since the yen's decline had a favorable impact on international operations.

A third indication of the way business has outgrown nation-states is the Euromoney market, a system the corporate powers formulated to create their own currency. That the financial world was able to establish and utilize this vast corporate finance scheme is evidence of the ingenuity and resourcefulness of the meganationals.

Financial experts understand that, as a tool, money has exceptional qualities. It is like wind and water—when it needs to go someplace, it carves its own path. The Euromarket erupted as a reaction to domestic regulations of bond markets and domestic tax provisions. Euromoney is currency deposited by corporations (and governments as well) outside their home countries. These funds are used to make international settlements, but financial instruments such as the Eurobond and Eurocertificate of deposit have grown up around it. This virtually unregulated system, in which the dollar and yen dominate, provided a convenient currency in which political bodies such as the USSR, Cuba, and others without formal trading ties to the United States—without the explicit ability to own dollars—could engage in trade without appearing to break diplomatic rules.

Euromoney, beyond a doubt, represents the escape of cash from national boundaries. The central banks can no longer effectively control the price of currencies, because of the huge activity in the Euromoney market.

"This supranational currency sloshes around the world more or less in complete indifference to the wishes of any central bank," wrote Heilbroner and Thurow.[7]

The Euromoney market has some advantages. It is too vast for manipulation by any one player or a cartel of players. This is the state European governments are attempting to achieve with the European Currency Unit, or ECU. In fact, the whole concept of the European Economic Community is an effort to counteract the predicament of being a small country with a currency too vulnerable to compete in international markets. The 12 EC countries are fervently proud nation-states, but Jacques Delors, president of the EC, was able to convince members of the dangers they face.

David Lawday, in the *Atlantic* magazine, described the dilemma this way. "Europe's established countries are, then, in an uncommon squeeze. The classic nation-state is too small for big things and too big for small things. The British political scientist David Marquand says that the growth of the EC—which could become a United States of Europe before the 1990s are out—has forced individual countries to recognize that they are too small to carry out their own separate economics, monetary, and environmental policies, let alone their own defense. Such matters used to lie at the jealous heart of sovereignty."[8]

The Jacques DeLors solution was to create a supracurrency, a financial tool that, like Euromoney, functions in the abstract realm, above and around the tangible francs, pounds, marks, and guilders.

The ECU is truly an advanced form of money. In the beginning, there was no paper that could be folded into a wallet or change to jingle in the pocket. Rather, it began as an invisible "basket" or value-weighted mix of the European currencies that could be used in paper or electronic transactions. There has been an ECU bond market for some time, competing with the Euromonies. The ECU is being used for credit card transactions, and in 1991 some 23,000 EEC officials and staff were to begin receiving their wages in ECUs. While there are few touchable ECUs in circulation, they will be available soon. Futurists tell us that in the next century actual cash will be obsolete anyway. By then we may be living in a cashless society where electronic ECUs will be perfectly appropriate.

As a testament to the socializing power of money, Fiat's chairman Giovanni Agnelli told his employees in a company publication, "European monetary union may well constitute the first real common language among 340 million Europeans and become the unifying element of a political and geographical entity of diverse cultures and languages."[9]

Agnelli recognized the political and technical difficulties of a single currency and a central bank, but he also welcomed it as a liberating force for capital.

The ECU and the monetary system to support it has been a hard-fought issue. Many European leaders, like Margaret Thatcher, find it difficult to hand over some of their authority to the EC. Yet the timing is perfect for the ECU to become a superior monetary force—a currency that fits to a tee the new world order of megabusiness. It could, in fact, be the dominant currency of the next century. At the very least the ECU will be able to compete with the Japanese yen and the U.S. dollar, creating an international monetary troika.

It is fascinating to watch the EC wrestle with the currency question as Europe moves forward into an integrated economic community encompassing upward of 325 million people. If all goes as planned, the EC will outsize the United States, still the world's largest economy. However, the EC isn't the only political/economic alliance under construction.

Other regions see the value of political and economic cooperation as well. At the northern end of South America, Venezuela, Colombia, Peru, and Bolivia decided to abolish virtually all regional tariffs before the end of 1991. Four other South American republics—Argentina, Brazil, Uruguay, and Paraguay—agreed on their own free trade zone, the Southern Cone Common Market. The market is dubbed Mercosur, a contraction of its name in Spanish, The scheme builds a market of 190 million citizens accounting for more than half the gross domestic product of Latin America and the Caribbean. The Andean region failed at earlier attempts, and most of the participating countries have severe economic problems that will strew their path with stones. Yet world conditions urgently call for nations to recreate themselves in mightier dimensions.

President George Bush already has negotiated a North American free trade agreement with Canada and Mexico, and is working toward his "Enterprise for the Americas Initiative." That plan would meld the two continents, from Alaska to Argentina, into a single trading federation.

Though the Bush plan was received with enthusiasm and moved quickly in its early stages, like Europe, the Americas will find actual implementation of the plan to be rough terrain. However, Americans are a step ahead of other regions in one respect. There is no need to concoct a new form of money. They have the still-powerful (though no longer almighty) U.S. dollar to use as a common denominator.

Chapter Nine

Meganationals versus Government: Round One

"It is only under the shelter of the civil magistrate that the owner of. . . valuable property . . . can sleep a single night in security."

Adam Smith

British Petroleum Company's predicament began with a good idea that since has spread to many nations of the world—privatization of government assets. It ended with a Middle Eastern government owning a substantial chunk of a company that the British government considers indispensable to its national interests.

In late 1987, Margaret Thatcher's Parliament set about to release a 32 percent stake in the oil company, an interest the government had held since 1914 when, as First Lord of the Admiralty, Winston Churchill bought half of the Anglo-Persian Oil Company. Anglo-Persian was renamed Anglo-Iranian in 1935 and christened British Petroleum in 1954. Churchill made the purchase to ensure fuel supplies for the Royal Navy in World War I, but over the years the government's ownership declined.

October 1987 was the target for ending all government involvement. As luck would have it, this was the month world stock markets took one of the most precipitous dives in history. Since the BP shares had been priced far above their postcrash level, it seemed unlikely that investors would be attracted to the shares at the official rate. Most were not.

The Kuwait Investment Office, the London-based arm of Kuwait's finance ministry, proved an exception. The KIO purchased BP shares in huge amounts, salvaging the ill-timed offering. Then the KIO kept on buying BP stock, until soon it owned 21.6 percent of the company. Though the investment office insisted that it wanted neither a voice in the management of the company nor a seat on the board of directors, Kuwait became BP's largest shareholder.

With an estimated investment cache of $100 billion to $116 billion, Kuwait held about $85 billion worth of stocks, bonds, and real estate in the United States, Canada, and Europe alone. The Kuwaitis owned 14 percent of the car manufacturer Daimler-Benz and a 20 percent interest in Metallgesellschaft, a mining, metals, and plastics company in which Daimler later acquired an equity.

After a period of high dudgeon and heated public debate, the British government demanded that the KIO cut back its holdings in the old-line British oil establishment to no more than 9.9 percent.

This was not BP's first acquaintance with Kuwait. Britain's influence in the Middle East stretches back to the Crusades; British Petroleum's history in the Middle East runs parallel to the history of the company itself. BP was the first to detect oil in Iran, just after the turn of the century.

Oil was originally suspected in Kuwait in the late 1920s. Daniel Yergin, author of *The Prize*, explained that "London had acquired 'responsibility' for Kuwait's foreign affairs in the late 19th century as an agreed-upon method to ward off Turkish Ottoman and German influence." Though Kuwait was anxious to produce oil and pull itself out of the Great Depression, the British government and Anglo-Persian had little confidence that oil would be located. They allowed American companies to do the exploration instead. When oil discovery appeared likely, Anglo-Persian changed its mind, and a whale of a fight ensued between the Americans and the British. In 1934, Anglo-Persian and Gulf oil agreed on a 50–50 joint venture. Oil was struck in 1938 though, due to World War II, the field was not brought into production until 1946. By the 1970s, Kuwait followed the example of other oil-producing countries and nationalized its oil. "Gulf and BP asked for $2 billion in compensation. They got $50 million," Yergin wrote. " 'Whatever you did, you got paid for,' one senior Kuwaiti told them."[1]

British Petroleum had experienced blunt dismissal in the Middle East before. William Knox D'Arcy, who had made a fortune in Australian gold mining, in 1901 was granted a concession by the Shah of Persia—now called Iran—to explore for oil.

Practically from that moment on, British Petroleum was caught up in continual episodes of drama and dark intrigue. The company grappled with Eastern emirates for oil field concessions and international competitors for control of properties, distribution systems, and markets. Britain's and BP's interests often appeared indistinguishable and Winston Churchill, for one, had no qualms about defending BP in any way that seemed necessary. As British colonialism waned around the world, however, BP's hold on the region slackened. Nevertheless, when the Middle Eastern countries first began nationalizing oil properties, it was felt to be an ignominious defeat for both BP and the Empire.

Under Brit-bashing Prime Minister Dr. Mohammed Mossadegh, Iran passed a bill nationalizing the oil industry in 1951. After winning the hard-fought vote, Mossadegh dispatched a representative to the headquarters of BP's Iranian subsidiary, where he sacrificed a sheep in front of the building. The emissary then announced to an enthusiastic mob that the Englishman's concession was canceled.[2]

"The British," wrote Yergin, "managed to mount an embargo by threatening tanker owners with legal action if they picked up 'stolen oil.' In addition, Britain embargoed goods to Iran, and the Bank of England suspended financial and trade facilities that had been available to Iran. In short, the expropriation was being met with economic warfare."[3]

After high-level diplomats failed to reach new terms with Iran, it seemed that BP had no choice but to surrender its leases and abandon the world's largest refinery, which BP had built at Abadan. Company employees packed up and, to the plaintive strains of the "Colonel Bogey" march, they sailed away.

British Petroleum was absent for only three years. Between the British embargo and the lack of trained employees to run the facility, Iran was unable to generate oil. British and American negotiators continued to haggle with a turbulent government. In the meantime, Dr. Mossadegh fell from power and, finally, an agreement was reached with a new regime. In a consortium with seven other oil companies in which BP held a 40 percent interest, the company returned to revive Iran's oil industry.

By then, however, BP had begun to enlarge its horizons. It explored for and was the first to discover oil in the North Sea. Strikes were made under the permafrost in Alaska and, after 10 years of exploration, a major field was discovered at Prudhoe Bay. In 1970, in return for a share of BP's Prudhoe Bay leases and other assets, British Petroleum acquired a 25 percent equity holding in Standard Oil of Ohio, John D. Rockefeller's original company. By 1991, BP owned all of Standard, from which the company derives one third of its profits. In 1988, Britoil was acquired for 2.8 billion pounds sterling, which put BP in the position of producing a quarter of Britain's offshore oil and 10 percent of its natural gas.

Still Britain's biggest company, the third-largest oil company in the world, and one of the world's greatest industrial corporations, BP has about 1,900 subsidiaries and 118,000 employees in 70 countries. The company is involved in the exploration, production, refining, and marketing of petroleum products. British Petroleum also operates in the chemical and food industries. As the result of BP's 1986 purchase of the U.S. company, Purina Mills, it is now one of the largest millers of animal feed.

Recently, the company began one of its periodic renewals. In the 1990s, BP has been undergoing considerable "rationalization," or reorganization under an ambitious new chairman, Robert B. Horton. The management structure was trimmed down and toned up, apathetic reserves were sold, and the employee base diminished by nearly 1,200. The company's image received a dressing up too, with greater emphasis given to the company's logo color—green— to make the company appear more environmentally friendly.

Like most oil companies, BP has not been perceived as particularly benevolent to the natural environment. BP, through a subsidiary, owns 50 percent of the Alyeska Pipeline Service Company which operates the oil terminal at Valdez, Alaska. The company must defend itself in no fewer than 170 law suits evolving from the 1989 Exxon Valdez oil spill. Early in the year following the Exxon Valdez spill, a chartered tanker carrying BP crude oil was punctured off the California coast, spreading oil over nearby Huntington Beach. It was " . . . an incident for which we were in no way responsible," said chairman Horton, but for which, " . . . the speed and thoroughness of our response won praise from quarters normally critical of the industry." In BP's 1990 annual report, Horton explained that he had taken steps to strengthen the company's health, safety, and environmental policy.[4]

Though he cut charitable spending in some areas, Horton also made a commitment to support community need, education projects in particular. About one third of the 18 million pounds sterling BP allocated for these projects was spent in the United Kingdom and the United States, where the company has most of its investments.

Most significant of all, BP in recent years has launched a campaign for new oil fields around the world to replenish its aging North Sea and Alaskan reserves. Again, BP called on its vast experience in dealing with precarious governments to establish ties with jurisdictions in regions of the world in which little oil exploration has taken place, such as China, Vietnam, West Africa, and the Philippines. Licenses also were gained in the Gulf of Mexico and new oil was discovered in Australia and Papua New Guinea. BP entered negotiations with the Soviet republic of Azerbaijan to invest in and revive part of Russia's deteriorating petroleum industry. Feasibility studies also were underway for Siberia.

There is no indication that the Kuwaiti ownership in British Petroleum (and BP's U.S. control of the former Sohio) or Kuwait's holdings of U.S. stocks, bonds, and real estate had any relationship to the overwhelming support that principality received from Britain and the United States in its dispute with Iraq. BP, at the time of Saddam Hussein's invasion, had few oil contracts in Kuwait. However, the fact that Britain had a prime minister with spousal ties to the oil industry and that U.S. President George Bush formerly earned his living in that business didn't hurt the Kuwaiti cause. At the very least, the petroleum industry had sympathetic ears in high places.

British Petroleum's story sketches the blurred lines between government and industrial sectors of the economy. Energy is essential to the survival of a modern nation. Commerce, public services, and national defense are contingent on its availability. But energy isn't the only commodity to fit into this category. The Japanese protect their rice farmers from the fear of not being able to feed Japan's large, island-isolated population. Americans worry that command of the computer chip industry by Japan could make U.S. defense systems, electronics, and other manufacturing industries vulnerable. "You can't be a military superpower if you are chained to a 6,000-mile supply line to Japan," said John Stern, head of the American Electronics Association's Tokyo office.

But the relationship between government and industry is even more complex, interwoven, and enigmatic than implied by those simple examples.

Without the economic base for taxation provided by business, governments could not last. Assessments paid by the mega-nationals, both directly and indirectly, are enormous. British Petroleum paid taxes worldwide amounting to 1,042 million pounds sterling. It is probably impossible to determine how much additional income tax was contributed by employees, business tax remitted by suppliers, or capital gains tax returned by investors.

Conversely, business depends upon government to protect private property and to maintain systems that expedite commerce, such as public health, education, transportation, and communications.

Adam Smith, the early economist, dispelled any doubt of the importance of government service: ". . . we should bear in mind that government provides one absolutely essential service in exchange for its taxes—a service without which no household or business could earn a cent. That is the service of the maintenance of law and order and the protection of property rights."[5]

As British Petroleum's ongoing success in British and U.S. oil production shows, those countries that protect private property with the greatest zeal tend to make the most attractive corporate domiciles. During free trade talks between Mexico and the United States, private business organizations repeatedly expressed the needs of the business community to be certain that company assets would be protected from one Mexican presidential administration to the next. They also insisted that Mexico must strengthen its patent and copyright laws.

Besides being a guardian of private property, government is a leading customer for business, as Churchill affirmed when he sought to secure an oil supply for wartime Britain. Philosopher Noam Chomsky pointed up the benefits that government extends to industry—and though Chomsky uses the United States as an example, similar conditions exist in both Europe and Asia.

"One function of the Pentagon system has been to ensure that the public provides the costs of R&D and a state-guaranteed market for advanced industry, while profits accrue to the private sector, a gift to the corporate manager," Chomsky wrote in an article for *The*

Nation. "Thus, business has always been troubled by what *The Wall Street Journal* calls 'the unsettling specter of peace,' and it grasps at the hope that a capital-intensive and high-tech military will still provide, as General Edward Meyer assured, 'a big business out there for industry.' "[6]

In 1990, John A. Young, president and chief executive officer of Hewlett-Packard, noted that the National Science Foundation funded about 17,000 research projects and the National Institutes of Health provided another 34,000 research grants. The U.S. space program, the Human Genome project, and the superconducting supercollider were also U.S.-government funded. Young, who also serves on the Executive Committee of Council of Competitiveness, claimed that only a small percentage of the U.S. budget for research has direct relevance to industry, because military technology consumes two thirds of the government's research funding. Chomsky probably would not have been surprised to hear that Young called for even greater government R&D spending, and closer links between industry and government-funded research labs.

General Electric, General Motors, AT&T, and Daimler-Benz are just a few of the meganationals that derive a considerable percentage of sales from military and nonmilitary government sources.

Thanks to the failures of the communist regimes, the privatization of government enterprise worldwide, and massive changes taking place in formerly controlled economies such as Mexico, it is now obvious that government command of industry damages production.

At the same time, the success of Japan, Korea, and Germany, each of which extends substantial patronage to industry, calls into question the superiority of American (and to a great extent British) models of capitalism that emphasize the independence of business.

Economist Thurow says Americans, in particular, get confused. "We say the American government shouldn't get involved with helping companies in the economy, that's wrong. And if the government does get involved, they screw things up. Then we get upset because the Japanese government helps its companies, and we think we ought to. I think the Japanese government is efficient and does in fact help Japanese corporations, but we as a society can't admit that. If we do, then we have to ask, what should we do?"[7]

This confusion is magnified because the international nature of business makes corporations more difficult to control. In fact, some say that giant, global business has escaped national boundaries, and the borders cannot be rebuilt.

Robert B. Reich, in *The Work of Nations* predicts the end of ". . . national economies, at least as we have come to understand the concept," he said. "In this world without economic borders, people will succeed or fail according to their market value—the skill and talent they bring to the workplace."[8]

One of the most heated debates of the 1990s has centered around the question: Is the nation-state dead? Historically it has been argued, and many traditionalists still insist, that government is the prevailing force.

"The irrelevance of the state is absurd," asserts Professor Chalmers Johnson of the University of California at San Diego. "Rules come from the legal system."[9]

Similarly, proclaims L. C. Van Wachem, chairman of Royal Dutch Shell, "The power of the sovereign state is paramount and no company has any similar power."[10]

Yet other experts are not so confident. They recognize that even in a so-called free enterprise system such as the United States espouses, the paths of political and economic power may be confused. There is increasing awareness that government is more than an impartial observer and regulator to a self-correcting economic system.

Certainly corporations make every effort to be heard when national policy is set. There are many hundreds of company and industry legislative offices in Washington, D.C. While companies are not permitted to contribute directly to political campaigns, they, along with labor organizations and other special interest groups, can establish political-action committees. The PACs seek donations from employees or members and pass those funds along to politicians of choice. In 1988, as national elections were heating up, PACs contributed more than $80 million dollars. AT&T (a heavily regulated public utility) has traditionally sponsored a generous business PAC—weighing in at $1.45 million in 1988. Foreign PACs contributed almost $3 million to the 1988 federal election campaign, nearly 4 percent of the total PAC contributions. ˉ

Pat Choate, in his thought-provoking book *Agents of Influence*, took Washington insiders and Japanese corporations to task for influence peddling. Japanese companies protested that their U.S. lobbying efforts were not as relevant as Choate claimed. "Choate is very naive to suggest that any country, by investing $100 million a year in lobbying in Washington, D.C., can become the third political party in the United States," said Toshio Yamaguchi, a former Japanese labor minister. The expectation of being a third political party perhaps is outlandish but, if Japanese corporations did not hope to wield influence, why did they spend so much money? Why did they spend any money at all?[11]

In Europe, corporations have been the driving force behind the EC unification program, with business leaders intimately involved in the process. Umberto Agnelli, vice chairman of the board of the Fiat Group and brother of Giovanni Agnelli, has served as head of the Committee of Common Market Auto Constructors in Brussels, the Common Market headquarters. Though Fiat officially champions open markets, the comittee is considered protectionist.

In *The Bigness Complex*, Adams and Brock write, " . . . it is no longer admissible to view government as an outside force regulating the economy in the same manner as a referee regulates the procedural aspects of an athletic event. The government has become an active participant in the economic game, and in some cases has a symbiotic relationship to the interest groups for which it makes the rules of the game. It can no longer be viewed as a countervailing force whose public policies constitute an independent, autonomous, and incorruptible judgment of what is in the public interest. Nor, incidentally, can it be viewed, with naive simplicity, as 'the executive committee of the ruling class.' It is far more accurate to view the state as part of a corporate-labor-government complex."[12]

So what is the correct future relationship between business and government?

Some go so far as to dismiss the role of government as adjunct to materialism. Japanese management consultant Kenichi Ohmae, in his book *The Borderless World*, maintains that the role of government today is simply to ensure that citizens have full access to the goods and services of the world. This view is startling on its own, but is even more so coming from a citizen of a nation that devotes intense energy to its industrial policy.

Robert Reich holds a loftier view. ". . . it is a nation's proper role to make sure its citizens have the education needed to compete," he says. While there is little doubt that education is important to a country's competitiveness, on its own, a high level of public education hardly seems sufficient. Industries are flocking to sites along the U.S.–Mexico border, where the wage rate is low but where Mexico's mostly poorly educated people can easily be trained to do assembly work. If education was the primary factor, the USSR, Cuba, and Ireland, which have reasonably well-educated populaces, would have stronger economies.[13]

Citizens of virtually every country in the world already are knowledgeable enough to understand one thing. To be well fed and dressed, to enjoy access to modern conveniences, health care, and personal liberties such as travel and appreciation of the arts, they must be economically proficient. In the United States, the European Community, the USSR, Mexico, and elsewhere, individuals are demanding that economic systems allow them to work and to achieve personal financial independence. Polish people voiced their will by internal revolution; Mexicans voted with their feet, fleeing north across the U.S. border. As a result of many forms of pressure from citizens, the contest to win new business investment for a country, state, or city has become so heated that the balance of power between government and commerce has shifted. Big business, and the meganationals in particular, have been able to gain important concessions.

"On the one hand, the multinational is in a position to win hard bargains from the host country into which it seeks to enter because the corporation is the main bearer of new technologies and management techniques that every nation seeks," explain Heilbroner and Thurow. On the other hand, they note, once a host country is selected, the company becomes a hostage to its laws.[14]

That was the case before the great mobility of business was established. Now, however, if the country does not offer the environment that a company needs, the corporation will simply go elsewhere. That, along with other forms of leverage, give corporations great influence over the law-making and legislative process.

Even when their cultural or other biases dictate otherwise, governments are being forced to cut taxes, privatize everything from telephone companies to prisons, and loosen regulations to allow a broader competitive field. The process is well underway.

New Jersey Governor James Florio, in 1991, signed legislation allowing foreign banks to establish back-office (those not related to customers) operations in his state. Sumitomo Bank immediately moved its computer and administrative offices from New York to New Jersey.

Prior to that change, Florio was not considered by foreign corporations to be their friend. Two years earlier, as a member of Congress, Florio sounded alarm bells in the international business community when he cosponsored legislation, the Exon-Florio amendment, that granted the President the right to veto investments in U.S. firms on national security grounds. In 1984, Florio also protested the establishment of NUMMI, a joint venture between General Motors and Toyota.

Yet, with 267 Japanese companies employing 22,727 people in his state, Florio must be keenly aware of the job-creating benefits of hosting foreign-based corporations.

Business Tokyo magazine expressed the incongruity this way. "It is ironic that while (U.S.) representatives rail against Japan on the floor of the House, officials from their states may be in Japan appealing for money. More than two thirds of the states have offices in Tokyo soliciting investment."[15]

Nations and states no doubt are confused by their changing roles in the economic process. Certainly citizens around the world are. While the French government cooperates on the EC agreement, French farmers protest the importation of meat from eastern Europe; while the U.S. government demands free trade through GATT, certain elected officials introduce protectionist legislation. Though Japanese carmakers contend that U.S.-made parts aren't up to Japanese standards of quality, Cadillac limousines carry Tokyo executives to and from assignations at the city's classiest hotels.

But what else is to be expected from an age of commercial reformation? Some visionary business leaders and social critics say that, for the most part, governments are irrelevant. They only interfere with the unfettered travel, trade, and discourse that will distinguish the next century from earlier eras.

Though the concept of nationhood may not be completely out of date, it does live in an altered state. Statehood continues for several reasons discussed earlier—paramount among them the need for protection of private property. The final reason nationalism persists is sentimentality. Even corporate leaders have some visceral connection to their cultural roots and to the soil from which they originate.

However, anyone who has lived in California, London, South Africa, or any other great migration center knows that loyalty to the home country sometimes is little more than sentimental. Home, in terms of national origin, is felt to be a beloved place. But when a nation no longer functions in the way its citizens require, they leave. While Irish-Americans may pour into the streets of New York to march on St. Patrick's Day, they usually return to their home country only to visit, to achieve a feeling of connectedness, to reaffirm their spiritual selves. While the "home" serves as an idealized concept, the citizen has given it up. Expatriate Japanese, Americans, and citizens of other economically and politically thriving countries almost always (in due course) return.

Yet, even citizens of the most functional economies such as Japan, the United States, or Germany (as described in Chapter one) can become disaffected. That is because of the growing conception that governments align with business, giving short shrift to interests that are of concern to individuals. The role of individuals (and labor) in the new government/business/labor order will be explored in the following chapters.

The fitting relationship between business and government will be argued for decades to come, especially in the United States where the disorientation is profound. Western Europeans are moving along in the debate and are negotiating their own new order. Japan reached consensus long ago, and whether the rest of the world likes it or not, is fairly satisfied with its own cultural arrangement.

While the Japanese model of government seems skewed at the moment toward the requirements of its corporate giants, the fundamental concept behind the Japanese method may offer a lesson for anyone trying to conceive of a better form of government. In *Politics and Productivity* by Chalmers Johnson and some of his associates, a Japanese businessman described his view of his government this way: "The state is thus a linchpin. Its power is not based on the concentration of legal authority sufficient to overwhelm recalcitrant groups. Rather it is derived from the state's strategic role as the indispensable linchpin that holds the functioning units of society together and permits it to act in ways that advance collective interests. Perhaps it can be called a "network" or "relational" state in the sense that its power is largely derived from the nature of its relationship as central coordinator of strong constituent groups in society."[16]

Regardless of the nobility of this debate, the meganationals are not willing to wait for various countries to decide what they are. They have a robust will to survive; they are tenacious and shrewd. As British Petroleum struggled to hold on to its Middle Eastern supply of oil, the company began to search the world for new supplies. As those new supplies dissipate, the company again launches a worldwide hunt for petroleum.

As the controversy of American competitiveness is debated, the most powerful American companies have quietly and willfully gone about what they must do to endure.

Before a free trade agreeement between the United States and Mexico was ever on the drawing boards, IBM, like many other meganationals, had established an impressive presence in Mexico. By 1990, IBM de Mexico had increased revenues by 20 to 30 percent annually to $730 million. General Motors de Mexico tripled sales to $2.1 billion a year. AT&T sold $130 million of fiber optic equipment to Telmex, the Mexican national telephone company. Mexico is of critical importance to corporate expansion, not just because it offers an inexpensive source of labor and raw materials. It also is an underdeveloped consumer market.

For these same reasons, no matter how trying it may be to settle political differences, British Petroleum, Coca-Cola, and dozens of other meganationals will pursue trade arrangements with Russia, China, and a greater presence in Africa and South America.

The will of the world's most powerful corporations to survive has meant uniting in joint ventures and technology sharing, engaging in borderless trading and international recruitment, and creating new systems for capital. The meganationals, with their uncanny smell for change, are leading government where business needs to go.

GOVERNMENT'S OBLIGATION
TO BUSINESS

Throughout the world, business leaders are pressing their demands on governments. Sometimes these include tax, development, or other benefits that erode the fiscal strength of governments and limit education, infrastructure, law enforcement, and other services. How can a government create a healthy business climate and at the same time fulfill its duties to its citizens? It does so by understanding its basic obligations and thoughtfully, warily examining any demands that go beyond these limits. Those obligations are:

1. Provide a stable form of government. Neither businesses nor individuals can build value or permanence without political stability.

2. Provide a balanced and fair legal system. Individuals and business entities must have equal access to justice.

3. Offer a high level of public education. The advanced state of technology requires knowledgeable, skilled executives and workers. Equal access to public education thwarts the extreme class differences that eventually create social chaos in which business and the individual cannot function.

4. Establish a satisfactory level of public health and welfare. Not only are healthy and decent living standards necessary to the maintenance of a reliable work force, there is a costly social price to be paid when public needs are not met. With modern travel and communications, it is no longer a secret that there are huge gaps between those who live in safety and ease and those who live in desperation. Unless an equitable balance in the human condition is found, the poor will always pose a threat to those with economic advantages.

5. Protect and perpetuate those natural systems which sustain life on earth. All human beings must be able to safely breathe the air, drink the water, and eat the food. That which kills off plants and wild animals eventually will kill the rest of us.

6. Create an efficient infrastructure, available for use by all sectors of the society. One of the joys of a viable political/economic system is that transportation, communications, and modern technology are widely available.

7. Allow the most open business environment and liberal trade climate possible. History has shown that too little guidance leads to turmoil and plundering, which damages all sectors of the economy. Too much intrusion stifles the entrepreneurial spirit. While some bureaucratic supervision is unavoidable, government regulations should be direct and simple.

8. Ensure freedom of expression. Without this fundamental right, it would be impossible to fulfill the first seven responsibilities.

Chapter Ten

The Global Corporation: Everybody's Child— Nobody's Child

"The forces of a capitalist society, if left unchecked, tend to make the rich richer and the poor poorer"

Jawaharalal Nehru

In the South African movie, *The Gods Must Be Crazy*, the plot revolves around a simple symbol of western culture that wreaks havoc among remote tribal members. There was never an explanation of what "the thing" that fell from a passing airplane was, but viewers around the world recognized it instantly. A Coca-Cola bottle.

Coca-Cola is the best known brand name in the world and one of the most uniquely American products that exists. Yet the Coca-Cola Company has been international since the 1920s and now generates 77 percent of its operating income from outside the United States. It distributes its soft drinks in more than 160 countries and uses approximately 40 different currencies. It is one of the handful of multinational companies with a foreign-born chief executive, and it employs a relatively small number of expatriate Americans abroad.

Considered one of the smartest marketing operations anywhere, Coca-Cola sometimes is described as a model of what a global corporation ought to be. The company's executives often detail with pride how the Atlanta-based corporation succeeds in such a diverse world. The picture isn't always as sunny as Coca-Cola executives imply; the company has made mistakes and enemies.

Yet the demand for its primary product, a 100-year-old elixir with a secret formula that the company only recently admitted does contain a small amount of defanged cocaine plant, is phenomenal.[1]

More than 45 percent of all the carbonated soft drinks sold around the world are Coke products—including the various Cokes, Fanta, Sprite, and sodas for specialized regions.

One of Coca-Cola's early presidents worked hard to equate the cola with the American way of life. During World War II, he vowed that every American in military uniform would be able to buy a 5-cent Coke, no matter how much it cost the company. At the urging of General Dwight D. Eisenhower, bottling plants were built near battlefronts in North Africa and throughout Europe. Thus Coca-Cola got a firm foothold abroad.

After the occupation of Japan, the commitment to servicemen gave Coke an early entree into that market. Unable to repatriate its yen earnings, the company instead invested within the country. A dozen of Japan's largest food and trading companies, including Mitsui, Mitsubishi, Kirin, and Kikkoman, became the bottlers. Coke now holds a 35 percent share of the Japanese beverage market. Its prime worldwide competitor—Pepsi Cola—holds only a 2 percent share.

Perhaps the mastery of Coca-Cola can best be portrayed by its experience with the Arab League boycott against Israel. For more than 20 years Coca-Cola, along with hundreds of other companies, was blacklisted from doing business in Arab countries because it also conducted business in Israel. However, consumers in those countries simply resumed buying Coke. Though the company was not officially taken off the boycott list until mid-1991, Egypt, Oman, Bahrain, and the United Arab Emirates permitted bottling plants to open in the late 1980s. Coca-Cola also sponsored a World Youth Soccer tournament in Saudi Arabia in 1989.

"U.S.-based companies of any size today think and act in international terms," Coca-Cola chairman Roberto C. Goizueta told the Town Hall meeting in Los Angeles. "They do so for the same reason Willy Sutton gave when asked why he robbed banks: that's where the money is."

About 95 percent of the world's five billion people live outside the United States, he noted. Goizueta also told his audience of some of the pitfalls of the unwary marketer in the global sphere.

"When we reentered China in 1979," he said, "we discovered that the literal representation of Coca-Cola in Chinese characters meant 'bite the wax tadpole,' We knew right away we had a problem, so we engaged an Oriental language specialist to experiment with alternatives. After looking into several dialects, he finally came up with four Mandarin characters sounding very similar to Coca-Cola and meaning 'Can Happy, Mouth Happy,' and we were happy with that."

Goizueta spared his listeners certain other tribulations of globalism, and there have been many. An earlier chairman, J. Paul Austin, felt that business was an effective vehicle to manage international relations and should be used to improve national economies. It was Austin who first introduced Coca-Cola into Russia and China. Developing his own ideas of business as a source of foreign aid, Austin initiated technological and educational programs in Third World countries where it did business. He imported clean-water technology and sponsored sporting programs in countries where governments and citizens were too poor to provide those services for themselves.

On the other hand, during Austin's regime, it was learned that Coca-Cola had made $1.3 million in illegal payments over a period of six years, mostly to executives and government officials in foreign countries.[2]

Then in the mid-1980s, the Coca-Cola bottling franchise in Guatemala was involved in the bloodiest labor union episode in Coca-Cola's history. Union organization in the Central American country frequently had been rocked by violence and, apparently, more than a dozen prounion workers were either kidnapped or murdered in a prolonged unionization effort at a bottling plant just outside Guatemala City. Despite the bloodshed, unionists persisted, saying that the Coca-Cola bottlers union had been at the vanguard of Guatemalan workers' attempts to organize. If it were to fail, the entire movement most likely would collapse. Charges flew that the franchise owner had enlisted the aid of the government and the national police to suppress the movement.[3]

"By this time the murders of Coca-Cola workers had attracted the attention of international church and human rights groups as well as the International Union of Food and Allied Workers, based in Geneva," wrote Anne Manuel in a 1984 piece in *The New Repub-*

lic. "The IUF began to press Coca-Cola headquarters in Atlanta to take action to stop the violence. Coca-Cola, however, insisted that it could not dictate labor relations to its franchise operator, and resisted IUF demands to revoke (the operator's) license."[4]

The IUF organized an international boycott of Coca-Cola. Workers barricaded themselves inside the Guatemala City plant until the parent company finally did step in and promise to find a new bottler. The action was unusual at Coca-Cola, which traditionally had allowed exceptional independence to its bottling franchise holders.

The arms-length relationship between the company and the public created by its franchise system has made Coca-Cola available in South Africa, though the U.S. parent bowed to international boycott pressures in 1986. The company sold its South African assets to investors that year. Other operations were shifted from politically white-dominated South Africa to the diminutive kingdom of Swaziland. Swaziland is surrounded by South Africa, does business with South Africa, and even uses the rand as its primary currency.

The company often has found its way around or through disputes with local and regional political bodies, even when that takes a long time. In India, the process has lasted more than a decade. India had demanded that Coca-Cola give up 60 percent of its local ownership to an Indian subsidiary. Even more unnerving, the government also demanded that it be told the secrets of the Coca-Cola recipe. Rather than comply, Coke left the country in 1977.

But economics will have its way. India's new government, in a strategy adopted to relieve India's chronic financial anguish, began wooing investments by multinational corporations in 1990. By the next year, Coke was negotiating to reenter the Indian market through a joint venture with Britannia Industries of India, a baking enterprise partly owned by RJR Nabisco Holdings Corporation.

Recently, turning away from its adventures into other lines of business (including a stint as owner of Columbia Pictures), Coca-Cola has altered its customary franchising philosophy and stepped up its expansionary course. Both in the United States and abroad, the company has busily bought back bottling franchises, especially those where performance was lagging and Coke thought its own people could do better.

Coca-Cola also formed joint ventures to expand business in Indonesia and other Eastern Asia countries. As chairman Goizueta pointed out, the global market is where the money is. In the United States, Coke earns less than 22 cents on a dollar of soft drink sales. But abroad, where competition is lighter and government policies sometimes keep the price of American sodas high to make them less affordable, Coke earns 54 cents on the dollar.

The company has invested hundreds of millions of dollars positioning itself for the 1992 deadline for restructuring European markets. In a joint venture with Nestlé, it will market canned drinks such as iced coffee and tea worldwide. Coke's new bottling plant at Dunkirk, France, opened in 1990. Located near the English Channel tunnel, the plant allows products to be delivered within hours to any point in the British Isles, West Europe, or East Europe.

Coke's new aggressiveness is most apparent in France and eastern Germany. After a court battle in which Coke claimed that its French franchise holder allowed Coke products to languish in favor of its own, the company ended a 40-year relationship. Immediately, Coke brought in a hard-driving U.S. manager, and Coca-Cola vending machines began popping up around France. Restaurant owners and their trade group in Bordeaux screamed in protest when dispensers were placed on the streets near their establishments, selling sodas for less than half the price the cafes were charging.

In keeping with J. Paul Austin's belief that private enterprise could lead the way to economic reform, Coca-Cola broke ground in 1991 on 3 soft-drink plants in Poland, the first of 11 to be built there. The initial $50 million investment was the biggest by any U.S. company since the collapse of Communism in Poland in 1989. When the Berlin Wall crashed down, Coca-Cola employees were at the old border checkpoints passing out free Cokes to East Germans who mostly had seen the soda advertised on western television. Before the wall collapsed, about 50,000 gallons of Coke products were sold each year in East Germany; by the end of 1990, just 13 months later, 31.7 million gallons of Coke, Fanta, and Sprite were consumed. Coke intends to spend $450 million building plants in East Germany, its largest foreign investment anywhere.

"This is the soft-drink equivalent of the Marshall Plan," said Emanuel Goldman, a beverage research analyst for Paine Webber Inc.

Considering the widening, international nature of business, it is time to abandon old prejudices toward outsiders, claim economists who are rethinking national priorities. "Public policymakers need to recognize that Honda U.S. can serve U.S. interests as well as Ford can," said Proctor P. Reid, who directed a study on globalization at the National Academy of Engineering. Coca-Cola is able to provide jobs and quench the thirst of Britons as easily as Orange Squash or, for Mexicans, as well as Panafiel.

Contemporary foreign corporations, these economists say, are less likely than they once were to treat their offshore plants as colonial outposts.

"It's not so much that world companies are abandoning identification with a single nation," wrote *Business Week* in a 1990 article on the stateless corporation, "as much as they're trying to become local companies in many countries. 'If I'm in Brazil, I am deeply concerned about the Brazilian economy, I get involved with the Brazilian school system, I get involved with Brazilian trade. I make myself as Brazilian as I can be,' said Colgate-Palmolive Co. executive Reuben Mark."[5]

There is no doubt whatsoever that meganational corporations expand beyond domestic borders in search of the growth opportunities provided by ripe markets. For instance, Mexico's population is increasing at about double the rate of the United States. Many other underdeveloped nations present similar demographics.

"We are now selling about 82 percent of our sales to the industrialized countries but these have only 15 percent of the world population," Helmut Maucher, chairman of Swiss-based Nestlé SA said in the late 1980s. "It is quite clear that population will grow and purchasing power will grow, despite some ups and downs, in the developing nations. That means tremendous possibilities for a food company."[6]

It is also plain that many companies search abroad for other conveniences—lower wages and easier union rules, governments that are lax in environmental enforcement, lower tax rates, and other concessions offered by countries anxious to expand their industrial bases. Roughly 45 percent of all Mexicans are under 14 years of age, and 1.2 million young people enter the job market each year. There are worker protection features in the Mexican constitution, and there are examples in Mexico of entrenched and abusive unionism. Yet, in reality, wages and working conditions for the majority of Mexicans are influenced by an oversupply of labor. While it is important for a government to provide fertile soil for business development, it is equally crucial that a government protect its citizens and environment from exploitation. It is easy enough to take advantage in a job market as desperately needy as Mexico's.

Most countries of the world—like Mexico—now welcome new businesses because of the additional jobs, new technologies, and tax revenues they bring. Once isolationist, Mexico is at the forefront of internationalization. Nestlé recently committed $300 million to expand its business in Mexico. Another meganational, General Electric, invested $200 million in a joint venture with a Mexican company to produce gas cooking stoves. The risk was high for GE, since this will be its only gas range factory.

Whether a company comes to open new markets, utilize cheap labor, or harvest raw materials, it invariably makes a mark on the society. Most often the changes are for the better. But when a corporation is established in a foreign country, the romance can afterward wear thin. A host society may discover that, by its own standards, the guest company is a rogue. And dealing with the scofflaw may not be easy.

Even the mighty U.S. government found itself in just such a corner when the Japanese electronics giant Toshiba was caught illegally selling restricted U.S. military nuclear submarine propeller technology to the Soviet Union. Japanese officials, their U.S. lobbyists, and lawyers, recalled Washington insider Pat Choate, mounted a "massive campaign" to derail sanctions against Toshiba. Toshiba's payments to beltway spin doctors were part of a $120 million lobbying campaign by Japanese firms between 1987 and 1989. Those who criticized Toshiba or the Japanese actions were described as racist or xenophobic. Even more perplexing for the government, Toshiba's distributors and other business associates in the United States protested, claiming that actions against Toshiba would hurt their business as well.[7]

Japanese businesses are not alone in playing the political game by a foreign country's own rules. The word "lobby" has a dirty connotation in Japan, but the Japanese have their own methods of accomplishing the same end. Many meganationals, including Mitsui, Du

Pont, and IBM, have added exbureaucrats and well-connected Japanese executives to their payrolls. It is the job of these "insiders" to help penetrate industry research programs, set up crucial government and business contacts, and plan market strategy.

Because Japan and the United States are the world's two largest economic powers, their disputes take on grand proportions. The United States has determined that foreign corporations, either by evasive but technically legal or by outright fraudulent tax practices, may have deprived it of billions of dollars in revenues. "By some estimates," wrote *Business Week* in 1990, "foreign-owned multinationals avoid $13 billion to $30 billion a year in U.S. taxes. But shuffling income from one jurisdiction to another to minimize taxes is as old as the multinational itself. And the outdated corporate tax codes of the industrialized nations can't keep up with the rapid changes in international commerce."[8]

The U.S. Internal Revenue Service brought tax charges against Hitachi America, Mitsubishi Electric, and Korea's Daewoo, to name a few companies. The U.S. Congress amended the 1990 budget to stiffen tax-reporting rules for subsidiaries of foreign firms. When he was Chancellor of the Exchequer, British Prime Minister John Majors called for a joint U.S.-British study of international taxation.

Industrialization and economic development bring more down-to-earth problems as well. Since the Maquiladora or cross-border assembly plant system started up along the U.S.–Mexican border, the area has become a dynamic economic zone and one of Mexico's healthiest regional economies. However, California beaches near the Mexican border now are often closed to swimming because of the untreated sewage spewing out of the inadequate Tijuana sanitation system. The rivers near Calexico and Nogales are strewn with cadmium, arsenic, and toxic metals. Supervision of waste removal and enforcement of existing regulations has been careless, but in negotiating the North American Free Trade Agreement, President Salinas de Gotari swore Mexico would not sell the environment for faster growth.

The environmentalist maxim, "Think globally, act locally," has been adopted by many business enterprises who vow to be as responsive to foreign operations as they would be in their native lands. Implementing the philosophy may be more difficult than echoing slogans, especially when business practices at home may be quite different from those found elsewhere. The Japanese, for example, only recently developed an awareness of the worldwide "green" movement. Japan itself is plagued with toxic waste and air- and water-pollution problems.

While Japanese corporations operate globally, the lifeline to home is securely knotted. Key employees are rotated to the foreign posts and, in most cases, key decisions are made only with the blessing of corporate headquarters. Often the Japanese companies themselves are working in accordance with the philosophies and policies of Keidanren, the Federation of Economic Organizations, which coordinates industrial planning in the Japanese economy.

The idea that Keidanren is losing its grip or that globalization is changing the way Japan does business is incorrect, says Chalmers Johnson, an expert on the Japanese economy and author of *MITI: The Japanese Miracle*. Keidanren's prominence is cyclical, Johnson says, becoming less evident in peacetime and prosperity. When crisis erupts, government and business again fall into step.

"When Japanese businesses go overseas, there is the idea that they slip the leash from Keidanren and the Japanese government. The evidence is not there. Toyota Kentucky acts no differently than Toyota Japan," Johnson contends.[9]

The federation, incidentally, serves as a business liaison and fundraiser for the Liberal Democratic Party, which has governed in Japan for more than 35 years.

Japanese companies, often reproached for discriminating against native employees in favor of imported-from-Japan management, are under pressure to change. Even so, it still merits special attention in the news when a Japanese company names a non-Japanese as top authority in a foreign division. Placing a foreign national in charge of an offshore operation is commonplace among other multinational corporations.

Though most have been abroad for some time, meganationals still face extreme suspicion in many countries. The leftist candidate in Mexico who captured a surprisingly high percentage of votes in Mexico's 1988 presidential election, Cuauhtemoc Cardenas, voiced the concerns of many Mexican citizens who recall that, in the past, the benefits of free and open trade did not trickle down to the masses. The North American Free Trade Agreement, which will swing the door wider for multinationals, Cardenas claimed, "doesn't amount to more than economic exploitation and political subordination."

Most of the meganationals acknowledge that, to atone for sins of the past and to win local confidence, they must be more integrated into the societies in which they are operating.

The meganationals frequently point out their generosity to local causes as proof of their commitment. Coca-Cola prides itself on being a good corporate citizen. Contributions by company officials allowed Emory University in Coke's hometown of Atlanta to fully develop its academic and medical programs. In Japan, the company has an annual good works allowance of $5 million. Coca-Cola sponsors unicycle competitions for children, aid programs for the handicapped, and cultural events like Tokyo's popular summer bonfire festival. The flowing Spencerian-script Coca-Cola logo was seen worldwide in 1991 when the company, along with Fiat and France's Credit Lyonnais bank, sponsored the popular Tour de France bicycle race.

But good citizenship goes beyond charity, especially charity that may double as an advertising or publicity vehicle, or may have other spin-offs to company profits.

There is a clear trend toward "corporate statesmanship," says Helmut Maucher, chairman of Nestlé SA, as chief executives are recognizing a responsibility to address societal issues beyond their narrow business interests.

Like Coca-Cola, Nestlé knows what it is to be nowhere a foreigner. Often called "the most multinational of the multinationals," Nestlé has operations and employees on all five continents and factories in more than 60 countries. Its canned and fresh milk, chocolate, frozen and packaged foods turn up on grocery shelves everywhere. At Nestlé headquarters, people of more than 50 nationalities work together. Half of the top management is not Swiss, and even Maucher himself is German-born.

Yet even Nestlé has come head-to-head with foreign antagonism. Following a 1986 presidential decree, Nestlé was forced to sell its 60 percent participation in the Peruvian company Gloria to Peruvian shareholders, who already held 40 percent of the capital.

Maucher often preaches the gospel that multinationals must behave in a socially responsible manner. Nevertheless, he has a blunt and clear-cut idea of why and how corporations should be going about their business.

"There is some apprehension that business will turn away from developing countries in favor of the opportunities offered in Eastern Europe," Maucher said. "For Nestlé, this is certainly not the case. For us, the only criteria will remain if there is a long-term return on our investment, regardless in which country."[10]

A meganationals's first obligation is to be a productive, profitable company, he said.

"Our main social responsibility and task," Maucher says, "is to invent, to make, and to sell products to consumers in a competitive environment which give real benefits to the consumer and make a contribution to overall prosperity in a free society—making a profit so that we can reward those people who have invested and have taken the risk."

With full realization on one hand that free enterprise is necessary for a healthy economy and on the other hand that public corporations must earn sufficient profits to reward investors—meganationals and governments everywhere are teetering on a balancing board for power.

Mexico unilaterally began to dismantle barriers to foreign investment in the late 1980s, and at the same time began reforms to improve its dreadful air and water quality. Perhaps looking to the experience of Middle Eastern countries, Mexico's leaders chose to maintain jurisdiction over oil production. The Indian government—which historically has taken pride in its self-reliance—intends to keep control of the manufacture of hazardous chemicals (after the tragic experience at Bhopal, who can blame them), motor vehicles, coal, petroleum, arms, atomic energy, and drugs. Only time will tell whether the cautious Indian approach will be workable.

These are decisions that evolve from a broader philosophical base. No matter how useful or benevolent a corporation may be, it cannot be expected or allowed to assume the functions of government. Business is not operated by a democratic process; by its very nature, management does not represent a majority view or public sentiment. In facing the rapidly changing nature and size of corporate activity, nations must identify and affirm their basic tenets. Otherwise, they will be embarrassed, cajoled, or bullied into doing things contrary to the long-range interest of their workers, consumers, investors, and their cultural identity.

Chapter Eleven

The Culture versus Meganationals

"Looking over the world on a broad scale, do we not find that public entertainments have very generally been the sops thrown out by the engrossing upper classes to keep the lower classes from inquiring too particularly into their rights, and to make them satisfied with a stone, when it was inconvenient to give them bread; wherever there is a class that is to be made content to be plundered of its rights, there is an abundance of fiddling and dancing; and amusements, public and private, are in great requisition."

Harriet Beecher Stowe, 1811–1896

Times were touchy in Leningrad, Gorky, and especially in Moscow. Citizens milled around in an agitated state, blocking off streets, stopping traffic, generating a tinderbox situation which at the drop of a match could burst into flames. The USSR was under enormous political stress in the summer 1990, but the anxiety was aggravated by a shortage of the very palliative that would quiet the nerves. Through a system failure of some sort, cigarettes were hard to come by and lines as long as 250 testy smokers waited at tobacco kiosks. Even the black market was tight, with Marlboros reportedly selling for 20 rubles or the equivalent of $32 per pack. The typical Russian earned only about 240 rubles per month.

One of the protestors confronted the deputy mayor of Moscow, according to the *New York Times*, and asked why the Soviet government didn't use some of its gold reserves to buy cigarettes from abroad.

"Gold reserves have nothing to do with this," the deputy mayor snapped back. "You see, there is a choice for us—either we spend money on medicine or on cigarettes. Now we have had to take the money for medicine and buy cigarettes.

"Tomorrow invalids will appear on the streets because they will not be able to buy important medicines they need. Then we will have to stop buying cigarettes and start buying medicines again."[1]

That kind of logic apparently went nowhere. A Moscow newspaper soon reported that one black marketer killed a buyer over a pack of cigarettes. President Mikhail S. Gorbachev angrily dismissed Vladilen V. Nikitin (no really, that's his name), the Soviet official responsible for tobacco production. The situation looked very grim until a month later when Philip Morris, the world's leading cigarette manufacturer and inventor of the Marlboro man, rode to the rescue.

Philip Morris, along with RJR Nabisco Inc., agreed to supply 34 billion cigarettes to the Soviet Union before the end of 1991. It was estimated that the 20 billion cigarettes provided by Philip Morris could add between $50 million to $100 million in operating profits to the company's international tobacco business. But that wasn't the real value of the deal.

U.S. tobacco companies would now have easy access to a market with 70 million smokers, at a time when smoking was on the wane in the United States and Western Europe was embarking on an anti-smoking crusade.

Philip Morris had known for some time that its enormously profitable U.S. cigarette business had a limited tenure. American cigarette consumption has been slipping at about 2 percent per year since 1981, when sales crested at 619 billion smokes. In addition to Russia, the company had been seeking markets in developing countries where, historically, smoking habits rise as the country becomes more affluent. As a result, the cigarette, beer, and food conglomerate increasingly focused its tobacco business on international markets. It bought the largest East German cigarette factory from the state, which gave Philip Morris 40 percent of the East German market.

Expanding the cigarette trade required some help from the U.S. government, which complied by threatening several foreign countries, including Taiwan, with retaliation unless they dropped trade barriers against U.S. tobacco products. Philip Morris and the two other leading U.S. tobacco companies are now selling about 3.7 billion cigarettes a year to Taiwan. The United States, worried about an intractable imbalance of trade, had plenty to gain. In 1989, total tobacco exports worldwide, both finished cigarettes and leaf tobacco, amounted to $5 billion and 125,000 American jobs, according to the U.S. Cigarette Export Association, In its 1989 annual report, Philip Morris noted that its sales outside the United States had increased 7.7 percent, including 78 billion cigarettes exported from the United States. "Our gross contribution to the U.S. balance of payments was $2.4 billion."

Philip Morris's gains abroad were not achieved without considerable opposition from antismoking advocates at home. One group went so far as to buy stock in the company and submit a shareholders' proposal that Philip Morris get completely out of the tobacco trade by the end of the 20th century. The proposition failed.

Health officials and consumer groups blamed Philip Morris and other giant cigarette manufacturers for the 75 percent growth in global tobacco use in the past 20 years. They were also faulted for encouraging the production of tobacco as a lucrative cash crop in developing nations. Between 1986 and 1987, tobacco production in China increased 10 percent.

Philip Morris stepped up its marketing campaign in Japan, targeting younger smokers and single women, market segments it knew had bountiful long-term potential. This was allowed to happen though death from lung cancer in Japan increased from 2.7 per 100,000 in 1950 to 20.2 per 100,000 in 1979. Such statistics, the American Medical Association insist, are the direct result of increased smoking.

Though his proposal to the Philip Morris board of directors that warning labels be placed on cigarettes sold in all countries even in the absence of local regulations failed, the Reverend Michael Crosby of the Province of St. Joseph of the Capuchin Order in Milwaukee made this point: "In Third World countries, where there is no information, there is no informed consent. People buy (Philip Morris) products and they just don't know the health risks."[2]

Despite the fact that the U.S. Surgeon General concluded in 1964 that smoking was not healthful, eventually linking it to fatal heart and lung disease (and addiction as well), Philip Morris stoutly defends smoking, presenting it as a personal rights issue.

"The tobacco industry continues to face a number of social and political challenges both in the United States and abroad," wrote the company in its 1989 annual report, in which most corporate officials were photographed with cigarette in hand. "Some of these stem from the agendas of antismoking activists; others, from the view that tobacco taxes are a simple solution to government budget deficits."

The company went on to say that it had supported legislation protecting those who choose to smoke from discrimination in employment, launched programs stressing accommodation of smokers and nonsmokers in public areas, and joined coalitions to fight unfair and regressive tobacco taxes.

To vividly associate its pro-choice campaign with civil liberties, Philip Morris underwrote the National Archives celebration of the 200th anniversary of the U.S. Bill of Rights. Though cigarettes cannot be advertised on U.S. television, the company's name was listed on television commercials for the anniversary. The message was impossible to disregard.

"The freedom to say and think what we believe. To express our individuality and diversity. That's our birthright, and it's ensured by this document. Join Philip Morris in supporting the National Archives' celebration of the 200th Anniversary of the Bill of Rights," intoned the commentator, as a picture of the revered document was shown. In a flourish to make the message both moving and global, Philip Morris's print advertisement displayed a photograph of Lech Walesa next to the quotation: "I've read your Bill of Rights a hundred times and I'll probably read it a hundred more before I die."

The disgusted editors of *The New Republic* asked, "How did the (Polish) Solidarity leader get roped into lending his name to this preposterous propaganda campaign? According to Guy L. Smith, the company's vice president of public affairs, 'He doesn't speak English and I don't speak Polish.' Apparently, however, both speak vigorish."[3]

In a peculiar turn of events, bans on tobacco advertising have worked to the advantage of large cigarette producers with well-known and premium brands such as Philip Morris's Marlboro, Benson & Hedges, and Chesterfield. Without mass advertising, it is more difficult to introduce new brands, and harder to market secondary and lesser known hallmarks. As a result, the established labels have captured a larger and larger share of the tobacco market.

Nevertheless, run ragged by continual attacks on its primary and immensely profitable main product, Philip Morris began decades ago to use its cash flow to expand into other product lines. Probably because it searched the world for items that are merchandised much like tobacco, its additional lines have been battered by health proponents as well. The gargantuan Miller Brewing Company has been impacted by anti-alcohol campaigns, especially in the United States. Even its Kraft food division, which provides cheese products, Jello, faux dairy cream, and numerous salad dressings, succumbed to pressure to reconfigure fat and cholesterol statements on packaging.

Despite the controversy over its corporate standards and public image, 126-year-old Philip Morris has assembled a recession-resistant, moneymaking group of companies. In addition to being the largest U.S. cigarette manufacturer, it is the second largest brewer and a looming presence in food processing. At the end of 1989, it held $2 billion in cash reserves, which financial analysts expected it to spend on international acquisitions. Accordingly, in 1990, Philip Morris strode deeper into the European market with the acquisition of Jacobs Suchard, a respected Swiss candy and coffee purveyor. Though firms of the size, nature, and quality that would appeal to Philip Morris are becoming scarcer, the company has plentiful resources remaining and is expected to continue to unfurl its flag the world over.

Earlier sections of this book addressed the emergence of pervasively influential meganational companies, their connections to one another, and their relationships to world governments. At the end of this natural chain (top or bottom, depending on one's philosophical bent) is the individual. It tilts many lives in a certain direction when a tobacco titan decides to provide and promote more cigarettes in a foreign country, a carmaker adds seatbelts as standard gear, or a paper mill cleans up its effluent before releasing it into a stream. As a result of these and many kinds of high-level decisions, the changing structure of business is being felt most keenly at the personal level.

The world still is an eclectic place with sparse, scattered populations in certain regions, masses of humanity in others. Economic maturity was reached in some areas decades ago, and now they are in a phase of regeneration. Other communities, often within the same national boundaries, are struggling to get started.

But even in the outposts of the globe, the giant corporations of the world now touch virtually every aspect of our lives from the vehicles we use, the food we eat, the clothes we wear, the health care and education we receive, and the work we do. Cigarettes probably are made by Philip Morris; the soda machine is likely to carry only Coca-Cola products; much of the food in the store is packaged by Nestlé or Unilever; the telephone system is either built by or connected to AT&T; the microwave oven in the cafe is made by Matsushita's Panasonic or General Electric. The list goes on.

In terms of jobs alone, the impact of the meganationals is awesome. If the employees of the 25 most powerful companies in the world were asked to stand together in separate groups, they would make a collection of small cities. Worldwide, Philip Morris directly employs 157,000 people. Nestlé's 48,027 U.S. employees alone would comprise a good-sized town. And it would be a community of well-educated, well-paid, probably well-traveled citizens. Many outsiders could be tempted to live in this pleasant community.

It is the marvels of affluence, mobility, new technology, and social and intellectual advancement that make the meganationals such desirable participants in most communities of the world.

But the currency of the meganational city is a two-sided coin. The battles over the environment typify the duality. On one side, corporate paperwork, product packaging, and mahogany-paneled offices the world over eat up the delicate and expendable northern redwoods and tropical rain forests at an alarming rate. On the other side of the coin, IBM, the world's biggest corporate donor, spent some $50 million dollars for good works outside the United States in 1990. Thanks to IBM, Costa Rica's National Parks Foundation will be using new computer equipment to develop strategies to preserve its rain forests.

IBM's commitment to this pressing environmental and social cause did not come about by accident, and it did not happen because the U.S. or Costa Rican governments demanded that someone do reparation for earth damage.

There has burst on the scene, beginning in the 1960s, a third influence on governance and the economy. While the personal voice in the recent past was expected to evolve naturally in the selection of a government or in consumerism, this is less and less the case. So in addition to the private (business) sector and the public (government) sector, from the shadows has emerged the citizens' movement or individual sector.

Consumers, members of religious sects, social activists, environmentalists, and even workers often feel they stand apart from both the corporate community and government representation. They believe that the partnership between government and business has left them out. The tightening alliance between business and government in the capitalist countries has made the traditional paths of political expression and change—the electoral process, political revolt, or even immigration—seem increasingly futile. Politicians seem more influenced by business backers than they do by voters. That, perhaps, is why in the United States so few people vote. Only the most dysfunctional countries undergo political revolt, since it leads to social and economic chaos that can take generations to correct. Only those from the most economically deprived regions have anything to gain by fleeing, and they are migrating to worldwide employment centers in incredible numbers. But individuals in the developed economies do fight for improved conditions and reform through the formation of grass roots organizations, citizen groups, through increasingly sophisticated watchdog societies.

In political capitals, these are sometimes called "special interest groups" and lumped together with organizations like the U.S. political action committees (PACs), which in fact are created by business interests to represent them. However, even when the citizen groups are commanded by a single charismatic leader, they can easily be distinguished from those that arise from corporate pursuits. Earth First, Mothers Against Drunk Driving (MADD), and countless other national and international organizations may solicit funds from various charitable sources after their founding, but initially they arose from a smoldering corpus of personal frustration.

Craig Smith, editor and publisher of the newsletter *Corporate Philanthropy Report*, recognizes the same trend, though he is viewing it from a purely American perspective. "The federal government has forfeited its responsibility for many of the problems that face America today," Smith said. "We are starting to witness the development of a consensus-based approach to problem solving through a coalition of civic, corporate, and nonprofit leaders." In this "post-federal" phase of America's development, Smith said, the unit of social change is the region.[4]

Corporations must respond to this form of social unrest, since no meganational is immune to pressure from private interest groups. Discussed earlier were the baby formula controversies that continue to plague Bristol-Myers Squibb, Nestlé, and the narrow range of producers of infant nutrition products; Mitsui Taiyo Kobe Bank and other financial institutions are the target of individuals and consumer groups who demand equal access to capital; Exxon, British Petroleum, Royal Dutch/Shell, and other petroleum companies are closely monitored by those whose resolve it is to guard the natural environment. The list of causes and concerns is varied and dramatic:

• For more than five years, the Infact group has waged a boycott against General Electric Corporation to coerce the company out of the nuclear weapons business. GE was an early leader in nuclear weapons production, though in recent years its nuclear business has mostly been focused on medical equipment and reactors that produce electric energy. The company still builds components for airplanes, missiles, and submarines for military use, and also conducts nuclear submarine research and trains personnel. Infact also was one of the leaders in the infant formula boycott.

• Several Japanese meganationals, including Sumitomo Bank and Dai-Ichi Kangyo Bank, have been accused in the United States of racial job discrimination against non-Japanese employees. Several law suits have been filed asserting that, in addition, Japanese executives sometimes slap around workers with whom they disagree.

• The National Environmental Law Center handed American Telephone and Telegraph 20,000 postcards from citizens asking the company to publish its entire environmental record. AT&T had been trumpeting its efforts to phase out ozone-destroying chlorofluorocarbons, but the advocacy group also wanted the company to tell of its violations of the Clean Water Act in New Jersey or any other environmental infractions.

• The Shell Oil Company was refused the right to operate gasoline stations along the New Jersey Turnpike allegedly because of the South African operations of its parent, the Royal Dutch/Shell Group. Religious organizations, students, union groups, and others pressed a boycott against any business working in segregated South Africa. "Were Royal Dutch/Shell to withdraw from South Africa, a strong voice against apartheid would be silent," the company responded in a statement. The company's mines and other assets cannot be removed from the country, the company said, so even if it did leave, the business would continue under South African owners, which could be much worse for the workers.

As the meganationals extend their presence into the lives of individuals everywhere, they will find that, in turn, they have greater difficulty with defiant individuals and with adversarial organizations. People will devise more and more power fronts as tools to vent their frustrations and to fight for chosen causes.

Helmut Maucher, chairman of Nestlé, seemed to be envisioning the same phenomenon when he told a New York audience that, in the future, global corporations would face problems with the ideas of "fundamentalism, utopia, absolute perfect solutions, no more the willingness of balanced proportionate views, some of the exaggerated views of the 'greens,' certain consumer protection policies, boycotting, etc."[5]

As irritating as the human interest movement may be to most corporate leaders, the great majority of the advocates are nonviolent. Their cost to a company can be counted only in money or time. Actions are limited to civil law suits, blocking traffic, boycotting products, or disrupting annual meetings.

Yet, as Theodore Roosevelt once observed, every reform movement has its lunatic fringe. This evolutionary, corporation-targeted drive is no different.

Unless the meganationals are sensitive to the individual and human aspects of the world in which they operate, these action groups can become as fervently hostile as any past revolutionary wave. It was to this extreme element that Deutsche Bank's Alfred Herrhausen fell victim. In Mexico City in 1991, IBM, Citibank, and McDonald's facilities were bombed; credit went to a Mexican leftist organization with roots back to the 1960s.

The citizen watchdog movements have their roots in a difficult terrain of issues as somber as fear of political and social domination, or as worldly as anger at increasingly similar and narrow job, lifestyle, and consumer choices. In most cases, the frustration is grounded in the world created by the oligopoly environment. Only by acknowledging and dealing with the origins of the discontent can the meganationals be truly conscientious global citizens.

Back in 1985, *Mother Jones* magazine published an article by Mark Dowie and Theodore A. Brown in which the authors attempted to list the 10 best and 10 worst American businesses. They were mimicking the obsession of business publications as well as the anti-business press for ranking and rating businesses on selected criteria. "We learn little from such rankings," the authors wrote, "except that the business press values growth, size, and fast profit, and the Left distrusts anything with *Corp.* after its name."

The authors set about to establish their own standards of good business, first of all, eliminating profits from the list. " . . . although we recognize the need for any enduring economic institution (or nation) to somehow generate a surplus, we decided not to make profit a criterion for evaluation, as profit alone does not seem to bring lasting social progress to American business."[6]

The *Mother Jones* measurements for good versus bad businesses, as it turned out, is a precise list of the six areas in which the meganationals are likely to encounter challenges from their various publics.

In order of importance, the public demands that corporations be accountable for the product, the workplace, the environment, the community, the consumer, and ownership.

Because of the essential changes coming in employment and work attitudes, and the profound impact of ownership, those issues will be the subjects of the following two chapters. The other four gauges of good business carry enormous cultural implications as well and are addressed throughout this book. However, they deserve special attention here.

Mother Jones asked these questions about a company's product or service: "Are (a company's) products of real social and economic value? Are they safe and of good quality? Are any of the business's products critical elements in machines or weapons of mass destruction?"[7]

As the situation with the Philip Morris tobacco division illustrates, products can be of economic value, but of questionable social consequence. They can be of good quality, yet not be safe.

They cannot be a weapon, yet be a means of mass destruction. Both alcohol and tobacco fall into this category, creating problems that go beyond personal health. *Worldwatch* magazine points out that alcohol abuse is both a health issue and a development issue in Third World countries, where "severe drinking lowers productivity, reduces agricultural output, and undermines progress toward improved health for women and children."[8]

Philip Morris's defense of its tobacco products shows how distressing it is for a company to abandon a product that is legal, desired by consumers, and a matchless source of revenue. Problems in tobacco-growing regions of the United States and Canada also demonstrate that ways must be pioneered to help workers find alternate means of earning a living when they find themselves involved in work that will be phased out.

The lessons learned from the American liquor prohibition of the 1920s and 1930s and the current war on illegal drugs is that completely outlawing a personally and socially destructive product is both costly and useless. Nevertheless, appropriate legislation, supervision, education, and medical treatment, as has been the route taken in the United States and other countries, can lead to a weakening demand for damaging products such as tobacco and alcohol.

As Nestlé's Helmut Maucher pointed out, the first obligation of a corporation is to make a profit. When the profits diminish, even the mightiest meganational will abandon a bad product and seek a more lucrative option.

"If the business is a manufacturer," asked *Mother Jones*, "does it protect the air, groundwater, and land it affects? If the business is financial, does it consider the environment in its lending, underwriting, or investment decisions?"[9]

Because the earth and sea and sky have always seemed so vast and omnipotent, some people have great difficulty coming to terms with the fouling and demolition of the planet. Many who long for the past, who live in isolated areas where the spoilage isn't so obvious, or whose livelihood is threatened, deny it altogether. Compulsive worriers or those who have seen the swiping claw of mutant nature believe the end of humankind is near. Even those with a more optimistic mindset have great difficulty in assessing the state of the environment. But they do know that as we go about our economic endeavors, as big business builds larger and larger oil tankers and constructs nuclear reactors that propagate more and more radioactive waste, as we slash down trees and send chemicals down the river into lakes, something important dies.

Economists, despite all their other failed forecasts, have seen this coming. The trouble derives from the difficulty capitalism has with what economists call "externalities"—the negative consequences or by-products of production such as garbage; traffic; or land, water, and air pollution. These externalities seem to be everybody's fault and nobody's fault. In the past, when populations were on such a scale that the environment could and would be self-cleaning and self-curing, the externalities were of little consequence. But from the Industrial Revolution until the present, the problems have become more complicated and perplexing. As governments have been unwilling or unable to clean up the burgeoning messes, citizen vigilante groups everywhere have applied pressure of their own.

While some environmentalist tactics seem extreme, they have caught the attention of many industrial companies, including most of the meganationals. Matsushita Electric Industrial in 1991 told all of its subsidiaries worldwide to set environmental guidelines in conformance to the rules of their host countries, making it the first Japanese company to do so. Hitachi, in its Japanese offices and factories, has switched to reusable plastic chopsticks in place of disposable wood. Fiat has taken an active role in the "greening" of motor vehicles, and since early 1990 has had an electric car on the market. Following numerous disastrous oil spills, Du Pont, owner of Conoco Oil, announced it would build new double-hulled tankers.

When *Mother Jones* inquired, "How does a corporation live within its community?," it posed questions that have been asked again and again in this book. "What kind of commitment does the business have to the local community, the national community? (What are the company's lobbying policies? Which politicians does it support? How much of its profits go to charity?) How does it behave in the international community? (Is the company a fair trader? How is it treating its overseas workers and consumers? Is it applying the same environmental and safety standards at home and abroad?)"[10]

Philip Morris learned that community practices which are at cross purposes to one another lead to discord. Building on its long tradition in funding the arts, in 1990 Philip Morris contributed about $15 million to arts organizations across the United States, making it one of the most lavish contributors to the arts. The company sponsored art museums, music academies, and dance troupes. The company also has been a long-time donor to Senator Jesse Helms, an archconservative Republican from North Carolina, a major tobacco-growing state. Helms is a vituperative critic of the National Endowment for the Arts, accusing it of sponsoring work Helms considers obscene. He especially assailed self-expressive works by homosexual artists. Several gay rights organizations and anti-AIDS coalitions started pressuring arts groups to reject funding from Philip Morris until the company ceased its subsidies to Helms.

"It is a clear case of corporate America playing both ends against the middle," William Waybourn, the director of public affairs for the Dallas Gay Alliance told the *New York Times*. "What happens in some cases is that you get burned, and in this case Philip Morris got burned."[11]

In the end, Philip Morris did not renounce Helms. Money, again, worked its magic. The company announced that it would substantially increase charitable contributions to AIDS medical research. The company didn't say how much it would give, but in the three years prior to the funding increase, Philip Morris contributed $1.3 million to various gay causes, including AIDS help organizations.

Mother Jones acknowledged the importance of consumerism in culture, but came up a little short in this department in terms of the global market. "Is consumer safety considered?" the authors asked, and "Are maintenance warranties honored?"

These are important considerations, of course. Most buyers, from homeowners to car shoppers to chewers of sugarless bubblegum, grapple with them on a regular basis. But there are larger questions as well. Do consumers get the choices they want, or only the choices the manufacturers present to them? Are goods distributed fairly? Are consumers in one part of the world given advantageous treatment at the expense of consumers elsewhere? Every company, large and small, promises to serve its customers atten-tively. That means different things at different companies.

To Kenichi Ohmae, author of *The Borderless World*, it means that consumers are in the driver's seat of the global economy. "Governments can still arbitrage information or otherwise protect their markets by forcing citizens to buy high-priced beef (as is the case in Japan) or poor-quality automobiles (the case in India and Brazil), but product labels are spreading all over the world and news of product performance is harder to suppress. Information has empowered consumers."[12]

While free trade does lead to a greater diversity of products—the U.S. car market is testament to that—the picture gets distorted when a few dominant companies govern any market. In Japan, where major corporations and their keiretsu conglomerates reign, prices are notoriously high. Golf clubs can be 21 percent to 42 percent cheaper in the United States than they are in Japan; men's jeans are 48 percent less. The phrase "Consumer empowerment has become an oxymoron in Japan," says Asia specialist Steven Schlosstein.

The ability to chart strategies on an international scale can give the meganationals enormous leverage. For example, in the United States in the past decade, no single item in the Consumer Price Index, the national indicator for price inflation, has gone up as much as cigarettes. A pack that cost 63 cents in 1980 was selling for $1.67 in 1991. As Philip Morris is swift to point out, rising sales taxes have contributed to higher prices. But the biggest advancement has come from factory markups by the manufacturers themselves.

The logic behind the U.S. increases seems to work this way. Cigarette smoking is declining at about 2 percent a year in the United States because the habit is perceived as unhealthy. A reduc-tion in the price of cigarettes will not reverse that trend. Since there is no hope of expanding the U.S. market, the only way to make more money is to hike prices. Since the prices go up slowly, at 5 cents to 6 cents a pack every few months, smokers don't resist. For a while smokers switched from premium brands to generics and other substitutes, but in recent years the price gap between premiums and second choices also has narrowed. In the meantime, cigarette companies are using profits—at Philip Morris, cigarettes earn more than twice what food and beer does—to transport themselves into foreign markets. By the time growth in the U.S. market is depleted, profits will be rolling in from other places.

None of the 25 most powerful companies in the world profiled in this book appeared on *Mother Jones's* Ten Best Companies list. Four of the 10 worst were meganationals: Philip Morris because it relies on a product that cannot be defended on moral terms; Du Pont for "consistently operating without regard for workers, the environment, or rights of the citizens of Delaware"; Citicorp for violations of its own business code of ethics; and General Electric, both because it is a major weapons manufacturer and because it was indicted for defrauding its own government. The article covered only U.S. corporations. No doubt a multinational survey would have presented a somewhat different picture.

In the meantime, while they await such a list, citizens around the globe continue to hope for the prosperity that the meganationals can bring to their homelands. Once they are blessed with the attention of one or more massive corporations, they begin to battle against their smothering authority, to preserve and enhance community and individual identities.

Chapter Twelve

Employees and the Meganationals

"The history of the world is the record of a man in quest of his daily bread and butter."

H. W. Van Loon, *The Story of Mankind*

In the 1970s in Great Britain, Sony began building color televisions. Sony was accompanied to the British Isles by Matsushita Electric, which opened a facility to build Panasonic television sets, by Toshiba, and belatedly by Hitachi, Japan's largest manufacturer of electrical and electronic equipment. There was a sweep of Japanese companies into Britain for use as a staging ground for European sales, thus mitigating Common Market protectionism. By 1981, Japanese companies had invested $2 billion dollars and some 13,000 Britons were directly employed by Japanese firms. Because of high unemployment, the companies were able to negotiate to their advantage with the infamous English unions; equally important, the Japanese companies found that British markets fell open to their products.

Then in 1984, British workers heard a message loud and clear that the Japanese had brought their assembly plants and merchandise to Britain, but not their workplace traditions. Certainly not the convention of lifetime employment.

Just before Christmas in 1984, Hitachi dispatched a letter to all its "company members," (i.e., workers) over the age of 35 at its plant in Hirwaun, Wales. The letter said that older workers were too slow, had failing eyesight, got sick too often, and were too resistant to change. Those who received the letter were offered about 1,800 pounds sterling ($2,160), tax-free, to take their leave. As an additional bonus, the discarded worker could nominate a 16-year-old who was finishing school, possibly someone in his or her own family, as a replacement. The letter did not mention that the older workers being encouraged out the door were likely to have accumulated pay increases to reach higher salaries. The young replacement would earn about $66 a week until age 18, when he or she would automatically get a raise.

The letter added insult to automation at the Hirwaun plant. Before the incident occurred, Hitachi's Hirwaun facility was building 300,000 television sets a year, but it was losing money. The company modernized the factory but found it then needed to lay off 500 of the 1,300 employees. After negotiating with the labor unions, Hitachi agreed to dismiss the workers with the least seniority first. Those, of course, were the youngsters. In the end, Hitachi found its average worker age was around 40, something of a problem in an assembly operation, which depends on low cost and high speed for profits.

Needless to say, Hitachi's (very) early retirement proposal did not fly well in England, reviving Britain's post–World War II image of the Japanese as mean-spirited and ruthless. But the country seemed to get over it, and so did Hitachi and other Japanese manufacturers. The local councils in Derbyshire fell to their knees in joy when, in 1989, they were told Toyota would build cars there. By 1991, Hitachi had contributed to the construction of a research facility at Cambridge University, where it will collaborate on microelectronics research.

Working on future technology with a partner like Hitachi is a real plum for British academicians and engineers. Though it is widely recognized for its televisions, VCRs, microwave ovens, and other consumer products, these largely have been spin-offs from Hitachi's more sophisticated undertakings. Hitachi also produces, among dozens of other products, hydroelectric turbines; state-of-the-art nuclear generators; advanced semiconductors; industrial robots; and electric locomotives, cars, and monorails.

Hitachi began experimenting early with computers, and in the 1960s built Japan's first on-line computer system. The company made rapid strides to catch up to International Business Machines and other world competitors, thanks to the Japanese Ministry of

International Trade and Industry (MITI) funding for technical research and development.

Hitachi has sometimes gone to extreme lengths to push into the big leagues of computers. In 1982, the U.S. Justice Department and the FBI caught Hitachi stealing trade secrets from a main rival, IBM. Eleven employees were indicted on charges of commercial bribery and theft. The company was required to pay hefty software royalties and to let IBM inspect its forthcoming products.[1,2]

As pleased as locals have been to be selected as sites for Japanese factories, Hitachi needed the new factories as much as England needed the jobs. As trade balances tipped too heavily in favor of the Japanese, it became ever more difficult to repatriate yen. The company found it had to move some production out of Japan, where it could be closer to markets and gain some protection from currency fluctuations. In the late 1980s, the strong yen helped curtail Hitachi's profits, which dropped 34 percent in 1987 alone.

Hitachi focused on increasing overseas manufacturing, promoting international procurement, and importing to Japan more products that Hitachi had manufactured abroad. In addition to its British facilities, Hitachi operates one of the largest border assembly plants in Tijuana, Mexico. It expanded its semiconductor production facility in West Germany and set up an Eastern Europe department for seeking new ventures there. By 1990, overseas manufacturing accounted for 23 percent of overseas sales, but it was Hitachi's goal to raise that to 50 percent.

"We want our overseas companies to be independent," said Hitachi chairman Katsushige Mita. "We don't want them to have to rely on Tokyo."

Since Hitachi started business in 1910 as a small machine shop, the company has been quick to adapt to change. It got its first big break in the manufacture of electric motors during World War I when foreign equipment was difficult to procure. When the Japanese military government came to power in the 1930s, Hitachi was pressured into manufacturing radar, sonar, and other war tools, though the company's founder prevented Hitachi from actually making weapons. Nonetheless, Hitachi was devastated by World War II and many of its factories were obliterated in Allied bombing assaults. Though the American occupation forces tried to disband Hitachi, the company was allowed to keep all but 19 of its manufacturing plants. Ironically, it was U.S. defense contracts during the

Korean War that set Hitachi back on its feet. In the years since, recessions and the 1974 OPEC oil crisis also have kept the company nimble.

Hitachi's ability to change seems to have helped it through the computer industry slump of the late 1980s. Sales increased 11 percent and net income rose 14 percent in 1989.

In spite of everything, Hitachi has continued to be an innovator. Its new flat-screen television shows great promise, as does its erasable compact disc and a video printer that produces extremely clear snapshot size prints from a television screen. There were even rumors in 1991 that Hitachi was, in emulation of Sony and Matsushita, looking for a Hollywood entertainment company to buy.

And despite its gaffes, Hitachi has been around long enough to know that it must make some effort to heal the damage of misunderstandings between Japanese companies and foreign workers and customers. In the late 1980s, Hitachi sent a senior representative to California to tidy up the company's bad-boy image. The emissary launched a crusade that included charitable contributions, cross-cultural events, and public forums on contemporary issues. Hitachi also sponsors a teacher exchange program in the United States, bringing American teachers to Japan and Japanese teachers to the United States. It might also help if Hitachi followed the example of some Japanese companies, which conduct similar cultural exchanges with their own workers, bringing foreign employees to Japan to help them understand the company and develop corporate camaraderie.

Less than 10 years ago, the Mexican border that divides San Diego and Tijuana was a farming plateau where tomatoes, cucumbers, barley, and celery were grown. Now close to 600 Hitachi workers assemble television sets and cabinets. Additionally, on both sides of the international border, major corporations such as Matsushita, General Motors, and scores of other U.S., Asian, and European companies pay workers less than $1 per hour to assemble computers, refrigerators, and dozens of other products. At the end of 1990, nearly 1,800 maquiladoras throughout Mexico employed 500,000 people, mostly young women who frequently work up to 10-hour days, six days a week.

The workers, most of them immigrants from the dusty, shack-ridden interior of Mexico, generated $2.5 billion in foreign investment in Mexico, making the maquiladora industry Mexico's second largest producer of foreign currency. Only Mexican oil is more lucrative.

The spawning of assembly plants in Mexico has led to profound social change. Feminists in Tijuana protested that young girls were being pulled out of school prematurely to report to work in the factories. Often their fathers could not find jobs at all. Work conditions in the huge, sheet metal warehouses were stultifying, breaks too short, and safety too often ignored. Decent housing near the factories is all but impossible to find. Turnover of workers is sometimes as high as 100 percent a year.

On the other hand, there *is* work, while none exists in many other parts of Mexico. Though conditions are slumlike, workers begin to claim land on the parched hills to build their own homes of tin, plywood, cement blocks, or whatever materials they can afford. Though the employers pay a housing fee to the government, federal housing projects are few. Former President Jimmy Carter's favorite organization, Habitat for Humanity, and even some employers, are building homes in areas that look like giant refugee camps.

Shops and businesses on both sides of the border thrive, as Mexican workers supply themselves with blankets, beds, radios, and rosary beads. In Tijuana, a sophisticated middle and upper class of professionals and business leaders has been cultivated. Some Mexicans have been made rich in the process, and Tijuana has become so large (at least a million residents) so quickly that nobody even knows how many people live there. The generator of all this activity—the maquiladora concept—has since spread to the interior of Mexico, and will no doubt receive special treatment under the North American Free Trade Agreement.

It has not been the world's largest businesses alone that have brought about this transformation of Mexico, but their influence has been undeniable. It was to lure the best capitalized, most technically oriented businesses that the Mexican government created the system of allowing material into the country duty-free for assembly and reexport.

The American meganationals have been particularly enthusiastic about the opportunities for low-cost manufacturing there. Following a dinner in Mexico City with the local heads of half a dozen Fortune 500 companies, General Electric chairman John Welch described it as ". . . one of the most upbeat meetings of Americans you'll ever have." Daimler-Benz and Siemens are established in Mexico, as are the major U.S. and European food companies. Both of the Japanese meganational manufacturing companies have plants, and the meganational Japanese banks either have a presence in Mexico or operations close enough to the border to serve Japanese companies manufacturing there.

And it isn't only in the rocky bean fields of Mexico or the pastoral home counties of England that people from distant and different cultures meet and work together. More than 80,000 jobs are said to have been created in California from the influx of some 500 Japanese corporations—including the meganationals and a multitude of companies financed by the Japanese meganational banks.

As the tempo of internationalization speeds up, workers in many lands find themselves under the management of massive corporations, often of foreign origin. Whether the experience is a good one, or whether it turns out to be exploitive and humiliating, often depends on the goals and attitudes of management.

In Japan, Merck was able to make one of the rare acquisitions of Japanese companies by an American corporation. Japanese workers were skeptical and anxious about what the change would mean to them. However, Banyu pharmaceuticals is doing even better than it did under Japanese ownership and the arrangement is comfortable.

Some companies have a particularly enlightened view of their role in the world. "Matsushita," the Japanese electrical giant said in its annual 1990 report, "is dedicated to becoming a truly international corporate citizen that contributes to the well-being of every community in which it operates. We believe that a company should be operated by local people for the benefit of their local communities. In the past year, the first American president was appointed to Matsushita Electric Corporation of America. Localization of R&D is the next area of priority for our globalization program. R&D facilities are being established and expanded in North America, Europe, and Asia to serve the needs of each region. One such example is Panasonic Advanced TV-Video Laboratories, Inc. which was newly established in North America."

The presence of Japanese companies has had positive repercussions in many places where they have set up business. *Forbes* magazine quoted a British worker in a 1981 article. "I was a shop steward in a typical British factory that had four grades of toilets and four grades of canteens, and as you worked your way up the company hierarchy you parked your car in a different car park. It was a situation tailor-made for class conflict. But the Japanese don't have that. They have the single-status employee approach, which we applaud."[3]

But, as happened with Hitachi in Wales, cultures sometimes clash, too. In 1988, 13 New York City women won a landmark $2.7 million suit in Federal court against Sumitomo Bank. The "Sumitomo Thirteen" claimed they had been discriminated against in working at the bank, and were denied opportunities for advancement. *Avagliano v. Sumitomo Shoji America Inc.* reached the U.S. Supreme Court before it was settled. The case supposedly put foreign corporations on notice that they must comply to equal opportunity laws in the United States. However, all 13 women either left Sumitomo voluntarily or agreed to leave, and are pursuing careers elsewhere.[4]

Yet the problems aren't all based on cultural differences. Many domestic companies find themselves in Sumitomo's and Hitachi's shoes. And no matter how well-meaning the meganational corporation involved, the growing size and the internationalization of business have ominous implications for workers everywhere.

"Globalization means a cut in wages," states MIT economics professor Lester Thurow. "If you don't have more skills than a Korean high school graduate, you will work for Korean wages. Those without education work for lower wage rates. Therefore U.S. wages (which have been among the best in the world) go down. This is the virtue of competition."[5]

The old solution for workers, unionization, is losing its force. It is true that unionism is alive and influential in some parts of the world, but it has been greatly diminished in the most developed countries. Part of the decay of unionism has come from within, incited by excessive zeal, poor management, or corruption. As swifter transportation and effortless communication allow business to seek labor anywhere, however, workers fear that strong union action will drive away jobs altogether.

UCSD professor Chalmers Johnson explained that the Japanese tamed their unions in a pragmatic way—by striking a deal.

"In the 1950s labor struggles were blood soaked," Johnson recalled. "What labor wanted was job security. The Japanese gave job career security to male heads of households who entered jobs starting from high school, in big companies. Male heads of households became labor aristocrats. But they also extracted a promise. Labor will play no role in politics. No labor parties, and just weak company unions. Nobody asks in Japan, how will it go down with the unions?"[6]

Once labor was turned into a fixed cost, Johnson said, Japanese corporations "got serious about manufacturing. They want workers to have lots of different skills so they can be moved around as needed. An assembly line worker can become a salesman when sales are off."

In their book *The Bigness Complex*, Walter Adams and James Brock sketch a different scene in the United States, but one with similar results.

"Whether we examine the role of the United Automobile Workers (UAW), or the United Steel Workers (USW), or the Communications Workers of America (CWA), these unions do not constitute a countervailing power with respect to entrenched corporate interests," write Adams and Brock. "In bargaining over wages, hours, fringe benefits, and democracy in the workplace, they may assume an adversarial posture toward corporate management; but, in a larger sense, they represent not countervailing but coalescing power in defending the parochial, short-run interests of their industry. In their Washington lobbying, their demands are indistinguishable from those of their corporate counterparts: 'the hand is the hand of Esau, but the voice is the voice of Jacob.'"[7]

Even in Europe, labor unions have beome institutionalized, though they still succeed in making their voices heard. The deputy chairman of Siemens' supervisory board is a company mechanic. Toolmakers, technicians, and electricians also serve on the executive council, giving some assurance that the high-level policy decisions are not made without consideration for the fate of employees.

Labor representation at the policy-setting level does not guarantee that labor and management always will agree. It was another meganational with labor officials on the board, Daimler-Benz, that battled with West German workers in the mid-1980s against the 35-hour work week. Daimler's tough stance set the tone for other German industries.

In the world of multinationalism, workers are the most vulnerable of all the stakeholders in business. While management may describe their employees as valuable assets, there is no denying they also are an expense. When costs must be cut, jobs are on the chopping block.

For example, in Du Pont Corporation's 1990 annual report, chairman Edgar Woolard talked of the company's "goal of becoming a great global company through people." He went on to describe, quite correctly, how Du Pont is considered a premier employer in many parts of the world, because of its generous programs and perquisites for workers. Six months after the annual report was published, however, a worldwide recession lead to a drop in earnings at Du Pont and Woolard announced a program to lay off 15,000 to 20,000 employees. Many of the jobs to be cut were in the United States, though some were in Du Pont's facilities in various parts of the world.

It's difficult for an employee to be loyal to a company when she or he no longer has a job. No matter how frustrating and tedious a General Motors employee may have found assembly line work, he isn't apt to like it when GM moves manufacturing to Mexico and shuts down his plant. Proponents of free trade and the internationalization of business often present a stack of technical studies showing that free trade creates more rather than fewer jobs, and benefits the economy overall. Nevertheless, joblessness and homelessness have become growing problems in the United States and, throughout the world, poor people are becoming even poorer.

However, those who can acquire the best, right education and the appropriate skills are more advantaged than ever. They can move throughout the world to where the high-paying jobs exist and their talents are in demand. If they are employed by a large, multinational company, their opportunities and income are especially enhanced. Employees of the 25 most powerful companies in the world, in particular, constitute an elite guard. It is at these companies that workers get the best hours, best assignments, best benefits, and highest pay. They are becoming the "Roman legions" of the working world.

In a five-page advertisement in *Scientific American* magazine, Nestlé described a scene at one of its laboratories. "A scientist in a white lab coat studies a tray of mosses and algae samples, grown in vitro. 'It seems to have proved a dead end,' he explains in English slightly accented by his native Norwegian."[8]

The scientist works at the Nestlé Research Center at Vers Chez-les Blanc, the world's largest food and nutrition research center.

"Almost five hundred such scientists and technicians from thirty-five countries work here," the Nestlé advertisement continued, "spending an annual budget of about SwF 100 million; they labor in near-utopian lab surroundings that cost SwF 200 million to build and another 75 million to equip, set amid the greenery outside Lausanne."

Perhaps Nestlé dresses up its image somewhat; certainly not all employees of the meganationals work in "utopia." But there is little doubt that to compete with the likes of Unilever, Philip Morris, and other large food conglomerates, Nestlé must invest in brainpower and technology. Nestlé's size, plus its edge in the marketplace, makes this level of investment possible.

"Oligopolies," Thurow says, "have often provided more agreeable working conditions, more handsome offices, and safer plants than have small competitive firms. Thus some of the loss of consumers' well-being is regained in the form of workers' well-being."[9]

The higher up the corporate ladder one of the elite employees progresses, the more he advances in the economic class system. In Japan, top executives earn around 17 times the pay of the average worker; in Germany the CEO average salary gap is 23 times; in the United States, the chief executive receives about 110 times the pay of the typical worker. The accumulation of better wages and benefits unquestionably ties an employee to an employer.

Thurow spurned the suggestion that workers, in the future, may become more loyal to their companies than they are to their countries. "People die for their countries," he said. "Not many people would die for their companies." Perhaps not directly or consciously, but many do toil under hazardous conditions, put up with stress that leads to heart attacks and other disease, and some even go to jail for illegal business practices that give their employer a competitive advantage. In Japan, a dreaded word has come into common usage among "sararimen" or male office workers— "karoshi" or death from overwork.

Despite perennial rumblings that young workers are changing the workplace, many individuals, once they have a career underway, identify closely with their work. If they are employed by a large, powerful, prestigious company, the bonding with an employer can be exceedingly strong. At IBM, where key employees are moved so often they chidingly say the company's initials stand for "I've been moved," there is exceptional loyalty to Big Blue.

Don Estridge, an executive who was instrumental in the development of IBM's personal computer, described his feelings when a stream of outside job offers came from other companies. "I guess I'll never leave IBM," Estridge was quoted in the book entitled *Big Blue*. "I can't describe what a kick it is when someone asks me who I work for and I tell them, 'IBM' and they are always impressed. Gee, that really means a lot to me—it's something money can't buy."[10]

Scarcity makes almost anything more seductive, and posts with the 25 most influential companies in the world are no exception. These jobs are becoming increasingly hard to come by.

"In terms of fraction of total employment, Fortune 500 companies employ less of the (U.S.) economy than they did 20 years ago," Thurow said. "However, the Fortune 500's fraction of the GNP is going up."

While the meganationals may grow in other ways, because these companies have access to the latest technologies, automation, robotization, and so on, the actual size of its labor force often shrinks.

- Although revenues still grew (albeit not as rapidly as before) between 1988 and 1990, IBM's employment level fell by 13,292 people. Further reductions of the workforce were made in 1991.
- General Electric in 1989 had 292,000 employees, down from 373,000 employees in 1986. Yet during the same period, revenues increased from $42 billion in 1986 to $54.6 billion in 1989. Total assets increased from $84.8 billion in 1986 to $128 billion in 1989.
- During that same period, AT&T was restructuring. It trimmed employment by 42,300 workers while revenues went up $3 billion.
- Fiat made similar changes between 1987 and 1989. Its employee base declined 14,578 but revenues rose 12.4 billion lire.
- Dai-Ichi Kangyo Bank, the world's largest financial institution, decreased its number of employees by 8.7 percent and, at the same time, doubled its income and boosted assets by 83 percent.

This trend speaks well for the efficiency of big business and for shareholder profitability. It does not look so good for those seeking stable, high-paying work.

As the perimeters of international business expand, the way people earn their livings also will shift. The welfare of working people everywhere was on the mind of Pope John Paul II when he gave his Centesimus Annus or One Hundred Year encyclical in 1991.

"The free market is the most efficient instrument for utilizing resources and effectively responding to needs," the Pope said. "But there are many human needs which find no place on the market."

Pope John Paul II explained that, "Whereas at one time the decisive factor of production was the land, and later capital— understood as a total complex of the instruments of production— today the decisive factor is increasingly man himself, that is, his knowledge, especially his scientific knowledge, his capacity for interrelated and compact organization, as well as his ability to perceive the needs of others and to satisfy them."

The Pope summarized the situation this way, "In our time, in particular, there exists another form of ownership which is becoming no less important than land; the possession of know-how, technology, and skill. . . . The fact is that many people, perhaps the majority today, do not have the means which would enable them to take their place in an effective and humanly dignified way within a productive system in which work is truly central."

The Pope called upon leaders of the business world to recognize that while profit is a regulator of the life of a business, "it is not the only one; other human and moral factors must also be considered."

The Meganationals
Employees Worldwide
(1991 Data)

AT&T   273,000 employees
Bristol-Myers Squibb   52,900 employees
British Petroleum   118,000 employees
Citicorp   95,000 employees
Coca-Cola   24,000 employees
Dai-Ichi Kangyo Bank   18,466 employees

Daimler-Benz   376,785 employees
Deutsche Bank   56,580 employees
Du Pont   143,961 employees
Exxon   104,000 employees
Fiat   286,294 employees
General Electric   292,000 employees
General Motors   761,000 employees
Hitachi   290,800 employees
IBM   373,816 employees
Matsushita   198,000 employees
Merck   36,900 employees
Mitsubishi Bank   14,271 employees
Mitsui Taiyo Kobe Bank (renamed Sakura Bank)
22,919 employees
Nestlé   199,000 employees
Philip Morris   168,000 employees
Royal Dutch Petroleum/Royal Dutch Shell   130,000
employees
Siemens   373,000 employees
Sumitomo Bank   16,476 (parent bank only, does not include
16 subsidiaries and affiliates)
Unilever   304,000 employees

Populations of Selected Cities:

Anchorage, Alaska, U.S., population 175,000
Belfast, Northern Ireland, population 303,000
Brazzaville, Congo, population 595,000
Geneva, Switzerland, population 161,000
Kingston, Jamaica, population 100,000
Muscat, Oman, population 85,000
Quebec, Canada, population 603,000
Raleigh, North Carolina, U.S., population 187,000
Reykjavik, Iceland, population 93,000
Suva, Fiji, population 69,000
Tegucigalpa, Honduras, population 550,000

Chapter Thirteen

Stakeholders of the Meganationals

"Two and two continue to make four, in spite of the whine of the amateur for three, or the cry of the critic for five."

James McNeil Whistler, 1878

It was the winter of 1991 when, from New York to New Zealand, Denmark to Delaware, managers of I. E. du Pont de Nemours and Company told employees about the good deal they were being offered. They would receive an option to buy 100 shares of company stock at a price of $38.25 per share. More than 136,000 employees in 53 countries on six continents were invited to participate in the program. The employees could exercise the options between 1 and 10 years from the time they were granted.

The stock option program "looks beyond the current economic downturn and recognizes the important role our employees will play in the future success of the company," said Du Pont chairman Edgar S. Woolard, Jr. "It's designed to help focus attention on our corporate vision of becoming a great global company through people and encourage employees to align their interest with that of our four key stakeholder groups—stockholders, customers, fellow employees, and society."[1]

In other words, the intention of Woolard and the Du Pont board of directors was to make employees feel like owners of the company, giving them an inducement to work hard and to make the value of their shares grow. Du Pont did not go so far, as some European companies have done, as to place a worker representative on the board. The 18-member board is comprised of prestigious representatives from other industries, plus delegates of the two factions who actually control the company. Edward B. du Pont speaks for the du Pont family's 22 percent interest in the corporation, and there are five representatives of The Seagram Company, which owns 24.3 percent of Du Pont. Two of Seagram's board members are members of the Bronfman family, who control Seagram.

Even if they could be voted as a block, the 13.6 million shares dedicated to the employee stock option plan could hardly stand up against the approximately 164.2 million shares controlled by the Bronfman family and the 148.7 million shares in the hands of various members of the du Pont clan.

Yet the option offering was more than symbolism. The company employees did stand to benefit financially from the endowment. After all, Du Pont's profitability since the company's birth in 1802 has created one of the wealthiest families in America—the du Ponts of Delaware. The Bronfmans, who got their shares in a 1981 swap for the stake they owned in Conoco, saw that $3 billion investment triple in 10 years. Du Pont's share price had grown at an average annual rate of about 10 percent in the five years that preceded the employee stock option offering. If that pattern were to repeat itself, an employee would realize a pretax gain of about $2,300 in 5 years, and more than $6,000 in 10 years.

Ironically, when six months later Du Pont announced plans to slash costs and severely reduce its work force, the value of the offering shot up. Du Pont's price rose $1.32 to $48.12 per share.

Additionally, the offering accentuated the increasingly international nature of corporate ownership, particularly among the meganational companies. The du Ponts are from the United States, the Bronfmans are Canadian, and the video tape Du Pont used to tell employees about the option plan had to be recorded in 14 languages. Du Pont stock is listed on the New York Stock Exchange, plus exchanges in Belgium, France, Germany, Japan, the Netherlands, and Switzerland.

Finally, in making the announcement, Woolard used a buzzword that had become increasingly popular in lofty corporate circles—"stakeholders." The word conveys the notion that the financial owners are not the sole proprietors of a company; a corporation has a wide range of people to whom it owes allegiance and responsibility. Woolard listed the stakeholders in what seems to be their rank of importance to management—stockholders, customers, fellow employees, and society. All four are essential to a company's survival, but business activity begins with those who take the risk and provide corporate capital—the stockholders. Ultimately, profits and losses flow back to the stockholders.

Ownership holds a singular place in the history of Du Pont. Few corporations in the United States can claim its patrician heritage. The company traces its ancestry back to an aristocrat who escaped the turmoil of the French revolution, then won his fortune in America by concocting explosives for the Civil War.

In his book, *Du Pont: Behind the Nylon Curtain*, Gerard Colby Zilg notes that the company, and the family it enriched, use their colossal might to influence local, national, and world events.

"The du Ponts own the state of Delaware. They control its state and local government; its major newspapers, radio, and TV stations; university and colleges; and its largest banks and industries, with four exceptions: Getty Oil, Phoenix Steel, and the Chrysler and General Foods plants, and even with these they've made profitable deals. The Du Pont Company alone employs more than 11 percent of Delaware's labor force, and when the family's other holdings are included, the percentage rises to over 75 percent. Throughout the United States, over a million Americans work to increase the du Pont fortune, and tens of thousands more work overseas at lower wages. Through one or more of their corporations, every nation in the 'free' world is touched by the silver hand of the du Pont family.[2]

"Predictably, the long arm of Du Pont can also be found in Washington, D.C. Du Pont family members represent Delaware in both houses of Congress. In the last 25 years Du Pont lieutenants have served as representatives, senators, U.S. Attorney General, secretaries of defense, directors of the CIA, and even Supreme Court justices.

"With their power, 'The Armorers of the Republic,' as they like to call themselves, have helped drive America into world war, sabotaged world disarmament conferences, built deadly arsenals of atomic weapons and nerve gas, flirted with Nazis, and according to charges brought before a congressional committee, once were even implicated in an attempt to overthrow the U.S. government— at the same time managing to avoid paying their share of taxes. A family ambition that was once limited to a total American monopoly, their vision of domination has now been extended to every corner of the world. As Irenee (du Pont) personifies, the power of the du Pont family is purposely subtle and quiet, but enormously effective."

It has been, however, more than a decade since a du Pont headed the company. Irenee du Pont retired from the corporate board in 1990, though other family members still serve.

Even Zilg, with his exhaustive research, wasn't able to clarify why the family and the company use the lower case "d" for du Pont, while in the popular press and in Du Pont's own literature, the upper case letter is used for secondary reference. The confusing practice, he noted, exemplifies the complexity of the company itself.

A durable and respected corporation whose name is virtually synonymous with the science of chemistry, Du Pont has a visceral problem. Founded on the explosives business (weapons in particular) and built even greater on chemicals, plastics, synthetic fibers, and oil, almost every one of Du Pont's major lines has a political, social, and/or environmental consequence. Among its 950 registered trademark brands, the company makes such environmentally perplexing products as plastics, chlorofluorocarbons, and pesticides. It manufactures Remington firearms, ammunition, and accessories. Du Pont also works strip mines and sells high-sulfur coal.

Yet the company has invented some of the most useful and ingenious products in the world, among them Nylon, Dacron, Lucite, Kevlar, and Teflon. In Du Pont's 1990 annual report, the company published a report card on its environmental efforts. Du Pont had reduced hazardous wastes, toxic emissions, and airborne carcinogens, and slashed energy consumption. Between 1990 and 1992, the company estimated it would spend between $500 million and $600 million annually for environmental control. But still, there are many incongruities.

While Du Pont announced it would work on a substitute for chlorofluorocarbons and convert to double-hulled oil tankers, the company is still frequently fined for environmental spoilage. It has refused to sign the Valdez Principles. This code of conduct was established by a group of environmental, investor, religious, and consumer interests called the Coalition for Environmentally Responsible Economies, and requires that companies not only respect the environment but always market safe products and services, and accept responsibility for environmental damage they may cause.

Despite its avowed dedication to shareholders and employees, Du Pont obviously isn't willing to be trampled by minority stakeholders. Shareholders' proposals to establish a review committee for Northern Ireland operations and to deliver a special report on South Africa business activities were opposed by management and were defeated.

While Du Pont pays respect to its various stakeholders, it is clear that the major stockholders still turn the keys to the kingdom. Du Pont's decision in 1991 to cut expenses by $1 billion and to dismiss up to 20,000 employees was in part prompted by the fear that, unless profits were fruitful enough to satisfy the Bronfmans, they might decide to sell their block of shares, making Du Pont vulnerable to an outside takeover.

The debate over the implications of the internationalization of business has been raging furiously in these final two decades of the 20th century. *Business Week* gave voice to the fundamental question in its 1990 article, "The Stateless Corporation."[3]

"Does it make any difference what a company's nationality is as long as it provides jobs?" After posing that question, the article went on to discuss several issues, such as what nation controls technology developed by a company in a foreign lab, and whose rules a company must follow when it is moving materials, employees, and services across multiple national borders. These are important issues, and perhaps will take a long time to clarify and answer. But to the first question, which *Business Week* left suspended, the answer is unmistakable.

It absolutely makes a difference where a corporation is domiciled. It is to the nation of ownership that profits ultimately flow. It is the headquarters country that is likely to reap the largest tax reward; where the highest paid employees are likely to reside, pay their own taxes, and spend most of their paychecks. Furthermore, through good times and bad, a parent corporation is likely to remain in the country where it germinated. While it is possible to switch headquarters, it is seldom done. In fact, in the case of the meganationals profiled in this book, it never has happened. Nestlé moved half its head office to Stamford, Connecticut, during World

War II. Though the company continued to operate in the United States, following the war management was reunited in Switzerland.

Michael J. Boskin, President George Bush's top economic advisor, and others have adopted the attitude that it doesn't matter who owns a company. "Whether it's American-owned, Japanese-owned, German-owned, or who-owned," Boskin said, "manufacturing in America in the '90s is going to be strong." His attitude has some merit. Every citizen needs a means of livelihood, and jobs are an important part of self-reliance. Furthermore, for a healthy economy, it is essential to allow a free flow of enterprise and trade. But it would be a mistake to discount the importance of ownership.

While jobs—whether they be in administration, manufacturing, or service—are good and useful to a local economy, never are they as lucrative as ownership. One simple way to determine the truth of that is to compare the lives and affluence of investor/owners with those of workers. The owner is more likely to drive an expensive car than is his assembly line worker. The same concept ripples along to cities, states, and nations. Cities like Minneapolis and St. Paul, where many large corporations are headquartered, have much richer government and cultural organizations than do cities like San Diego, which is home to many large plants, but head office to few big corporations. This is the reason that the United States, Germany, and Japan—along with other important industrialized nations—continue to be better off than those countries or regions which simply attract economic ventures because of raw materials or cheap labor. The wealthiest countries invariably are major seats of ownership.

Furthermore, jobs—even technical ones—can be quite transitory. Again, *Business Week* described practices in a business world without borders. "Some world companies make almost daily decisions on where to shift production." If the demand for a product declines in one country, production can be transferred somewhere else where demand is still strong. If labor or other problems erupt in one location, work can be moved to a friendlier or more compliant environment.

"When West Germany's BASF launched biotechnology research at home," the magazine explained, "it confronted legal and political challenges from the environmentally conscious Green movement.

So in January (1990), BASF shifted its cancer and immune-system research to Cambridge, Massachusetts, and plans an additional 250,000 square-foot facility outside Worcester, Massachusetts. The state is attractive because of its large number of engineers and scientists but also because it has better-resolved controversies involving safety, animal rights, and the environment."[4]

While it is true that the best-trained workers will be able to move with industry, or to seek out other work at home, shareholders face no such inconvenience. They can be owners from anywhere.

Only a few meganational corporations are controlled by a single individual or family; Fiat and Du Pont are the most notable among them. More often, ownership is dispersed in the hands of many shareholders, meaning that the company is under the supervision of no shareholders except management itself. Professional managers make the corporate decisions, including nominating those outside board members who ostensibly represent shareholders. As a result, even an incompetent chief executive officer who may have angered many investors has a tight hold on his job. When a CEO is ousted, the pressure is more likely to come from creditors who refuse to lend money unless management is replaced.

Even so, to ensure that investors are willing to buy new shares or debt instruments when they are issued, management must make certain that investors are satisfied with the return on their capital. The rewards to shareholders can be gleaned from share-price appreciation, by dividend payout, or by both. The blue chip companies aim for both. Except during periodic difficulties that each has been able to overcome so far, the meganationals have repaid shareholders reliably and generously.

Over the long term, the 25 most powerful companies in the world—the meganationals—have been exceptional investments. AT&T has paid dividends steadily for 113 years; Exxon for 110; Coca-Cola, 99 years; and Royal Dutch, 45 years. Understandably, dividend and share-price performances for European and Japanese corporations were disrupted because of World War II. And, granted, not all of the companies have been among the highest earning publicly traded stocks. Yet even the dawdlers are remarkable for their steadiness, longevity, and tenacity in rebounding from hard times. And despite their conservative tendencies, the return on these companies often is relatively high.

At the company's 1991 annual meeting, Merck chairman Dr. P. Roy Vagelos offered this comparison. "On average, one dollar invested in the Standard and Poor's Industrials at the beginning of 1985 was worth $2.38 at the end of the first quarter of this year, yielding a compound growth rate of 15 percent. One dollar invested in the other leading health-care companies at the beginning of 1985 was worth $4.07 on March 31, 1991, a compound annual growth rate of 25 percent. The same dollar invested in Merck," Vagelos said, "was worth $6.73, for a compound annual growth rate of 36 percent."

Du Pont has paid dividends without interruption for 88 years and even though some major investors may have been disgruntled, at the peak of the 1990–91 recession, Du Pont was among the 10 highest-earning U.S. companies. In fact, 9 of the top U.S. earners in the second quarter of 1991 were meganational stocks—Philip Morris, General Electric, Exxon, AT&T, Merck, Du Pont, Bristol-Myers Squibb, and Coca-Cola. Only one U.S. meganational—General Motors—was among the 10 biggest losers.

Though they all are mature companies, many of the meganationals—because of their customary cycles of renewal—offer the share-price appreciation usually expected of youthful growth stocks. Most recently Philip Morris, Coca-Cola, Daimler-Benz, and Merck have been among the frisky meganationals.

It isn't surprising, given their experience and value, that many meganational shares have been at the forefront of the globalization of stock markets.

Investors, both institutional and private, have responded to the trend toward internationalization, and have placed their investments accordingly. In the decade just past, foreigners tripled their U.S. shareholdings. American shareholders, meanwhile, quintupled their ownership of foreign stock.

Most U.S. meganationals trade on foreign exchanges, as do many of the meganational corporations of other countries. Philip Morris, IBM, Exxon, and many others can be found on the Tokyo stock exchange. In addition to trading on eight Japanese regional exchanges, Matsushita is listed on the New York, Pacific (California), Amsterdam, Frankfurt, Dusseldorf, and Paris stock markets. Unilever trades on exchanges in Amsterdam, London, New York, Austria, Belgium, France, Germany, Luxembourg, and Switzerland. Even stocks that are not listed on foreign exchanges frequently are available for purchase abroad through the larger brokerage houses.

As eager as investors around the world have been to invest in these companies, it hasn't been easy for some of the world's oldest and most powerful corporations to open up ownership. For years, Nestlé operated under a dual stock system that limited non-Swiss ownership to one third of all shares outstanding. The limited number of foreign shares traditionally traded at a much higher price than the Swiss shares. Finally, in the late 1980s, Nestlé decided that, to be truly multinational, and perhaps to vindicate its accelerated push into foreign markets, it must allow equal access to ownership. In a controversial move that abruptly drove down the price of the foreign shares and elevated the price of domestic shares, Nestlé abandoned the vestiges of xenophobia. Anyone could buy the registered Swiss shares, and since they cost less than the non-Swiss stock, many investors made the switch. For a time, foreign institutional investors who saw their Nestlé share price plunge blackballed the stock. Soon, however, investors couldn't resist the possibilities the shares offered. Now Americans are the largest single group of Nestlé owners after the Swiss.

Discrepancies in regulations covering the disclosure of financial information sometimes prevents corporations from expanding into global stock markets. Mitsubishi Bank, in the early 1990s, broke from the pack and became the first Japanese bank to acquiesce to U.S. financial disclosure rules so it could trade on the New York Stock Exchange.

No German companies are listed on the NYSE, though it is the world's largest investment market. This is largely because U.S. disclosure of investor information is so different from that required at home. In his 1989 annual report, Edzard Reuter, chairman of the Daimler-Benz board of management, gave a different, but equally interesting reason.

"Against the backdrop of standardized European accounting standards," Reuter wrote, "we are planning the introduction of Daimler-Benz shares on important stock markets of the world, primarily in London and Tokyo. We remain, however, highly skeptical about the practice of quarterly reports and payment of dividends because we also want to assure that your company continues to give priority to a business policy which is geared to the long term."

This appears to be an oblique reference to why Daimler did not seek listing on an American exchange. If a stock's price doesn't appreciate or dividends don't increase regularly, it is quickly abandoned by U.S. shareholders. Reuter did find enough long-term stability in U.S. industry, however, to form strategic alliances there, including one with United Technology Corporation.

As any investor who follows the news has discovered in the past few years, international equity investing is not without risk. There are plenty of shenanigans on the U.S. exchanges, even with their strict regulations and extensive surveillance. The securities industries in other countries have their own rules and traditions, which aren't always understood or appreciated by outsiders. Some of the practices are colorful, to put it mildly.

An annual meeting of a Japanese corporation can take on the farcical extremes of the Kabuki theater, thanks to the infamous "sokaiya." The maneuvers of the sokaiya or harassers at Japanese shareholder meetings is described in *Inside Japanese Financial Markets* by Aron Viner.

"Under the guise of consultants or market researchers, it is the habit of the sokaiya to ferret out personal information, often embarrassing, about top executives of the company, and threaten to stand up at a shareholders' meeting and shout it out,"Viner wrote. "They subsequently are paid consulting fees or subscriptions bought to their bogus publications to keep them quiet. It's extortion or blackmail. To gain entrance to the meeting, the sokaiya buys shares in the company. The payoff takes various forms. The amount may be small, or as much as $100,000."[5]

Keeping a lid on the sokaiya has grown quite costly over the years.

"A 1981 police survey (cited in Kaplan & Dubro's *Yakuza. The Explosive Account of Japan's Criminal Underworld*) revealed 6,800 sokaiya in 500 separate groups extorting as much as $400 million annually," Viner said. Though Japan's commercial code was rewritten to make payments illegal and to impose prison terms for violation, ways around the law have been found and the payments continue.

"Individual shareholders also are endangered by sokaiya antics," said Viner.

"The sokaiya operate in groups, the larger groups usually belonging to one of many underworld organizations," he explained. "The biggest sokaiya groups sell their services to companies in another way. They function as 'guards' intended to intimidate dissident shareholders. Thus, a shareholder attempting to express an opinion or raise a question embarrassing to management would encounter a sokaiya response. Such responses range from loud heckling by sokaiya to physical abuse."

Several years before the Japanese markets were swamped with scandals of preferential client treatment, self-dealing, and links to organized crime, Viner posed these questions. "Systematic cooperation of Japan's major industrial and financial institutions with extortionists and thugs raises more general questions about the conduct of the firms themselves. Can a corporation that hires sokaiya to shout down shareholders be trusted to provide accurate financial data regarding corporate performance? Can a corporation, which by bowing to corporate blackmail breaches the Commercial Code, be trusted in other instances? The international reputation of Japan's most eminent blue chip corporations is impugned by their willingness to cooperate with blackmailers and thugs who are often members of organized crime syndicates."

Shareholders elsewhere seldom face such unruly obstacles in making their wishes known to corporate management, yet neither are they encouraged to express their views.

To appreciate that global business activity is amassing in the hands of a relatively few (and often cooperative) corporations is alarming in itself. To realize that those few corporations are dominated by a small group of people (who also maintain business and social ties among themselves) adds to the consternation. Yet it is within the sphere of ownership—the very culprit that we tend to fear—that individuals the world over find the highest prospect for governance over the burgeoning global corporations.

There are three recent trends that offer an opening for improved shareholder jurisdiction over corporate affairs.

The first is internationalization of ownership, which was discussed earlier in this chapter. Americans have sometimes taken offense at the growing Japanese investment in U.S. real estate and corporate assets, which reached $78.5 billion in 1990. The resentment is provoked by the sense that American investors do not have the same freedom to acquire Japanese assets. If American investors

have placed investments in Hitachi, Mitsubishi, or any of the leading Japanese banks, they are less likely to feel threatened, to believe
that their country is owned by a foreign entity. Conversely, Japanese investors who acquire IBM shares will be pleased to see their
company prosper, no matter where it does business. The same is
true of Nestlé or Siemens or Royal Dutch/Shell. Those who own
the company are unlikely to consider it a hazard to their own
national interests. At the same time, a company with many foreign
shareholders is more apt to be sensitive to the countries in which it
does business.

Yet again, free enterprise hits snags where shareholdership is
concerned. As described earlier, Fiat was pressured by a customer,
the U.S. government, to disassociate itself from the investment of
Libya and its leader Moammar Khadafi. The British government
took no more kindly to substantial Kuwaiti investment in British
Petroleum. Both Fiat and British Petroleum represent unique circumstances, however. In most cases, cross-national investments
can help stabilize economic progress and settle world opinion.

The European Community has redressed some of the legal differences that once kept investors apart in its member countries and,
as globalization of investments progresses, other nations also are
reaching greater consensus.

The democratization of the multinational corporations is being
encouraged by two other recent phenomena—the evolution of
employee ownership and an uprising of shareholder activism.

While employee ownership reverberates of the old socialist
dream of worker-run enterprises, it also vaunts a capitalist twist.
These are shares employees have earned by higher productivity or
purchased with their own money. The compensation of employees
by conferring on them shares in the company is not as widespread
as it might be, but the practice is catching on. In 1980, in the United
States, there were just over 5,000 companies with 4 million employees participating in employee stock option plans. By 1989, 10,000
companies joined the movement with 10 million employees taking
part. A 1991 study showed that worker-owned stock in public corporations probably exceeded $150 billion, including about 12 percent
of the shares of 1,000 large, publicly owned companies.

The exact value of employee holdings is impossible to calculate,
since in many cases the number of shares held by individuals is so

small it need not be reported to regulators. In Europe, where bearer stock is common, ownership can be anonymous.

However, it is estimated that AT&T employees own 11 percent of the company's outstanding shares. At both Exxon and General Motors, employees hold a 9 percent stake in the company.

About $53 billion of worker-owned shares in the United States are held in Employee Stock Option Plans (ESOPs), which are trusts that hold stock for workers.

"The most intriguing aspect of this trend," said a *Business Week* editorial, "is the possibility that workers who own a significant share of their companies will want a voice in corporate governance, as has already happened in the case of several companies contemplating mergers. Employers who prepare for this development by setting up mechanisms for dialogue can lay the groundwork for productive cooperation between labor and management in future decision making. Those who don't may find worker ownership is a mixed blessing."[6]

The serendipitous side of the picture is that, since employees are concerned with job security, they are less likely to rush the company into risky ventures for the sake of short-term profits or to vote for an unfriendly takeover unless they are completely disillusioned with existing management. The darker side is that employees as a group are easy to locate. They have in the past found themselves courted in proxy fights. Who they side with no doubt will depend on how they believe they have been treated.

So far, the voices of employee shareholders, like those of other investors, have been muted. The attitude of management has been that it would direct the corporations, and if shareholders didn't like it, they could sell. The only alternative to abandonment, even for someone with a relatively large interest in a company, has been a 500-word resolution to be placed in the company proxy statement. Some investors, especially employee shareholders, professional investors who manage pension funds, and others with fiduciary responsibility, are asking for more of a voice.

"If you want shareholders to behave as owners," said Sarah Teslik, executive director of the Council of Institutional Investors, "you want to create inexpensive, nonconfrontational ways for that to happen." Teslik looked favorably on the recommendation of one corporate adviser that major investors be encouraged to present their suggestions to the board of directors in person. "It beats putting something into 500 words on a proxy statement. Instead you can have a civilized conversation with the board."[7]

Despite the obstacles, shareholders increasingly are learning how to make themselves heard. The issues brought up by shareholders range from social causes to excessive compensation of management to workplace and environmental safety matters. The Coalition for Justice in the Maquiladora, as an example, is threatening shareholder tactics against companies refusing to adopt "responsible standards" in their Mexican operations. One member of the coalition is the Interfaith Center on Corporate Responsibility.

As limiting as the proxy route may be, many investors are using it as an economic or social forum. Unfortunately, many shareholders resort to redress through the courts, with the shareholder class action suit becoming virtually an industry of its own.

In a speech before the Social Investment Forum, lobbyist and former Abbot Laboratories vice president David Jones described the potential clout of the shareholder rights movement. "It is my belief that shareholder activism is the most powerful force for change in the corporate sector."[8]

Jones went on to show that management has learned tricks of its own. "Corporations have become very good at managing activists. What used to be purely defensive (public relations) strategies have evolved into elaborate initiatives. Industry deflects attention away from itself and absorbs the energy of activists by financing large, professionally managed organizations to deal with issues. Individual companies keep activists busy through meaningless meetings with issue managers trained to be credible and noncommittal."

Nonetheless, shareholders often have prevailed. Jones cited the infant formula wars. Activist organizations, using share ownership as a lever, forced Nestlé, Bristol-Myers Squibb, and some of their competitors to change the way nutrition products for babies were sold, both domestically and abroad.

"Corporations," Jones concluded, "are not going to change because we walk away and invest somewhere else. They will change if the owners demand it. The owners can do that if they will work hard and be smart and stick with it."

Chapter Fourteen

Unruly Laws

"If we would guide by the light of reason, we must let our minds be bold."

Justice Louis Brandeis, *New State Ice Co. v. Liebmann*, 1932.

The 1991 Paris airshow was excitement on the tarmac. The Kuwait/ Iraq war had been wrapped up and the clever, powerful tools that routed the invader were there for the world to see. Furthermore, the restored government of Kuwait was on a shopping expedition that made the embattled international aircraft industry stand up and salute.

"We lost about two thirds of our fleet during the Iraqi invasion," explained Ahmed al-Mishari, chairman of the Kuwaiti Airways Corporation, "and most of our maintenance facilities, engine workshops—the whole thing." According to Mishari, Iraqi forces stole 15 aircraft, including 8 Airbuses, 3 Boeing aircraft, and 4 smaller executive jets.[1]

Adding to the airshow clamor was the fact that the two leading U.S. aviation manufacturers, Boeing and McDonnell Douglas, were slinging epithets in a verbal scuffle with Airbus Industrie, the first serious non-U.S. competition they'd encountered. Airbus, claimed the American firms, now had a well-developed line of aircraft on the market and was making money, yet continued to be subsidized by the four European governments that established it 21 years earlier.

"There is no more blatant example in the world today of a tax-supported entity engaged in unfair and predatory trade," charged John F. McDonnell, chairman and chief executive of McDonnell Douglas in an *Aviation Week & Space Technology* essay that ran several months after the Paris event but was a continuation of the same quarrel.[2]

"During the last two years," McDonnell continued, "Airbus has captured 29 percent of the world orders for civil aircraft, up from 13 percent in the early 1980s. Airbus has been able to 'buy' market share by pricing its products far below their real cost. And it has hurt McDonnell Douglas Corporation and the Boeing Co. in other ways as well. Airbus has undercut our prices and profits, and with that the consortium has undercut our ability to shoulder the risk of new programs."

As the international airshow progressed, the competition between the U.S. manufacturers and Airbus intensified, with Airbus solidly holding its own. Not only did the European upstart win sizable orders from U.S. companies, it copped a $1.9 billion requisition from Kuwait for up to 24 jets. The Kuwaitis ordered only three commercial airliners from Boeing. To muffle any U.S. insinuation that the Kuwaitis seemed ungrateful for the support they'd received from the United States in ousting Saddam Hussein's army, Europeans pointed out that they too had sent troops to the Middle East.

There was another twist, however, to the Kuwaiti order from Airbus. While the Airbus consortium was originally sponsored by the governments of France, Germany, Britain, and Spain to combat the U.S. dominance of aviation, the ownership is not purely governmental. Precisely to privatize its interest in Airbus, the German government in 1989 sold a controlling interest in its consortium partnership to Daimler-Benz. So where does this circular dance lead? Because the state of Kuwait owns 14 percent of Daimler-Benz, the Kuwaitis (at least in part) were buying the airliners from themselves.

Messerschmitt-Bolkow-Blohm (MBB), which brought with it Deutsche Airbus, was only one in a series of acquisitions that Daimler-Benz made beginning in the mid-1980s. The ambitious purchases startled many business experts and alarmed not a few. In 1985 Daimler acquired the 50 percent it did not already own of Motoren und Turbinen-Union, a maker of aircraft engines and diesel motors for tanks and ships. Several months later Daimler spent $130 million for 65.6 percent of Dornier, manufacturer of civilian aircraft, space systems, and military equipment such as the "fliegerfaust 2," the European version of the Stinger missile. The following year Daimler launched into high-technology electronics, robotics, and household appliances with the acquisition of AEG A.G. As the purchase of aviation, computer-related, and other firms continued, Daimler-Benz soon burst forth as Germany's largest industrial company. It also became a formidable contender in other world industrial markets.

Speaking to a large extent of Daimler-Benz, Dr. Erich Riedl, German government coordinator for Aerospace and Space Affairs pointed out to readers of *Interavia Aerospace Review,* "The regrouping of German aerospace industrial capacity opens the way for the industry to grasp opportunities offered by the emergence of a Europe-wide aerospace industry."[3]

Even before the wall between East Germany and the West was ripped down, Daimler had formed joint ventures with several co-operatives in East Germany. But once the barrier collapsed, Daimler moved even more rapidly into territory it had been compelled to abandon following World War II. The company committed itself to invest more than 2 billion marks or $1.11 billion in the eastern regions of Germany by the mid-1990s. Its electronics subsidiary, AEG, will set up shop there, and a truck assembly plant will be built. By 1991, Daimler had 9,000 employees in eastern Germany, and planned to have 20,000 by mid-decade.

It is the profitability of Daimler's acclaimed Mercedes-Benz motor vehicles—not to mention the sustenance of 28-percent owner Deutsche Bank—that provide the base for this expansion. The cars, trucks, and other vehicles bring in about 72 percent of Daimler sales. Mercedes-Benz and its sterling reputation also make Daimler the exemplary German company.

Carl Benz and Gottlieb Daimler, from whom the company derives its name, never met in their lifetimes. Yet both were at the dawning of the automobile as a practical form of transportation and as a romantic image. The company's history is adorned in legend affectionately repeated by automobile buffs everywhere. Certainly, taken back to its dual origins in 1885 and 1886, Daimler-Benz qualifies as the oldest auto company in existence. The economic difficulties following World War I led to the 1926 merger that made Daimler-Benz a single company. The company achieved international fame early, in part due to its conquest of international motor sport racing.

As the Third Reich emerged, Adolph Hitler claimed the

Mercedes-Benz as his official parade transportation. Later the state took over the company to produce trucks, tanks, and planes for military service. Little remained of Daimler-Benz factories following the relentless bombing of German industrial sites in 1944. At the conclusion of the war, the loyalty of the German workers to the company was extraordinary. Though there were virtually no factories to return to, Daimler-Benz employees reported for work anyway. Soon they were producing cars of exceptional quality.

Daimler-Benz's return to greatness in the 1950s unfolded with the investment and leadership of convicted war criminal Friedrich Flick. Though Flick lost an estimated 80 percent of his steel fortune in the war, he had enough money left to acquire 37.5 percent of Daimler. His $20 million investment soon swelled to $200 million, making Flick Germany's second wealthiest industrialist. Flick was convicted of crimes against humanity (among them using slave labor) by the tribunal at Nuremberg and spent five years in prison. However, unlike Siemens and other companies that later paid compensation to ill-treated workers, Flick refused. It wasn't until his son sold Friedrich Flick Industrial Holdings Co. to Deutsche Bank in 1986 that reparations were made. At that time the Flick group still owned 10 percent of Daimler-Benz, though Deutsche Bank sold the shares.

During the postwar years, Daimler built a reputation for being a conservative company, committed to a strategy of step-by-step growth. In the late 1980s, the vehicle maker jumped that track in favor of a hard-driving management style. Though the company is intimately linked with Airbus Industries and will be looking to the consortium for expanded profits in the decades ahead, that has not prevented Daimler from forging confederations with some of Airbus's coolest competitors.

In fact, Daimler wove such an intricate pattern of joint ventures, it has pacts with its competitor's competitors.

• Led by Deutsche Aerospace, France's Aerospatiale and Italy's Alenia in 1991 joined in a new consortium called International Commuter, to build an 80- to 130-seat commuter aircraft. The new plane will compete in a market similar to the Boeing 737 and McDonnell Douglas Corporation's MD87 and, to the bafflement of Airbus, with the 130-seater it has on the drawing boards. Between 1991 and 2006, airlines are expected to buy $40 billion worth of planes of this "regional jet" size.

• A furor flared in the press when Daimler agreed that Messer-schmidt, builder of German World War II fighters, would explore mutual work with Japan's Mitsubishi group, builder of Japan's World War II Zero fighter planes. Ghosts of World War II leapt to life.

• Motoren und Turbinen-Union is working with both General Electric and GE's competitor, Pratt & Whitney, on jet engine ventures.

• Through Deutsche Airbus/Deutsche Aerospace, Daimler signed a five-year agreement with Airbus archrival Boeing to study and develop a supersonic commercial transport.

It is too soon to tell where this tangled web of agreements will lead, but certainly they link Daimler-Benz with some of the most entrenched, influential, and innovative companies anywhere. The agreements also serve another function. The U.S. government has implied that it might levy trade sanctions against Airbus products, and perhaps even Daimler-Benz goods, if Airbus doesn't begin operating without government subsidies and show more resolve about paying back past loans. Considering the joint venture arrangements, and considering that the United States is Mercedes-Benz's largest market, it will become increasingly difficult to lash out at Daimler-Benz without at the same time flogging a U.S. venture partner or a Mercedes-Benz dealership.

"Surely," said the old radical Rose Pastor Stokes, "there is not a capitalist or well-informed person in this world today who believes that this war is being fought to make the world safe for democracy. It is being fought to make the world safe for capital."[4]

Stokes was referring to World War I when she made this bold appraisal. She could have easily been talking about the trade conflicts that are erupting at the end of the 20th century and are likely to dominate world affairs for decades into the future. Capital, after all, is transforming the globe.

While few economists, politicians, or social observers would be crass enough to think that commerce alone will set people free, it has become impossible to ignore another reality. It is much easier to enslave those who are bound by poverty and the tenuous personal health, limited education, and paucity of opportunity that invariably attend impoverishment. Freedom and prosperity go hand in hand.

Looking to those countries and regions that have achieved first world status—the United States, Japan, Germany, Great Britain, Canada, and a handful of other nations—it is also easy enough to decide that it is vigorous international trade that fires up the economic machinery.

Is it any wonder that corporations—and the governments that succor them—plot trade strategy and protect their territories with warlike fervor?

In response to American warning of trade retribution over the Airbus subsidies, Airbus president Jean Pierson at the 1991 Paris Airshow drew his sword. "Whoever starts a war is going to find himself in a war," Pierson declared. "If the Americans take some action, I can assure you the Europeans will respond."

Business practitioners in all phases of trade are faced with fierce competition that borders on combat. "The trade picture in electronics pits all the global giants against each other in the struggle to capture the same markets. Canada's Northern Telecom, West German's Siemens, Japan's Hitachi and NEC, respectively, and a bevy of U.S. corporations are reaching what an analyst at Dataquest terms 'unprecedented aggressiveness,'" noted Julian Weiss in *The Asian Century*.

There is a growing sense that the world of international commerce is out of control, said Weiss, and it is probable that trade and other national alliances, including the U.S./Canadian pact and the drive to create the European Community have been reactions to the unmanageability of events.

Even the United Nations has acknowledged this sense of disorder in the rapidly changing world. "The General Assembly on 17 November declared the period 1990–1999 as the United Nations Decade of International Law," reported the *UN Chronicle*, "thus heeding a growing worldwide recognition of the need to strengthen the rule of law in international relations."[6]

Despite the globally recognized importance of trade, there is no single, overriding body of law to handle trade and finance issues. The General Agreement on Tariffs and Trade is the closest thing to it, and despite the lip service given to the tenets of free trade, GATT represents managed, rather than free, trade. Even in that context, GATT has not always accomplished the job it was formulated to do.

"Nowadays many businessmen, while proclaiming their belief in free trade as a theoretical ideal, tell you at the same time that as a matter of practical fact, free trade is myth," wrote *The Economist* in

London, in an exhaustive 1990 essay on trade practices. "Everybody is cheating. Trade agreements are meaningless. Competing means beating the successful exporters (especially the Japanese) at their own game—by promoting the domestic industries that matter, and by telling foreign governments to buy more imports, or else."[7]

Most countries recognize the importance of guiding principles, fair standards, or, at the very least, a mutual understanding on how trade *should* be conducted. Meganational leaders constantly remind them that the patchwork quilt of trade treaties is inefficient.

"We're . . . hobbled by the tortuously slow pace of trade agreements," said AT&T Communications Group Executive Victor Pelson. "Agreements are often reached on an ad-hoc, bilateral basis that's unbefitting today's environment. In an era of instantaneous information, we're eking out an agreement here, a principle there. In the process, we beach the benefits of technology that could invigorate world production and trade."[8]

Even so, attempts to modernize and expand the scope of GATT have been slow and ridden with conflict.

The issues discussed at the GATT meetings are indeed important. And in the evolving world of the meganationals, where oligopolies are increasingly dominating market segments, many of the GATT issues are critical. Most of the theories that demonstrate the value of free trade are based on the assumption that there are many players or potential participants in the market, which in many fields of enterprise is no longer the case.

One of the most hotly debated points in the free-trade argument has to do with dumping, or, by conventional thinking, selling a product at a price below that which it cost to produce. Some view antidumping rules as thinly veiled protectionism. Others consider dumping as egregious economic trickery. (Dumping is sometimes defined as selling products abroad at a lower price than they are sold at home, but that definition brings up a whole other round of arguments.)

Dumping, as a trade tactic, is bound to succeed when a larger player can afford to underprice in a market long enough to drive competitors out. The Airbus story illustrates the point.

But first, Airbus's side of the story. For years, a handful of U.S. commercial aircraft manufacturers held a grip on the world market. Because the upfront costs (research, design, development) are so exorbitant in aircraft manufacturing and the time required to produce a plane is so long (up to a decade), the number of competitors in the aviation market is inevitably small. Conditions are ripe for an oligopoly, and that's exactly what exists. Though components and materials are provided by a network of suppliers in both the United States and Europe, the predominant players in the commercial airliner business have been Boeing and McDonnell Douglas.

The Europeans, however, insisted they could not accept the U.S. domination of the market. The British government, on its own, first consolidated its smaller companies into one stronger entity, then helped get British Aerospace going. Finally, British Aerospace was privatized under the guidance of former Prime Minister Margaret Thatcher. In the 1970s, Airbus Industries was created. Aerospatiale of France and Messerschmitt-Bolkow-Blohm of Germany each hold a 37.9 percent stake in the venture; British Aerospace, a 20 percent; and Construcciones Aeronautics of Spain (CASA), a 4.2 percent interest.

It is estimated that $13.5 billion ($26 billion when interest is added) in government subsidies have gone into the development of the company. While subsidies were given in the form of loans, competitors complain that the company has not been forced, as they were, to pay market interest rates. Because loan repayment is tied to profits made on planes, the payback time is extended indefinitely. Competitors who finance operations through the capital markets have a fixed payback time, 10 years on the average, regardless of profitability. Though Airbus does not release figures, it was estimated that by 1989 only about $500 million of the subsidies had been repaid. As the pressure mounted from outside and as the company reached profitability, Airbus did escalate its payback pace. The company said it would repay $900 million of the debt in 1991.[2]

The government investment obviously allows Airbus to offer planes at highly competitive prices. The scheme has succeeded in giving Europe its own aircraft industry. The effect also has been to severely cripple the U.S. manufacturer whose products most closely resemble its own—McDonnell Douglas.

Though the United States officially protested the Airbus subsidies to GATT, the treaty's structures against subsidies are somewhat weak and, at any rate, the countries involved claim it is their sovereign right to subsidize key industries. Further, they insist, the American aircraft industry is indirectly subsidized by government military spending.

In short, the argument is prolonged and complex, and likely to continue for some time. However, U.S. manufacturers are feeling some urgency in the matter. Between 1990 and 2008, it is expected that about 11,500 commercial jets will be purchased, worth approximately $600 billion. Additionally, Airbus is exploring the idea of bringing out a 600- to 700-seat airliner, even bigger than Boeing's 747. The development costs for a new plane could be as high as $4 billion, and it is expected that, again, the costs will be government-subsidized. The mighty Boeing, which also was contemplating a larger airliner, could be disabled in the large jet market if Airbus's plans for a jumbo-jumbo jet proceed.

Economists say that, in real terms, subsidizing Airbus is not to the advantage of the nations involved, since it means the Airbus airplanes are costing Europeans more than they should. This is because the citizens of the participating nations, on top of the price their airlines pay for the equipment, also pay for the planes through their taxes. Furthermore, these countries are subsidizing the airlines of foreign countries as some of their taxes are transferred—as a gift—to nonconsortium Airbus buyers.

Additionally, economists claim that Americans will be losers in this game, no matter what course of action they choose. The U.S. aircraft industry is bound to wither, since Boeing and McDonnell Douglas will be able to sell fewer and fewer planes at a price based on the full cost of production. After all, airlines can get similar equipment for less money from Airbus. If the U.S. government retaliates by denying Airbus the right to sell in U.S. markets or by placing a high tariff on the planes, U.S. airlines will be forced to buy higher priced equipment than their foreign competitors. The higher costs eventually would be passed on to customers, making the U.S. airlines more expensive to fly than the foreign competitors. Furthermore, the Europeans are likely to strike back in some way, which could reduce or block the sales of some other U.S. product abroad. As in all wars, all sides risk casualties in the international trade wars.

In the near term, at least, the winners in this high-stakes game are consumers, especially consumers in those countries without an aircraft manufacturing industry. They have no aircraft jobs or revenues to lose, and yet they can buy airplanes at lower than expected prices.

These artificially low prices are the reason some analysts like dumping. Selling below the cost of production, they point out, allows consumers to acquire goods at a highly advantageous price.

The rewards to consumers, however, are short term. When the competition has been eliminated, or sufficiently crippled, the dumping producer inevitably raises prices. When there are few or no other competitors, the surviving company is then free to set prices wherever it chooses. And as Airbus well knows, in the aircraft industry capital costs discourage young, innovative companies from getting a foothold in the market. Other countries, such as Japan and China, are now entering the aircraft business, but through joint ventures with industry leaders, and, even then, only with considerable government guidance and support.

While GATT can provide the larger framework in which the Airbus and numerous other disputes can be settled equitably, GATT itself is not free from manipulation. The major corporations of the world have painstakingly followed the GATT negotiations, lobbying for measures that will protect them from what they consider to be unfair trade.

Critics claim the meganationals also have lobbied for provisions that will ensure their future market dominance.

Writing in *The Nation*, Robert Weissman, editor of *Multinational Monitor,* charged that GATT embodies a hidden agenda. The industrialized nations through GATT, have "sought to encourage the Third World's growing export dependency and to tighten multinational corporations' control over Third World markets and resources."[9]

That is why, Weissman claims, the United States has insisted on agricultural trade reform and the inclusion of three new areas in the GATT rubric: intellectual property, services, and investments.

New trade rules in agriculture and textiles, he said, would encourage the poorer nations (predominantly found in the southern hemisphere) to concentrate on products best suited to export, at the neglect of crops needed for internal consumption. "In agriculture, this is likely to be associated with the creation of large plantations, intensified use of pesticides, displacement of peasants who produce for local consumption, and clearing of rain forests."

Furthermore, he says, "Proposals from the industrialized countries in the area of intellectual property alone could foster a massive transfer of resources from the South to the North. The

U.S. proposal calls for all countries to adopt and strictly enforce U.S.-style patent, copyright, and trademark laws. It attempts to address claims by multinational corporations that they lose $40 billion to $60 billion each year to Third World 'pirates' who counterfeit their goods and infringe on their patents."

From the perspective of the U.S. meganationals, these infringements represent robbery, pure and simple. Often, this point of view is accurate. Merck, in its company literature, points out that the pharmaceutical industry, where a new prescription may take 7 to 10 years and cost $125 million to develop, is especially vulnerable to replication.

"The pirates who steal these priceless intangibles easily find ways of profiting from their misuse," Merck said. "Trademarks are copied. Films, books, recorded music, and computer programs are duplicated inexpensively with no loss of fidelity. A medicine that resulted from the work of hundreds of Ph.D. scientists and M.D. clinicians, and took years to win regulatory approval, may be copied inside of a week by a single chemist with little more than a master's degree. The patent holder will be unaware that a theft has occurred until the product of the theft appears on a market. And within a year, the pirate may be able to produce enough to drive the patent holder's product from the market."[10]

But to the poor countries who see no hope of catching up to the technological and other achievements of the developed countries, copying a costly drug or reprinting a textbook may seem like a simple question of survival. They believe that the rules, which follow the U.S. and European pattern, are too stringent. The protection time for intellectual property is too long and perhaps covers too broad a field, they insist.

Weissman claims that the new GATT rules also are rigged in other ways to favor the developed nations. Naturally occurring products, such as plants and minerals, understandably, cannot be protected as intellectual property. However, it is common practice for the multinational pharmaceutical and other companies to send representatives to folk medicine practitioners or herbalists in poor countries to learn the natural capabilities of plants, soils, insects, and other organic matter. Once the scientists understand what these natural products can do, the company then genetically engineers the product into a new form, which then can be protected as intellectual property. The knowledge of the Third World practitioners has been confiscated, and the poor countries have no way of protecting one of the few unique forms of information they possess.

The GATT proposals for protecting intellectual property have been promoted by pharmaceutical and other trade groups, and backed strongly by an informal group called the Intellectual Property Committee (IPC). The IPC is a coalition of 13 major companies including International Business Machines, Du Pont, General Electric, and Merck. Intellectual property will be protected, probably under GATT, because private property is one of the pillars on which capitalism is built. The incentives to work, achieve goals, and excel are based on the possibility of controlling and using assets, including intellectual property.

Big business also has manipulated the latest GATT negotiations to undercut regulations that protect consumers, workers, and the environment, charges investigative reporter Daphne Wysham, also writing in *The Nation*. "Under GATT an obscure panel of scientists based in Rome called Codex Alimentarius will be empowered to review existing environmental, health, and safety standards in all the signatory nations, with the goal of 'harmonizing' regulations according to Codex's application of 'sound science.' Regulations deemed too stringent would be cited as unfair trade practices subject to heavy penalty."[11]

For example, Wysham continued, "Codex would likely overturn the international standard governing the marketing of infant formula. This standard was adopted by the World Health Organization (WHO) in 1981 after charges that Nestlé Corporation's campaign to convince Third World women to substitute infant formula for breast milk may have resulted in increased infant disease and death."

The Codex panel, in effect would be in the position to be the ultimate authority on what constitutes "sound science" on a particular matter. Even among highly qualified experts, however, opinions have varied on the scientific truth in such far-reaching but complex subjects as the safety of the bovine growth hormone, the proper application of genetic engineering, or the environmental importance of old-growth forests. Furthermore, Wysham noted that the attention of Codex would be focused on "science" as it relates to trade practices, to the exclusion of social, political, or moral issues.

And while Codex officials say that membership on the Codex panel is open and diverse, Wysham claimed the panel is not constituted with objectivity in mind.

"It is a body stocked with industry handmaidens from the USDA and FDA, wide open to lobbying by U.S. and transnational corporations. For example, a recent official U.S. delegation to Codex included three corporate executives from Nestlé; one each from Coca-Cola, Pepsi, Hershey, Ralston Purina, Kraft (Philip Morris), and CPC International; as well as representatives from several food-processor associations, including the Grocer Manufacturers of America and the American Frozen Food Institute. In all, nearly half—12 of the 28—of those attending were from industry."

As the GATT agreements have progressed, Codex has been granted even greater powers, following GATT's declared intent of raising international food standards to the highest level. That, for the most part, has meant adoption of the food standards and regulations of the United States. Codex was established in 1962 by two United Nations organizations, the Food and Agriculture Organization and the World Health Organization itself.

There are signs that Codex will hold to the healthiest standards available. Those hopes received credence in the summer of 1991 when the panel rejected the use of certain controversial livestock growth hormones.

Despite the probability that GATT doesn't measure up to the purest ideals of free trade, and despite the dangers that Weissman and Wysham warn against, if properly formulated and fairly instituted, GATT could provide the great guiding principles needed in the new world of meganational business.

The original GATT agreement, though far from perfect and often disregarded, was of great value to world commerce. " . . . GATT did a fine job during its first 30 years," explained *The Economist*. "In a series of trade rounds, governments cut the average tariff on manufactured goods from 40 percent in 1947 to less than 10 percent by the mid-1970s. Since then the average tariff has fallen even further, to roughly 5 percent. In addition, by the late 1950s, the industrial country governments had established a modern system of international exchange and payments, with fully convertible currencies. As a result, tariff liberalization spurred remarkably rapid growth in world trade. Between 1950 and 1975 the volume of trade expanded by as much as 500 percent, against an increase in global output of 220 percent."[12]

It is estimated that an additional one-third reduction in manufacturing–trade barriers could increase the combined gross national products of the United States, Canada, Japan, and the European Community by $4 trillion through the year 2000. About $1.1 trillion of that amount would occur in the United States. Even if figures are overstated, which sometimes happens, the freer flow of money into the world economy would be considerable.

GATT negotiators often proclaim that trade will collapse without a new agreement. "What we're doing here is building a trading system for the 21st century," proclaimed U.S. Trade Representative Carla Hills of the Uruguay round of talks. "If we don't succeed in reaching an agreement, nations will turn inward and trade will contract. It will be a tremendous mistake that historians will mark."[13]

The trade picture without a reworked GATT isn't quite that hopeless. The Dark Ages need not repeat themselves. Trade at least at the current level would continue. The meganational corporations, with their vast, well-established network of international trade, would see to that. The far greater danger is that a twisted, manipulative GATT emerges, and is observed by the nearly 100 GATT signatories without appropriate refinements.

If GATT falls short or fails to meet the approval of the 100 participating nations, there still are alternatives.

Regional agreements offer one alternative, perhaps serving as a predecessor or test ground to freer trade in disputed areas. The Association of Southeast Asian Nations (ASEAN) set the example several years ago by simply going forward independently with a regional agreement on certain points of trade. Self-preservation was their motivation. The European Community pact and the North American Free Trade Agreement could well be mere interim structures allowing countries to explore ideas and test practices for more open trade, before extending the concepts to the broader world market.

And there is another truly radical alternative, one available to most nations. Given the propensity of many countries, the United States included, to intercede in trade disputes, it is clear that neither governments nor the corporate world entirely trust the concept of free trade. In fact the freer it is, the more frightening trade tends to become.

If all else fails, however, nations of the world could honestly give free trade a try. They could follow the example of Mexico and begin to drop barriers unilaterally. *The New Republic* columnist Michael Kinsley wrote, "Free trade purists (I'm one) believe that open borders are the best route to national prosperity no matter what policies other countries pursue."[14]

Kinsley said that after contemplating the mind-boggling complexity of contemporary trade issues, he always comes to the same conclusion: "End these tedious fights. Drop out of the GATT negotiations. Repeal the 'Super 301' (U.S.) trade retaliation laws. Stop worrying about what is and isn't 'dumping.' Allow American citizens to buy foreign goods and services without hindrance whether or not foreign countries extend their own citizens the same freedom. Yes, we will give up a sometimes useful stick for beating down foreign trade barriers. But we'll get some mighty advantages, too."

The benefits include, Kinsley said, a higher standard of living since consumers will enjoy the cheapest goods available, plus a greater competitiveness at home to produce the cheapest goods.

"We'll be the saviors of Africa, Eastern Europe, Latin America, developing economies everywhere. They, more than Japan, are victims of U.S. protectionist rules. Free access to the American market would mean far more to them than any conceivable amount of aid or development loans."

In calling for the United States to lower hidden trade barriers for Eastern Europe, James Bovard, author of *The Fair Trade Fraud*, made a similar point. "Are we so rich that we can afford to give Eastern Europe handouts, yet so poor that we cannot allow them a chance to honestly earn a few dollars? Charity is no substitute for opportunity."[15]

Truly free trade would, mercifully, put thousands of lobbyists and lawyers out of business, Kinsley added. "Now the huge cost of conducting trade disputes gets passed along to consumers of products both imported and domestic, no matter which side wins." And finally, Kinsley said, if the United States were to follow this course it would set a proper example for the rest of the world.

Freer trade, the high ground of economic policy, is no panacea though. Displacements do take place; inefficient industries in certain countries will die a painful death and individuals who do not find a way to adapt to change may never secure worthwhile employment again. A liberal trade agreement with the United States did not save Canada from a recession in the early 1990s. Free trade will not bring all people in the world up to the highest standard of living, though it does tend to make people better off than they otherwise would have been.

As for the meganational companies, they would find themselves competing in a world that offers them no special favors. But by virtue of their experience and worldwide book of business, they are better positioned to survive and flourish than are most of their smaller competitors.

Chapter Fifteen

Corporation, Heal Thyself

"We demand that big business give people a square deal."

Theodore Roosevelt

When Helmut O. Maucher grasped the reigns at Nestlé SA in 1981, the Swiss food giant was under siege by social and political activists from around the world. The company had made a forceful drive into Third World regions. Of Nestlé's 303 factories, the 81 in developing countries contributed 21 percent of total production. Then, in 1977, a boycott against all Nestlé's products arose in the United States and spread. The issue, again, was babies. The protestors claimed that the company's sophisticated marketing campaigns made Third World mothers eager to switch to infant formula from breast milk even though they were ill prepared to use the formula properly. Poor and often illiterate families mixed the canned concentrate with the available water, which often was unsanitary and made the baby ill. To stretch the formula to last longer, they sometimes added more water than called for, which gradually starved the child.

Nestlé's infant food was developed originally to save the lives of newborns who could not be breast fed, and the company insists that the formula still fills an important nutritional function. Nevertheless, it is estimated that the boycott, which lasted into the 1980s, cost Nestlé as much as $40 million.

Maucher made the settlement of the boycott one of his first missions when he assumed command of Nestlé. He met with boycott leaders and agreed to comply with the World Health Organization's demand that Nestlé stop promoting the infant formula through advertising and free samples. Though the dark shadow of the baby milk controversy still hung over the company, Maucher made long strides to restore the image of an old and respected establishment. But the truce didn't hold. Critics claimed that Nestlé, the world's largest infant formula maker with more than 50 percent of the non-U.S. formula market, almost immediately broke its pledge. The boycott was revived in 1988. "It was reinstituted to finish what we started," Nancy Gaschott, a consultant for Action for Corporate Accountability, told the *New York Times*.

The incongruity in the Nestlé case is that Maucher remains outspoken on behalf of the multinational corporation's role as a responsible world citizen. He implies in his speeches that social reformers sometimes "exaggerate" their claims and he emphasizes Nestlé's important contributions to a safer and better-fed world. Indeed, Nestlé's corporate mandate requires it to specialize in products "that contribute to human well-being."

Maucher expressed his belief that meganational corporations can help solve many of the world's problems—especially the elimination of world hunger—in a 1989 speech before the Council on Foreign Relations in New York.

"It is clearly industry's duty to speak up, as it is our duty to understand what is happening around us and to make our business decisions in the context of society as a whole. We should actively seek an open dialogue with government, if we want to foster mutual understanding. Government leaders need to understand the microeconomic decisions that businessmen are faced with daily; executives should know that their survival and success in the long term depends on their making decisions within the context of larger issues. The better we understand each other, the more successful our system will prove in the future," he said.

But business, Maucher indicated, sometimes can achieve more than governments because business people know better how to get things done. "Private enterprise is generally much more efficient, and is also experienced in logistical matters and reducing waste," the German-born Maucher insisted.

Maucher's perspective no doubt has grown from his experience at Nestlé in working in distant venues. The Anglo-Swiss Condensed Milk Company was established in 1866 by a pair of American brothers who hoped to sell plentiful Swiss milk to the rest of Europe, including Britain. At about the same time in a nearby town, chemist Henri Nestlé formulated a milk food for babies. By 1905, the two competing companies decided to merge, and even today, Nestlé claims both Cham and Vevey, the towns where the companies were founded, as registered offices. Switzerland, almost from the beginning, represented a very small market. Only 2 percent of Nestlé's business is done in its home country. A holding company for more than 200 operating units, Nestlé today trades in a vast range of goods including chocolate, tea, coffee, dairy products, baby food, frozen foods, ice cream, pet foods, pharmaceuticals, and grooming products. Its hundreds of familiar brands include Friskies pet food, Kit Kat, Baby Ruth and Butterfinger candy bars, Stouffer and Lean Cuisine frozen dinners, and Nescafé coffees and teas. A major player in many countries, Nestlé holds 33 percent of the British market for frozen foods and is among the top three food companies in the United States. For 75 years, Nestlé has been selling evaporated milk and chocolate in Japan and it is the second largest foreign company there, behind IBM.

While Maucher insists that his company has plenty of competition, Nestlé's major adversaries are other meganationals—Unilever and Philip Morris with its Kraft General Foods division. The company executive realizes, however, that a dominant position comes with solemn obligations. "We cannot continue to ask for a bigger role for private enterprise without being willing to shoulder some responsibility and integrate ourselves with other parts of society," he said.

Maucher has taken specific steps in this direction. He has, among other things, appointed an executive to coordinate environmental efforts throughout the company. Perhaps alluding to the nurturing, "Mother Earth" traits of the job, Maucher calls his female appointee "Mrs. Environment."

A recurring theme for Maucher is that feeding the burgeoning world population is technically possible—despite a growing rat population (three rats per person in India) that eats food which humans should be consuming, wars, and inefficient economic systems.

"We know that we cannot feed a world of 5 to 10 billion people in the future in the same way we are eating now in the United States and Europe, with 60 to 70 kilos of meat per capita," Maucher explained in a 1989 interview with the International Management and Development Institute. "That method is too costly, because animal proteins cost seven times as much as proteins taken directly from a plant. Feeding the whole world this way will never be possible. So we have to work more directly out of raw materials— out of plants—to develop interesting products such as cereals and pasta, where we arrive at a very good quality of food without the costly process of going through the animal."[1]

An important part of the mechanism for eliminating world hunger, Maucher explained, is helping to build an economic base in underdeveloped countries. Nestlé not only sells its traditional products in the developing world, but when possible draws supplies from local farmers and uses local raw materials. Products also are adapted to native taste patterns. Maucher expects, of course, that Nestlé will also profit from this sort of development aid. Without incomes, consumers have no money to spend. "People must be able to buy our products," he said.

" . . . we are proceeding with our efforts as a private enterprise because feeding the hungry will be an important part of our business strategy in the future," Maucher continued, "This is where I see Nestlé's role and our contribution. Of course, we expect that we will obtain a return in exchange for our efforts—but if we are allowed to do this, we will also contribute manyfold more to the world at large."

Despite Maucher's international mind set and Nestlé's global reach, until 1989 two thirds of Nestlé's shares (the registered shares) were reserved for Swiss citizens only. However, as part of what Maucher described as the company's "liberal, multinational, cooperative strategy," ownership of registered shares has been extended to global investors.

Maucher's pragmatic, matter-of-fact view of business and society has spurred rapid growth for the company. By the end of 1990, Nestlé had a total of 423 factories extending across 62 countries. Poorly performing subsidiaries were sold, the lagging U.S. operations reorganized, and new acquisitions and joint ventures embarked upon. It is not unrealistic to expect Nestlé to have sales of 100 billion Swiss francs by the year 2000, Maucher said. In 1990, sales were half that—50 billion Swiss francs. Along the way, he contended, Nestlé has increased communication and understanding among peoples of many nations.

Maucher ended his speech to the New York Council on Foreign Relations by twisting his listeners' minds one more revolution into the future—a future where the citizens of the world see each other in a more brotherly light.

" . . . perhaps one day, ladies and gentlemen, you will decide to rename this distinguished institution from the Council on Foreign Relations to the 'Council on Global Relations.' Such a decision will then reflect a reality that is forming under our eyes in these fascinating times," he said.

What is the truth? Is Nestlé the scrupulous corporate citizen it claims to be? Does Nestlé valiantly combat world ignorance, poverty, and hunger? Or are its critics correct? Does Nestlé foist socially destructive practices and unhealthy products on people already living in intolerable situations?

There is truth on both sides of the argument. Nestlé does, in fact, offer jobs to willing workers, hope for afflicted infants, and relief to many grateful parents. On the other hand, in its baby bottle formula, Nestlé does have a profitable and readily marketable product to protect. Sometimes the company's selling tactics are cast in shades of gray. By supplying free samples to mothers leaving the hospital, the company encourages parents to get hooked on a convenience that may not be best for their child. Also, many young, inexperienced, and insecure mothers assume that the sample formula given to her is the nutrition source recommended by the hospital and her physician. Once the infant is comfortable taking the formula, parents hesitate to make any change that could disrupt the baby's progress.

Many companies, large and small, suffer from the Nestlé syndrome. Their executives may intend to be good corporate citizens and may believe they are responsible members of society, but they also have a devil of a time convincing certain segments of the public that they do the right thing. Like Nestlé's Maucher, executives today generally acknowledge their public obligation. The dilemma that corporate leaders must resolve is how best to satisfy their contract to sustain a going, growing concern—and at the same time make sure everyone in the company is operating within legitimate bounds.

Nestlé and nearly all other meganational corporations provide statements of ethical guidelines with which they expect their employees and associates to comply.

"To be successful into the long term," Royal Dutch/Shell Group

chairman L. C. Van Wachem has said, "any commercial enterprise, big or small, multinational or national, must I believe have,
and demonstrate, a good sense of responsibility to all its stakeholders, viz. shareholders, employees, customers and suppliers,
and society as a whole. Shell companies do have such a sense of responsibility, codified in our Statement of General Business Principles . . . "[2]

These ethics declarations give both insight into corporate con-
victions and some understanding as to what the meganationals are
striving for. Perhaps understandably, those corporations that routinely come under attack, such as the oil and tobacco companies,
have generated the best-refined statements of responsibility.

Sometimes it isn't what is said, but the way it is said that speaks
the loudest. Like most other codes of this type, Shell's is clearly
presented, starting out with a general statement of intent.

"The objectives of Shell companies are to engage efficiently,
responsibly, and profitably in the oil, gas, chemicals, coal, metals,
and selected other businesses, and to play an active role in the
search for and development of other sources of energy. Shell companies seek a high standard of performance and aim to maintain a
long-term position in their respective competitive environments."

Compare that to Exxon's introductory paragraph in its 17-page
Standards of Business Conduct: "Exxon's primary objective is to be
the world's premier petroleum corporation. Accomplishing this
ambitious goal means achieving operational excellence, technological leadership, and superior financial results not only in the oil and
gas business, but also in chemicals, coal, and minerals. Attainment
of this objective should provide an attractive and secure return to
Exxon shareholders while meeting the corporation's responsibilities to society."

The difference in actual content of the two statements may be
barely discernible, but the underlying message fairly leaps from the
page. In the Shell statement, market dominance is soft-pedaled,
and social responsibility is introduced early and integrated into the
whole of the statement. In the Exxon proclamation, the last three
words, "responsibilities to society," come almost as an afterthought
to the objectives of superiority and profitability. The subliminal
message seems to be: "We aim to be number one . . . and oh, yes,
we also try to be good."

The best companies, meganationals among them, have earned public respect by a long-term dedication to commendable standards. Due to the multifarious nature of the business, however, high ideals haven't always guarded a company from grief.

Merck & Co., on the eve of its 100th anniversay, is consistently honored as one of the most admired corporations and one of the best places to work in America. The words of its founder George Merck are frequently quoted in company literature. " . . . we try never to forget that medicine is for the people. It is not for the profits. The profits follow; and if we have remembered that, they have never failed to appear . . ."

Merck produces vaccines for children's diseases, medications to fight heart disease, cancer, diabetes, Alzheimer's disease, and dozens of other ailments, and is searching for an AIDS remedy. The company has instituted programs to make affordable medications available to low-income, elderly, and other needy Americans. Along with Du Pont and other companies, Merck has backed former U.S. President Jimmy Carter in his medical missions to impoverished countries.

"Merck has always maintained a long-term focus. The company has always been, and continues to be, driven by the challenge of unconquered diseases. Responding to that challenge affords Merck, we believe, the single best way of meeting its obligations to patients, shareholders, and employees," recounts its corporate literature.

Modern technology, though ingenious, sometimes surprises and disappoints even the most sophisticated minds. Merck, along with other pharmaceutical companies, has been the defendant in the diethylstilbestrol (DES) lawsuits brought by some 350 women and their daughters who seemingly contracted vaginal cancer following treatment by the synthetic estrogen drug. DES was prescribed from the late 1940s through the 1960s in the belief that it prevented miscarriage. The victims are seeking damages totaling about $350 billion.

Even aside from human fallibility, there can be genuine differences of opinion about the most suitable way to do business. Management may see things one way; customers, suppliers, or even workers may see it another. Merck, despite its reputation as a good place to be employed, has had difficulties with labor relations and at times has been crippled by employee strikes. Executives and engineers at General Electric may very well see nuclear power as safely manageable and nuclear weaponry as a patriotic contribution to national defense, regardless of how antinuclear factions view the issue.

Further, when a company engages many thousands of workers in a multitude of subsidiaries, employees and their practices can be extremely difficult to monitor. After all, even a trained and disciplined army that moves like a single, purposeful unit is only a group of nervous young men and women, each of them trying to remember what they are supposed to do. Invariably, somewhere in the tidy columns, there is a bumbler or renegade. "Out of the crooked timber of humanity," observed the philosopher Immanuel Kant, "no straight thing was ever made."[3]

Matsushita Electrical Industrial Co. employees are regularly reminded of the inspirational writings of the company's wise and thoughtful founder, who is sometimes described as Japan's Thomas Edison. In the spirit of Konosuke Matsushita, the company's annual report says, "Matsushita views management, technology, products, and services from the people's standpoint. Our ultimate goal is to contribute to society. Through our corporate activities, we strive to promote social welfare and enhance the overall quality of life." Nevertheless, Matsushita has been accused by the U.S. International Trade Commission of dumping personal computers in U.S. markets below cost and criticized for adhering to the Arab boycott against Israel. Matsushita also has been implicated in several recent scandals in Japan. In one, an employee of a leasing subsidiary was arrested for causing $365 million in losses to his own company by helping a restaurant owner obtain massive loans using faked documents as collateral.[4]

The various functions of massive companies like Matsushita, Nestlé, and Merck are so diverse and spread so far geographically that promises—especially if they are not essential to the task at hand—are difficult to keep.

For example, when hearings were conducted in California in the mid-1980s as to the wisdom of permitting oil drilling leases off the sensitive Pacific coastline, spokesmen for numerous oil companies testified that oil drilling, pumping, and transport had improved so dramatically in recent years that the public's fear of oil spills was unfounded. Their presentations were extremely convincing; yet since that time there have been several large West Coast spills involving the oil of British Petroleum, Exxon, and other major producers. The oil companies frequently blame a subcontractor or some unseen difficulty for the spills, but the oil ended up in the water, on the wildlife, and on the beaches nonetheless. And despite the barrage of negative publicity following the Valdez, Alaska, and Long Beach, California, accidents at the turn of the decade, sea pollution continued. A 1991 report by the Alaska Department of Environmental Conservation said tankers operated by Exxon, British Petroleum, and other companies routinely pumped toxic sludge and oily ballast water into the ocean from Panama to Alaska.

As the oil disasters unfolded, two things became apparent. First, the executives who sincerely swore that accidents and environmental pollution could be avoided were not the same ones who hired and supervised rig workers or oil tanker crews. Second, human beings do the work and, even using the foremost technology, people can err.

The "shalls and shall nots" found in the conduct codes of Royal Dutch, Exxon, and other meganationals are likely to get little attention unless the company continually restates and reinforces the message. Seminars on professional conduct, reference to the goals in speeches by corporate executives, exploration and expansion of the concepts in employee newsletters, and other communication outlets are among the possible tools of communication.

Philip Morris, General Motors, and several other companies set a valuable example by interjecting their declarations of corporate responsibility into their corporate annual reports.

In its statement, Philip Morris made a pledge to produce high-quality products, be sensitive to the environment, adopt conscientious food labeling, and study world hunger. In its 1990 annual report, the company also confronted head on its most onerous ethical dilemma. While the company stood on ground that didn't please critics, it nevertheless made its policy clear:

"We have acknowledged that smoking is a risk factor in the development of lung cancer and certain other human diseases, because a statistical relationship exists between smoking and the occurrence of those diseases," former chairman Hamish Maxwell wrote to shareholders. "Accordingly, we insist that the decision to smoke, like many other lifestyle decisions, should be made by informed adults. We believe that smokers around the world are well aware of the potential risks associated with tobacco use, and have the knowledge necessary to make an informed decision."

If a company is truly committed to being answerable for its decisions and the actions of its employees, public articulation of its position and conduct codes is necessary. The corporation must also expect to be held to those statements.

In *Economics Explained*, Heilbroner and Thurow mention several moves that governments could take to improve corporate citizenship. They suggest the widening of legal responsibility of the corporation to include areas of activity for which they now have too little accountability. These areas include environmental damage and consumer protection.

It would also help to increase public accountability through disclosure—or the so-called "fish bowl" method of regulation. Companies might be required to make public all sorts of information on health, safety, employee, political, social, and other activities. At the present, there is considerable information in company documents, especially for companies trading under the U.S. Securities and Exchange Commission rules. Companies worldwide voluntarily print a compendium of admirable works, including contributions to sports, entertainment, and charity. Fiat distributes pages and pages on its "cultural policy," detailing how the company sponsors Venetian art exhibits, finances renovation of important royal sites, and offers prizes for academic inquiry.

Unfortunately, for almost every meganational, it takes extra digging to find the information that casts a company in a lesser light. In most annual reports the situations where society has decided the corporation has been remiss can be found buried in the footnotes to financial information under "other liabilities" or "contingencies," or some other ambiguous heading. The sentence or two that spells out the trouble often is inadequate. There is no question that further frankness is needed. Heilbroner and Thurow go so far as to suggest that disclosure rules might include public access to corporate tax returns.

Corporations could defuse the growing tension between business and private interests by seizing the initiative. Any number of voluntary steps demonstrate a willingness to respect the needs and wishes of the societies in which they operate. In Japan, the debate over corporate ethics became vigorous in the early 1990s, following a parade of public scandals.

In a two-part article that appeared in the *Japan Times*, Osaka University economics professor Iwao Nakatani analyzed Japan's problems and offered advice for improvement. While his words were directed at his countrymen, the principles apply universally.

"First," Nakatani said, "moral conscience must be established among the top echelon of corporate management. As John Maynard Keynes said, the market will become corrupt beyond saving if it has no moral basis."[5]

Nakatani pointed out that Japan's laws and the punishment for violations are too vague, considering the global nature of Japan's capital markets, and must be made more understandable. "The big Japanese securities houses are not the only ones affected by (Japanese) law," he noted. "The entire world is."

The big corporations, he added, "have a strong influence. They can and do move trillions of yen. They can do almost anything. Managers have a great responsibility in seeing that their efforts are sustained by a firm moral conscience."

Corruption, Nakatani emphasized, "cannot be prevented by clearly stated regulations alone. The brakes lie in the human heart."

Certain meganationals, though there are few Japanese corporations among them, already have adopted some of the following practices and with good results:

• Not only should the meganational corporations publish their statement of conduct in the annual report each year, they should regularly evaluate their own compliance. In the United States, corporate ethics programs have become increasingly common, due to a 1991 change in the sentencing guidelines for crimes such as fraud. Under the new federal rules, those companies whose ethics programs meet federal standards and who cooperate in investigations will be sentenced more leniently should they wind up in court.

• All corporations should make a commitment to unobstructed communications. Open communication builds confidence among stakeholders that a company intends to operate in a way that will withstand public scrutiny. "No part of a corporation should remain hidden from public view," insisted Kyocera's Inamori.

• Communication must flow in both directions. This can be accomplished by accepting representatives of adversarial interest groups on boards of directors—as Exxon recently did following the Valdez oil spill—and by adding worker members. While outside members now are recruited from academia or the professional investment community, these delegates too often are selected because of their compatibility with management, rather than their ability to voice unwelcome ideas.

• Encourage public debate. When public interests and corporate interests are at odds, the proper course of action may present itself naturally through widespread discussion. Meganational corporations may be able to avoid costly mistakes by listening. Citicorp learned this lesson when it introduced a point-of-sale data system that tracked buying habits, brand preference, and other information on shoppers through retail cash registers. Consumers complained that the POS system was an invasion of privacy, and especially didn't like the idea that the information could be sold to third parties. Giving up six years of research and $20 million in investment, Citicorp finally shelved the project.

• Allegiance should be paid to two international voluntary codes for business conduct—the Organization of Economic Cooperation and Development (OECD) Declaration and Guidelines for International Investment and Multinational Enterprises, and the International Labor Organization (ILO) Tripartite Declaration of Principles.

The OECD guidelines were developed for multinational corporations and adopted in 1976. They cover a wide range of activities including disclosure of information, competition, financing, taxation, and science and technology. The OECD code are not laws, but rather moral obligations that call for public debate and monitoring to encourage compliance. Though the OECD often is reproached for being a "rich man's club," the declarations recognize corporate responsibility to workers, Third World societies, and to those most vulnerable to meganational authority.

The ILO conventions, at the moment, put only gentle pressure on the signatories who break the rules. They do, however, have the potential for power. Founded in 1919 and passed along to the United Nations from the League of Nations, the ILO has a unique structure: each country's delegation includes representatives from governments, labor groups, and employer organizations. In the early 1980s, the ILO introduced secret balloting, which offered greater liberty to delegates from repressive regimes. The ILO standards, covering worker safety, health provisions, maternity benefits, and so on, have been a critical force for workplace reform.

It does little good to talk about an extensive "stakeholder" community, and at the same time to limit the voice of that community to such weak steps as shareholder proposals or to the pugnacious acts of product boycotts, strikes, or lawsuits. By taking the steps listed above, the meganationals could resolve some of the conflicts that exist between capitalist endeavors and private interests. These steps could pave the road to a better integrated and more peaceable global economy.

Though some are loathe to do so, the leaders of the world's largest and most powerful businesses must acknowledge another truth. Ultimately, corporations are like governments. Both are institutions that society needs, and in fact until some superior mechanism is invented, *must* have. But tyranny, abuse, and inefficiency can creep in and destroy all that was formerly good and useful. Individuals will continue to keep watch over both government and corporate activities, press for suitable checks and balances, and demand accountability. "Eternal vigilance is the price of liberty," warned Wendell Phillips in 1852.

Chapter Sixteen

Looking Around and Looking Ahead

"Nothing in life is to be feared. It is only to be understood."

Madame Marie Curie

The world is caught up in the most extraordinary period of economic transformation it has experienced since the Industrial Revolution of the 19th century. Propelled by strides in transportation, communications, and other technology—nations and peoples everywhere are jousting for position in a coming world in which every country must think for itself. The venue of competition looks more like a video game screen than a football field, except that, like football, the players are hulking giants. Because the somewhat twisted experiments with communism have run amok, those countries with the most successful economic histories are home to the big league teams—and a new capitalist energy is rampant.

With their strong and stable traditions of commerce and trade, the United States, Europe, and Japan inscribe the rules.

"The countries of the Trilateral area (again, North America, Europe, and Japan) produce over 70 percent of the world's income and are, politically, the world's most advanced in terms of freedom and democracy," Fiat chairman Giovanni Agnelli told the Trilateral Commission in 1989. "They possess the economic and political strength necessary to guide the world toward more orderly economic relations, more relaxed political dealings, and the conferring of greater powers of intervention on international organizations."

In particular, a select group of corporations from these countries play leading roles in this struggle for market dominance and profits.

The 25 most powerful are the meganational corporations described in this book. They range from Dai-Ichi Kangyo Bank, the world's greatest private-sector bank with $470.2 billion in assets to swift and smart Merck & Co. with sales (in 1990) of $7.6 billion. Making the most of their accumulated experience, their bankrolls, and their elaborate commercial networks, this pack of prestigious corporations has constructed a stone-solid footing in international business. This foundation has been built with remarkable sophistication.

"The giant corporation—as (John Kenneth) Galbraith notes, with somewhat Pickwickian exaggeration—has achieved substantial control over its environment and considerable immunity from the discipline of exogenous control mechanisms, especially the competitive market," wrote Adams and Brock in *The Bigness Complex*. "Through separation of ownership from management it has emancipated itself from the control of stockholders. By reinvestment of profits, it has eliminated the influence of the financier and the capital market. By massive advertising, it has insulated itself from consumer sovereignty. By possession of market power, it has come to dominate both suppliers and customers. By judicious identification with the manipulation of the state, it has achieved autonomy. Whatever it cannot do for itself to assure survival and growth, a compliant government does on its behalf—assuring the maintenance of full employment, eliminating the risk of and subsidizing the investment in research and development, and assuring the supply of scientific and technical skills required by the modern technostructure. In return for this, the industrial giant performs society's planning function."[1]

Warnings such as the one above have been sounded for decades—an aristocracy of powerful corporations was guiding our lives. The idea has been routinely disparaged by business and political leaders because they dread a public backlash. None of the meganational companies, however, are shy about asserting their global ambitions. And rather than apologize for collaborating with governments, most meganationals, even those in the United States, are open about it. This coziness with bureaucracy takes on an ironic twist when coming from the likes of AT&T, which during the 1980s was carved up by U.S. government antitrust enforcers.

"Last year," AT&T group executive Victor Pelson told the 1990

Asian Society Symposium, "we bid on a switching contract in Indonesia, with a potential value of $2 billion. In the process, the president and other top administration officials intervened to neutralize competing political pressures. It was a role *The Washington Post* called 'unprecedented.'" In that AT&T Indonesian proposal, the U.S. government used the Export Import Bank and the Agency for International Development to assemble a financing package for the Indonesian government—if Indonesia bought the AT&T system. AT&T, though it is a huge and financially sound company, said it could not compete with the credit arrangements underwritten by other countries for their telecommunications industries. Additionally, AT&T's chairman, Robert Allen, has called for "bold, cooperative action between business and government" to undergird emerging technologies in the United States.[2]

It is encouraging to see Pelson use "we" when talking of AT&T, and to see action attributed to an individual, rather than "the company." It's all too easy to speak of business enterprises as though they were robotic, dehumanized machines, which of course they are not. The quickening of big business has been attended by the emergence of powerful executives such as Robert Allen. While the role of these executives in the concentration of business has been monumental, they are merely building on a tradition as ancient as the Roman Empire. Not everyone looks kindly on the jobs these modern-day Ceasars do.

"Karl Marx looked ahead and saw this competitive anarchy as the seed of capitalism's destruction," wrote Paul Solman and Thomas Friedman in *Life & Death on the Corporate Battlefield.* " . . . And although history has thus far shown him wrong, by the 19th century there arose a breed of men whose existence Marx had predicted. These men believed deeply that *their* self-interest would prevail, because bigger was better and biggest was best, and they had—or would have—the biggest companies and fortunes to prove it. Given that capitalism was not indisputably paramount both economically and socially, the most successful business strategy seemed to be the simplest; the best way to keep one's business fat and profitable was to make it the only business in sight."[3]

At the helm of these corporate juggernauts are some of the smartest, best-educated, and shrewdest men in the world. Unlike many leaders of the past, few of these potentates actually were born to their seats of power. None were elected by popular vote. Some inherited a smaller company and moved it into the league of front-runners. Most fought through the ranks to the top of their corporations, and their skills have been tested in battle. These men have had to be aggressive and tough; as their companies grow, so do other contenders in this high-stakes crusade for world markets.

Through mergers, acquisitions, joint ventures, and other acquisitive business practices, the network of dominant corporations has built exceptional strength at home and abroad. The mega-nationals have consolidated their money-making armies in the developed economies, and are looking to the less developed parts of the world for their next campaigns. On top of that, the most advanced companies are joining forces to refine and adapt existing products, invent the tools of tomorrow, and tackle new markets. They are the new industrial colonizers.

The players may be bigger and may be converging from all parts of the globe—but the absolute number of competitors is shrinking. The world economy is becoming dominated by a limited number of companies in most of the major industries. Many countries or regions of the world are unprepared for the proficiency with which these oligopolies will be able to orchestrate their activities. Antitrust rules, trade regulations, labor, safety, and other laws are not adequate for the challenge, though there is a scramble to make ready.

The new regional alliances, such as the European Community, seem to be a counteraction to these massive corporate machines. The European nations sense that, alone in their cherished sovereignty, they are too small to withstand the pressures of the new economic order. Only by joining forces can the European nations nurture their own economies, exert monetary prerogatives, promote domestic industries, and guard the public interest.

Trade alliances, such as the North American Free Trade Agreement, are attempts by states to create a regional power axis, not just to vie with other regions for new business investment but to safeguard the very right to govern. Political leaders have recognized that national autonomy has been eroded by corporations that can jump borders and escape unwanted dominion.

One of the simplest ways to sustain a vital economy and to hold tight to power, it now seems, is to become a steward of business. In the past 50 years, the American/European self-reliant form of capitalism has prevailed, but this won't necessarily be the case in the next century. Capitalism is under pressure.

"I think capitalism is not bankrupt," said economist Lester Thurow. "Between 1945 and 1990 we had an economic contest between capitalism and communism and capitalism won. Now (the contest) is between two very different forms of capitalism. It is the Anglo-Saxon, antitrust form versus the communitarian version of capitalism, ala Germany and Japan. It is a very different conception of how things should work."[4]

While closer alliances between government and business are to be expected, the drive also will continue to erase trade barriers between nations. In theory, freer economies lead to more work on the average, though some regions will lose jobs and others will gain. Those areas with cheap labor and capital costs, such as Mexico, are undergoing the same transformation that percolated through Asia three decades ago. While the economies of these industrializing nations will become more affluent, their unique cultures will wear away.

Workers, in particular, face dramatic changes. If free trade agreements work as they do in theory, countries and regions will specialize in the goods and services they can furnish most efficiently and cheaply. They will trade with others for the merchandise that is produced more efficiently elsewhere.

This means greater specialization of work, with less variety in employment options and less autonomy within a region. Japan will wield its vast capital resources and fiscal expertise to dominate in financial affairs, but its rice production will decline. The United States may turn to Japan for money, but will excel in scientific development and food production. Europe, while contributing both capital and technological know-how, will be the guiding light for style, culture, and intellectual pursuits. Europe will continue to show the rest of the world how to live graciously.

Further specialization of tasks also means that routine work will migrate to the region with the lowest wages. On the other hand, the meganationals, to be nearer and better tuned to customers, are doing more research and development, engineering, and even high-level manufacturing abroad. Fortunately, this allows a more even spread of knowledge.

Because of their vast resources and drive to competitiveness, the meganational corporations will seek the best and brightest workers. They will pay well for this talent in terms of salaries, fringe benefits, and working conditions. Though the life of a "company man" may not appeal to every person, jobs with the meganationals will be increasingly prestigious and sought after.

These companies are generous to investors as well. While at any given time a particular company or industry may be in a low cycle (probably because it is undergoing a period of shedding and rejuvenation), the top 25 meganational corporations have demonstrated an uncanny ability to survive. Their stock prices tend to be stable (with a few exceptions) and share-price appreciation and dividend payout often are exceptional.

These are companies people believe in. Therefore, the world will adjust to their burgeoning power in several ways. A number of inventive ideas have been suggested, though some have little chance of being implemented.

Kyocera's Inamori called upon Japanese corporations to curtail their own growth. Expressing his grave concern over the trend toward overexpansion of large corporations, Inamori warned Japanese companies that if they did not restrain themselves, they may live to regret it. "It may be unwise for huge corporations to move so ambitiously into so many new areas," he wrote in a 1990 essay. "With their financial and human resources and technology, they will have free rein in any industry, driving out small businesses and venture enterprises or excluding them from the outset."[5]

While recessions, military conflict, and other disruptions certainly will slow corporate growth from time to time, corporate expansion is unlikely to end. When growth exceeds a corporation's ability to manage, investments will become purely financial in nature. As in the case of Sumitomo Bank and Goldman Sachs, there is no management involvement by the parent company; the role of the junior company is to supply profits to its parent.

Not only will acquisitions continue, more industries are likely to face consolidation, creating oligopoly in a wider range of enterprises. Kenichi Ohmae, author of *The Borderless World*, insists this expansionary trend calls for a higher government power. "Inevitably, as these patterns of choice make themselves felt, some nations will be more badly hurt than others," claims Ohmae. "That is why, inevitably, there must be a supragovernmental body of some sort that can monitor such developments and cushion the worst of their effects." Ohmae envisioned something along the lines of a magnified European Community. He would like to pay one third of his taxes to such a council to deal with global problems, one third to his own nation, and one third to his community to solve local problems.

Whether a world that has yet to fully trust the United Nations or bow to the World Court is ready for a "supragovernment" is debatable. Regional organizations such as the European Community may be experimental steps in that direction, but the development of the EC and similar systems is lagging behind the need for them. One format for worldwide regulations and standards already exists under the General Agreement for Tariffs and Trade. While far from perfect, GATT has been functioning for decades and has much of the mechanism in place for review, regulation, and enforcement. Furthermore, GATT has a cadre of experienced leadership.

The revision and expansion of GATT is underway, though the process has been touchier and more turbulent than expected. Even when GATT and other agreements are adapted to the new world economic conditions, they won't reply to all of the questions. Refinement and modification of regulatory bodies, treaties, and so on must continue as more experience is gathered in this unfolding business environment.

Here are some of the things already known about this yet-to-be-traveled world:

• The United States will lose some clout in the world of capital. This is not because of any humiliating national failure. On the contrary. It is because the Great Depression, which damaged the world balance of trade, and World War II, which finished the job and gave great advantages to unbombed North America, are over at last. Europe and Japan have fully rebuilt. The world is a more balanced place, with the major regions of the world competing with greater equality for a share of the economic pie. The United States—where the majority of the meganational corporations are domiciled—will compete energetically in world markets, but it is unlikely that the former U.S. economic dominance will be revived.

• Democracy is in for a rough go. Even in the United States, many citizens now advocate the Japanese model, which ostensibly is based on democracy. In fact the Japanese system depends on a potent business/government coalition and a subservient populace. U.S. Secretary of State James Baker also has called on developing countries to look to Mexico as a prototype. While Mexico has implemented impressive economic reforms, the country operates under a strong centralized government and human rights abuses are commonplace. And both Japan and Mexico still manage their economies—a practice that wears a more respectable imprimatur when it parades under the flag of "industrial policy."

The challenge that the old capitalist states face is to reinvent themselves in a fresher form that acknowledges the new structure of the world economy. "We are discovering that there are different ways of organizing capitalism," wrote Chalmers Johnson and his coauthors in *Politics and Productivity: How Japan's Development Strategy Works*. "It is not a matter of whether the United States can or should imitate its competitors. The task will be for the United States, in its own way, to develop new capacities that are equal to its new challenges."[6]

• While the Eastern European countries have cast communism aside, there is no guarantee that their next form of government will be representational, or that the economic system will be capitalism as practiced in the United States or similar countries. Nevertheless, citizens of these countries will hasten into the consumer society and will quickly industrialize. As some validation of that concept, officials in Berlin report that garbage in East Germany has tripled since unification, overwhelming manpower, equipment, and budgets. Most trash derives from overly packaged consumer goods.

• Public activists, following the archetypes Ralph Nader and Jeremy Rifkin, will arise as 21st century heros. Activism, as a defense against overwhelming corporate authority, will become more potent. These charismatic activists will be seen as the chief advocates of individual political rights.

• Shareholder activism also will evolve as a balance for meganational power. Broader international ownership of corporate shares and a rising level of employee ownership will energize the shareholders' rights movement.

• Conflicting ideologies are likely to arise within individual countries and among the global establishment. Throughout the early 1990s, President George Bush's administration pursued a North American Free Trade Agreement and pressed GATT negotiators to broaden its scope and diminish trade barriers. At the same time, military officials at the Pentagon crusaded for controls on the export of formidable yet inexpensive computer workstations that possibly could be adapted to military weaponry. Similar equipment, according to computer makers, could be purchased from manufacturers in England and Japan, and was expected to be available soon in Taiwan and Korea. Worlds never click over from old to new in an orderly fashion. These conflicts point to the ragged edges where old-world thinking prevails and where ancient adversities remain unsettled.

• Despite attempts to preserve and promote ethnic qualities, a sameness will continue to spread throughout the world. Some of this standardization is desirable, such as the uniform technical standards being proposed for the telecommunications industry. Not only will such guidelines make worldwide communications networks easier to operate, they can raise quality standards and reduce costs. But homogeneity in other areas makes the world less colorful and fascinating. Teenagers in the remotest islands of Scotland wear similar hair styles and listen to the same musical beat as teenagers in Puerto Rico, Alaska, and almost everywhere. No matter what trouble spots Cable News Network television camera crews visit, they find someone to interview in English. "Trendcaster" John Naisbitt contends that people will continue to assert their distinctiveness in many ways, in what he calls "cultural nationalism." There always is hope that Naisbitt is correct.

• Sadly, terrorism will proliferate, spreading even deeper into the corporate realm. Those individuals who feel alienated from the stainless steel, reverberating, affluent world of meganational business will search for a more trusted voice. Because this faction is small, it will struggle to be heard. The greatest resonance, unfortunately, is achieved through violence.

Despite the disheartening news, there are propitious aspects to the increasing eminence of the meganational corporations. More and more, society will turn to the business sector to assuage human pain and suffering, to sponsor cultural enrichment programs, and to establish and monitor standards of behavior. Because working in a corporate environment has become central to the lives of so many people, the companies will be forced to respond.

• The meganational corporations are becoming leaders in the "greening" of industry. Siemens builds much-needed systems for purification of effluent. AT&T established a goal of reducing its own manufacturing waste by 25 percent and increasing paper recycling by 35 percent by 1994. The company is modifying its manufacturing process so that fewer harmful substances will be released into the earth's ozone layer. Admittedly, attitudinal changes toward the environment have been inspired by citizen and government pressure. But when big companies fall into compliance, standards are set for others in the same industry, scientific data are accumulated, and an industry springs up to provide the necessary equipment and services to make clean air, water, food, and land a reality.

• Through richly funded and well-targeted research and development budgets, the large corporations will usher in some amazing new products and make many old ideas work better. Solar cars, drugs that ease mental illness without zombielike side-effects, interactive television in remote parts of the earth—these are some of the advances so far. AT&T is working on hearing computers, "thinking" computers, and "smart cards" that contain easily retrievable medical records, special instructions, or other live-saving information. AT&T, Siemens, and other electronic communications companies are putting the final touches on a scamless, uniform worldwide communications network that links the "global village" anticipated by Marshall McLuhan in *Guttenberg Galaxy*.

• The meganational corporations, with profit in mind of course, will cushion the shocks of political and social change. Deutsche Bank, Daimler-Benz, Siemens, Coca-Cola, and other companies made immediate investments in East Germany when it was reunified with its western half. The investments brought jobs and an anchor for many people living in a troubled economy that will take some time to revitalize.

• Through corporate activities, relationships are being built among the nations and peoples of the world that will transcend national and cultural differences. When Siemens conducts a joint venture with Matsushita and another with IBM, cross-cultural relations are formed at the personal level. AT&T employees, who often compete with Siemens, are working on cooperative projects in

Japan, Spain, Singapore, the United Kingdom, and dozens of other countries. Granted, intimate human contact hasn't always resolved problems of racial and cultural discrimination or built a bond of understanding, at least not in the early phases. But the American experience shows that, given enough time, people become more tolerant of personal differences, especially if they aren't squabbling over scarce resources.

What course should enlightened people and governments follow, in light of the mushrooming size of multinational corporations?

• *Embrace change.* The rise of the meganational corporations will bring far-reaching alterations in the way people live and work, but many of the new ways will be superior. Food, medicine, information, and equipment will be of higher quality and more readily available throughout the world. Workers will gain new skills and enjoy safer working conditions.

• *Be inventive.* The smaller companies that will fare the best are those that can serve some ancillary, subcontracting or complementary or service function for the meganationals. However, a counterculture will thrive to serve the segment of society that insists on going its own way. Entrepreneurs who can best anticipate the needs of the independent, contrarian thinkers will be able to build their own business empires.

• *Resist the temptation to idealize capitalism and big business.* While there are many admirable, ethical people in the world of business, there also are tyrants, frauds, and deceivers. Like government, big business can be a marvelous mechanism for human beings to achieve fulfillment, or it can be repressive, elitist, and abusive of the environment. Unless individuals are committed to thinking objectively about the role of business and at times fiercely defend themselves and the world in which they live, this universe could become a disagreeable and dangerous place.

• *Champion civil rights.* "The weakening of state power is also a sign of the advent of a borderless world, brought about by the power of the people, in the area of politics," claimed Kyocera's Inamori. "Like underground springs that bubble up here and there, this economic and political tide is spreading throughout the world and will result in the simultaneous reassertion of popular will everywhere, not just in communist societies. The 1990s is therefore bound to be a turbulent decade."[7]

References

Adams, Walter and James W. Brock, *The Bigness Complex*. New York: Pantheon Books, 1986.

Bock, Betty; Harvey J. Goldschmid; Ira M. Millstein; and F. M. Scherer, eds. *The Impact of the Modern Corporation*. New York: Columbia University Press, 1984.

Brandeis, Justice Louis, *The Curse of Bigness*. New York: The Viking Press, 1934.

Burstein, Daniel, *Euro-quake*. New York: Simon & Schuster, 1991.

Choate, Pat, *Agents of Influence*. New York: Alfred A. Knopf, 1990.

Chposky, Jim and Ted Leonsis, *Blue Magic*. New York: Facts on File Publications, 1988.

Colby, Gerald (see Zilg entry).

DeLamarter, Richard T., *Big Blue: IBM's Use and Abuse of Power*. New York: Dodd, Mead, 1986.

Derdak, Thomas, ed., *International Directory of Company Histories*. Chicago: St. James Press, 1988.

Grossman, Peter Z., *American Express: The Unofficial History of the People Who Built the Great Financial Empire*. New York: Crown Publishers, 1987.

Heilbroner, Robert L. and Lester Thurow, *Economics Explained*. A Touchstone Book, New York: Simon & Schuster, 1987.

Johnson, Chalmers, *MITI and the Japanese Miracle: The Growth of Industrial Policy*. Stanford University Press, 1982.

Johnson, Chalmers; Laura D'Andrea Tyson; and John Zysman, *Politics and Productivity: The Real Story of Why Japan Works*. New York: Harper Business, 1989.

Magaziner, Ira and Mark Paterkin, *The Silent War: Inside the Global Business Battles Shaping America's Future*. New York: Vintage Press, 1990.

Marx, Karl, *Capital: A Critical Analysis of Capital Production*. Moscow: Foreign Language, 1961.

Ohmae, Kenichi, *The Borderless World: Power and Strategy in the Interlinked Economy*. New York: Harper Collins, 1990.

Porter, Michael E., *The Competitive Advantage of Nations*. New York: The Free Press, 1990.

Reich, Robert, *The Work of Nations: Preparing for 21st Century Capitalism*. New York: Alfred A. Knopf, 1991.

Slater, Robert, *The Titans of Takeover*. Englewood Cliffs, N.Y.: Prentice-Hall Inc., 1987.

Smith, Adam, *The Wealth of Nations*. Indianapolis: Liberty Classics, 1981.

Smith, Roy C. *The Global Bankers*. New York: E. P. Dutton, 1989.

Solman, Paul and Thomas Friedman, *Life and Death On The Corporate Battlefield*. New York: Simon & Schuster, 1982.

Tarbell, Ida, *The History of the Standard Oil Company*. New York: Harper & Row, 1966.

Taylor, Wayne C., *The Firestone Operations in Liberia*. New York: Arno Press, 1976.

Viner, Aron, *Inside Japanese Financial Markets*. Homewood, Ill.: Dow Jones-Irwin, 1988.

von Wolferen, Karel, *The Enigma of Japanese Power*. New York: Alfred A. Knopf, 1989.

Weiss, Julian, *The Asian Century, and What It Means for the West*. New York: Facts on File, 1989.

Wilson, Charles, *The History of Unilever*, vols. I, II, and III. New York: Praeger Publishers, New York, 1968.

Yergin, Daniel, *The Prize: The Epic Quest For Oil, Money and Power*. New York: Simon & Schuster, 1991.

Zilg, Gerard Colby, *Du Pont: Behind the Nylon Curtain*. Englewood Cliffs, N.Y.: Prentice-Hall, 1974. (This book was republished in 1984 under a new author and a new title: Colby, Gerard, *Du Pont Dynasty*, L. Stuart.)

Endnotes

Chapter 1

1. Mike McNamee and Catherine Yang, "Deutsche Bank Nabs a Plum—But It Didn't Come Cheap," *Business Week*, December 11, 1989, p. 102.
2. Leonard Silk, "Economic Scene: The Rich Legacy of an Economist," *New York Times*, January 4, 1991.
3. Alexander Cockburn, "War and Class," *Anderson Valley Advertiser*, October 10, 1990.
4. Fred Gardner, "Roamin Noam in Marin," *Anderson Valley Advertiser*, March 20, 1991.
5. William Holstein, Stanley Reed, Jonathan Kapstein, Todd Vogel and Joseph Weber, "The Stateless Corporation," *Business Week*, May 14, 1990.
6. Kazuo Inamori, "Can Capitalism Survive," *Intersect*, PHP Institute, International Editorial Division, October 1990.
7. Richard Loun, "Ex-Emcon Workers Say Promises Broken," *San Diego Union*, October 18, 1981.

Chapter 2

1. "Alaska House Rejects Exxon Spill Pact as Too Low," *New York Times*, May 3, 1991.

Chapter 3

1. "A Colorful D.C. Tale," *New York Magazine*, May 27, 1985.
2. "Formula for Controversy," *Time*, January 14, 1991.
3. David Rockefeller, "The Trilateral Commission Explained," *Saturday Evening Post*, October 1980.
4. Darrell Delamaide, "The Duetsche Bank Juggernaut Will Keep On Rolling," *Euromoney*, January 1990.

Chapter 4

1. Aron Viner, *Inside Japanese Financial Markets* (Homewood, Ill.: Dow Jones-Irwin, 1988).
2. Andrew Tanzer, "The Other Banks Feel Threatened," *Forbes*, October 2, 1989.
3. Charles P. Alexander, "Scandal Rocks General Electric," *Time*, May 27, 1985.
4. "Mitsui and Taiyo Kobe Banks to Merge," *San Diego Union*, August 29, 1989.
5. AT&T Annual Report, 1989.
6. Professor Lester Thurow, interview with author, 1990.
7. "Letter to Shareholders," Exxon Corporation Annual Report, 1991.
8. "Japanese Amassing Huge Corporate Reserves for Takeovers," *Business Tokyo*, November 1989.

Chapter 5

1. Charles Wilson, *The History of Unilever*, vols. 1, 2, and 3 (New York: Praeger Publishers, 1968).
2. Thomas Derdak, ed., *International Directory of Company Histories*, vol. 1 (Chicago: St. James Press, 1988).
3. "Inside Japan's M&A," *Business Tokyo*, November 1989.
4. Robert Heller, "A World of Difference," *AT&T Reports*, January 1991.
5. Jonathan Kapstein, "GM's Swedish Fling Is Causing Headaches," *Business Week*, February 4, 1991.
6. "Message to Shareholders," General Electric Annual Report, 1989.
7. Maryann N. Keller, "Streetwise: The Joint-Venture Adventure," *Motor Trend*, April 1990.
8. "Message to Shareholders," Daimler-Benz Annual Report, 1989.

Chapter 6

1. "200 words—Beauty and the Man," *Lear's*, January 1990.
2. "Protect and Survive," *The Economist*, September 22, 1990.
3. Richard I. Kirkland, Jr., "Fiat's Unsung Roman Hero," *Fortune*, January 5, 1987.
4. Victor A. Pelson, AT&T, speech before the Asia Society Symposium, Los Angeles, November 1, 1990.

5. "Globesmanship," *Across the Board*, January/February 1990.
6. Neil Gross, Otis Port, and Richard Brandt, "Making Deals—Without Giving Away the Store," *Business Week*, June 17, 1991.

Chapter 7

1. John Markoff, "Chief Reads Riot Act at I.B.M.," *New York Times*, May 29, 1991.
2. "IBM: As Markets and Technology Change, Can Big Blue Remake Its Culture?" *Business Week*, June 17, 1991.
3. Richard Thomas DeLamarter, *Big Blue: IBM's Use and Abuse of Power* (New York: Dodd, Mcad, 1986).
4. Ibid.
5. Robert Slater, *The Titans of Takeover* (Englewood Cliffs, N.J.: Prentice-Hall, 1987).
6. Professor Lester Thurow, interview with author, 1990.
7. Carla Rapoport, "Why Japan Keeps On Winning," *Fortune*, July 15, 1991.
8. Ferdinand Protzman, "Market Place: German Unity Favors Siemens," *New York Times*, March 28, 1991.
9. Steven Greenhouse, "European Antitrust Agreement," *New York Times*, December 22, 1989.
10. Walter Adams and James W. Brock, *The Bigness Complex* (New York: Panthcon Books, 1986).
11. Kazuo Inamori, "Can Capitalism Survive," *Intersect*, October 1990.
12. A. E. Cullison, "Tokyo's '89 Prices Found 16% above Those in New York," *Journal of Commerce and Commercial*, July 24, 1990.
13. Tim Smart and Ronald Grover, "Pumping Up a State's Power to Bust Trust," *Business Week*, January 15, 1990.
14. Inamori, "Can Capitalism Survive?"
15. Justice Louis Brandeis, *The Curse of Bigness* (New York: Viking Press, 1934).

Chapter 8

1. Tom Fox, interview with author, 1991.
2. Gilda Haas, interview with author, 1991.
3. "Mitsui and Taiyo Kobe Banks to Merge," *San Diego Union*, August 29, 1989.

4. James Flanigan, "Europe's Message about the U.S. Economy," *Los Angeles Times*, October 10, 1990.
5. Peter Grier, "Many Nation States Face Fragmentation in New World Order," *Christian Science Monitor*, May 6, 1991.
6. Robert Heilbroner and Lester Thurow, *Economics Explained*, a Touchstone Book (New York: Simon & Schuster, 1987).
7. Ibid.
8. David Lawday, "My Country, Right . . . or What?" *Atlantic*, July 1991.
9. "European Monetary Union," *Made in Fiat*, Fiat corporate publication, April 1991.

Chapter 9

1. Daniel Yergin, *The Prize* (New York: Simon & Schuster, 1991), pp. 647–648.
2. Ibid., p. 455.
3. Ibid., p. 462.
4. "Letter from the Chairman," British Petroleum Annual Report, 1990.
5. Adam Smith, *The Wealth of Nations* (Indianapolis: Liberty Classics, 1981).
6. "Radicalism in Ember," *The Economist*, March 14, 1988.
7. Professor Lester Thurow, interview with author, 1990.
8. Robert Reich, *The Work of Nations: Preparing for 21st Century Capitalism* (New York: Alfred A. Knopf, 1991).
9. Professor Chalmers Johnson, interview with author, 1990.
10. L. C. Van Wachem, letter to author, July 1, 1991.
11. "Guilty as Charged?" *Business Tokyo*, November 1990.
12. Reich, *The Work of Nations*.
13. Walter Adams and James W. Brock, *The Big Business Complex* (New York: Pantheon Books, 1986).
14. Robert Heilbroner and Lester Thurow, *Economics Explained*, a Touchstone Book (New York: Simon & Schuster, 1987).
15. "Florio Flip-Flops on Investments," *Business Tokyo*, July 1991.
16. Chalmers Johnson, Laura D'Andrea Tyson, and John Zysman, *Politics and Productivity: The Real Story of Why Japan Works* (New York: Harper & Row, 1989).

Chapter 10

1. "Trade Secrets," *U.S. News & World Report*, July 11, 1988.
2. Thomas Derdak, ed., *International Directory of Company Histories* (Chicago: St. James Press, 1988).
3. Anne Manuel, "Unions and Terror in Guatemala: Coke Battle," *The New Republic*, September 17 and 24, 1984.
4. Ibid.
5. William Holstein, Stanley Reed, Jonathan Kapstein, Todd Vogel, and Joseph Weber, "The Stateless Corporation," *Business Week*, May 14, 1990.
6. "Beyond Globalization: Corporate Strategies for the 1990s; an Interview with Helmut Maucher," *International Management and Development Institute*, August 1989.
7. Pat Choate, *Agents of Influence* (New York: Alfred A. Knopf, 1990).
8. Howard Gleckman and Ted Holden, "Can Uncle Sam Mend this Hole in His Pocket?" *Business Week*, September 1990.
9. Professor Chalmers Johnson, interview with author, 1990.
10. Helmut Maucher, "The Role and Responsibility of the Multinational Corporation in a World in Crisis," speech before the Council on Foreign Relations, November 27, 1990.

Chapter 11

1. "Smokers' Revolt Succeeds in Moscow," *New York Times*, August 23, 1990.
2. "Proposals Fail at Philip Morris," *Associated Press*, April 23, 1990.
3. "Notebook: Blech," *The New Republic*, June 19, 1990.
4. Jonathan Lloyd-Owens, "Corporate Giving," *Intersect*, Fall 1990.
5. Helmut Maucher, "The Role and Responsibility of the Multinational Corporation in a World in Crisis," speech before the Council on Foreign Relations, November 27, 1990.
6. Mark Dowie and Theodore Brown, "Taking Stock: The Best and Worst of American Business," *Mother Jones*, Foundation for National Progress, June 1985.
7. Ibid.
8. Robert Zimmerman, "Alcoholism Booms with Drinking Promotion in Developing Countries," *Los Angeles Times*, July 21, 1991.
9. Dowie and Brown, "Taking Stock."

10. Ibid.
11. Mervyn Rothstein, "Uneasy Partners: Arts and Philip Morris," *New York Times*, December 18, 1990.
12. Kenichi Ohmae, *The Borderless World: Power and Strategy in the Interlinked Economy* (New York: Harper & Row, 1990).

Chapter 12

1. James Daly, "Hitachi's Goodwill Campaign Banishing Bad-Boy Image," *Computerworld*, August 27, 1980.
2. Frederick Hiroshi Katayama, "The Mountain Priest," *Fortune*, August 3, 1987.
3. Lawrence Minard, "Look Who's Building Plants in Britain," *Forbes*, March 16, 1981.
4. Catherine Breslin, "Working for the Japanese," *Ms.* Magazine, February 1988.
5. Professor Lester Thurow, interview with author, 1990.
6. Professor Chalmers Johnson, interview with author, 1990.
7. Walter Adams and James W. Brock, *The Bigness Complex* (New York: Pantheon Books, 1986).
8. Nestlé special advertising supplement, *Scientific American*, 1990.
9. Richard T. DeLamarter, *Big Blue: IBM's Use and Abuse of Power* (New York: Dodd, Mead, 1986).

Chapter 13

1. "Du Pont to Offer New Stock Option Program to More than 136,000 Employees," *PR Newswire*, February 18, 1991.
2. Gerard Colby Zilg, *Du Pont: Behind the Nylon Curtain* (Englewood Cliffs, N.J.: Prentice-Hall, 1974).
3. William Holstein, Stanley Reed, Jonathan Kapstein, Todd Vogel, and Joseph Weber, "The Stateless Corporation," *Business Week*, May 14, 1990.
4. Ibid.
5. Aron Viner, *Inside Japanese Financial Markets* (Homewood, Ill.: Dow Jones-Irwin, 1988).
6. "The Real Strengths of Employee Ownership," *Business Week*, July 15, 1991.

7. Judith H. Dobrzynski, "If Stockholders Bang on Boardroom Doors, Open 'Em," *Business Week*, December 3, 1990.
8. David Jones, "Romantics, Radicals and Realists," speech delivered to the Social Investment Forum, April 10, 1989 (full text in *Vital Speeches of the Day*).

Chapter 14

1. Steven Greenhouse, "Kuwait Picks Airbus to Rebuild Fleet," *New York Times*, June 18, 1991.
2. John F. McDonnell, "Subsidized Airbus' Below-Cost Prices Undercut U.S. Transport Aircraft Firms," *Aviation Week & Space Technology*, August 5, 1991.
3. Dr. Erich Riedl, "Watershed for German Aerospace Industry," *Interavia Aerospace Review*, May 1990.
4. Rose Pastor Stokes, Labor organizer, speech, 1917.
5. Julian Weiss, *The Asian Century and What It Means for the West* (New York: *Facts on File*, 1989).
6. "1990s Declared UN Decade of International Law," *UN Chronicles*, March 1990.
7. "World Trade: Jousting for Advantage," *The Economist*, September 22, 1990.
8. Victor A. Pelson, AT&T, speech before the Asia Society Symposium, Los Angeles, November 1, 1990.
9. Robert Weissman, "Prelude to a New Colonialism," *The Nation*, March 18, 1991.
10. "Health Care Innovation: The Case for a Favorable Public Policy," Merck & Co., Inc., August, 1988.
11. Daphne Wysham, "Big Business Hijacks GATT: The Codex Connection," *The Nation*, December 17, 1990.
12. "World Trade."
13. Art Pine, "Global Trade Talks Entering Key Final Year," *Los Angeles Times*, December 19, 1989.
14. Michael Kinsley, "TRB from Washington," *The New Republic*, March 4, 1991.
15. James Bovard, "For the U.S., a Repeated Trade Slip," *New York Times*, August 18, 1991.

Chapter 15

1. Helmut Maucher, "The Role and Responsibility of the Multinational Corporation in a World in Crisis," speech before the Council on Foreign Relations, November 27, 1990.
2. L. C. Van Wachem, letter to author, July 1, 1991.
3. Immanuel Kant, *Selected Works: Critique of Practical Reason and Other Writing in Moral Philosophy* (New York: Garland, 1976).
4. Jack Robertson, "ITC Clears Way for Duty on Japan WPs," *Electronic News*, August 12, 1991.
5. Iwao Nakatani, "Corporate Ethics Require," *Japan Times*, September 16, 1991.

Chapter 16

1. Walter Adams and James Brock, *The Bigness Complex* (New York: Pantheon Books, 1986).
2. Victor A. Pelson, AT&T, speech before the Asia Society Symposium, Los Angeles, November 1, 1990.
3. Paul Solman and Thomas Friedman, *Life and Death on the Corporate Battlefield* (New York: Simon & Schuster, 1982).
4. Professor Lester Thurow, interview with author, 1990.
5. Kazuo Inamori, "Can Capitalism Survive?" *Intersect*, October 1990.
6. Chalmers Johnson, Laura D'Andrea Tyson, and John Zysman, *Politics and Productivity: The Real Story of Why Japan Works* (New York: Harper & Row, 1989).
7. Inamori, "Can Capitalism Survive?"

INDEX

R

S

Also Available from Business One Irwin . . .

AMERICA'S HOLLOW GOVERNMENT
How Washington Has Failed the People
Mark L. Goldstein

Delves into the inner workings of our government and shows how rollbacks in regulations have reduced the government's capacity to accomplish important tasks. Goldstein provides insight into the consequences our "Hollow Government" will have on the nation's governance and prosperity. *America's Hollow Government* reveals the failure of federal agencies to fulfill their mandates and uphold the law. Goldstein shows how Congress and its focus on political survival cripples agencies and fuels the budget deficit. He explains how the "Hollow Government" was created and details how it impacts ordinary citizens, cities and states, American industry, and the future.

ISBN: 1-55623-467-8 $24.95

SECOND TO NONE
How Our Smartest Companies Put People First
Charles Garfield

Discover how you can create a workplace where both people and profits flourish? *Second to None* by Charles Garfield, the best-selling author of *Peak Performers*, gives you an inside look at today's leading businesses and how they became masters at expanding the teamwork and creativity of their work force. Using this unique mix of practical strategies gleaned from our smartest companies, you can respond to the challenges of today's global marketplace, provide superior service to your customers—and your own employees, maintain a competitive edge during times of rapid transition and restructuring, and much more!

ISBN: 1-55623-360-4 $24.95

THE DISNEY TOUCH
How a Daring Management Team Revived an Entertainment Empire
Ron Grover

A Fortune Book Club Main Selection!
Grover, one of Hollywood's best business reporters, reveals how Michael Eisner, Frank Wells, and the members of Team Disney engineered the turnaround that continues to amaze business people everywhere. You'll get the inside story of how they increased earnings 741 percent in six years!

ISBN: 1-55623-385-X $22.95

THE DOMINO EFFECT
How to Grow Sales, Profits, and Market Share through Super Vision
Donald J. Vlcek and Jeffrey P. Davidson

Details the proven techniques Domino's Pizza uses to target and maintain a 50 percent annual growth goal. This unique, behind-the-scenes look reveals how virtually any company can efficiently implement the same winning management strategies.

ISBN: 1-55623-602-6 $24.95

WORKFORCE MANAGEMENT
How Today's Companies Are Meeting Business and Employee Needs
Barbara Pope

Provides practical advice for organizations struggling to respond to ongoing change. Pope shows how to integrate business and employee needs in order to recruit and retain the best employees. She shows how you can manage work force problems before they become critical, work collaboratively to develop human resource programs and policies that match business plans, jobs, and people, and much more!

ISBN: 1-55623-537-2 $24.95

SURVIVE INFORMATION OVERLOAD
The 7 Best Ways to Manage Your Workload by Seeing the Big Picture
Kathryn Alesandrini

Gives you a step-by-step action plan to survive the information onslaught and still have time to effectively manage people, increase productivity, and best serve customers. You'll find innovative techniques, such as Priority Mapping, Context Analysis, Visual Organization, and the use of a Master Control System to manage details by seeing the big picture.

ISBN: 1-55623-721-9 $22.95

Prices quoted are in U. S. currency and are subject to change without notice. Available at fine bookstores and libraries everywhere.